PLA
AME
FOOTBALL
ANNUAL 1987-88

Macdonald
Queen Anne Press

A *Queen Anne Press* BOOK

© NFL Properties 1987.

Officially Licensed Product by NFL Properties

First published in Great Britain in 1987 by
Queen Anne Press, a division of
Macdonald & Co (Publishers) Ltd
Greater London House, Hampstead Road
London NW1 7QX
A BPCC plc Company

Cover photograph: Phil Simms of New York Giants (All Sport)

British Library Cataloguing in Publication Data
  Playfair American football annual —
  1987-88
  1. Football, Periodicals
  796.332'05   GV937

  ISBN 0-356-14438-0

Typeset by Visage Typesetting Ltd., London SW19
Reproduced, printed and bound in Great Britain by
Hazell, Watson & Viney Limited,
Member of the BPCC Group,
Aylesbury, Bucks.

CONTENTS

AMERICAN FOOTBALL

What is American Football? It's not all that different from rugby, indeed, that's how it all started in the American Universities round about 1870. Just like rugby, it's a game of gaining territory, moving down the field and somehow getting the ball across the opposing team's goal line.

How does a team move the ball? *The 4-Down system:* The team in possession (the Offense) is allowed four downs (attempts) to gain 10 or more yards' progress towards the opposing goal line. These 10 or more yards may be gained on just one down (attempt) or, if necessary, by using all four downs. The immediate reward for gaining the 10 yards is that the offense retains the possession of the ball and is allowed another series of four downs to gain 10 or more yards, and so on.

Scoring *Touchdown and Conversion:* Of course, the object is to score more points than your opponent. The most valuable score is a Touchdown, rather like a try in rugby. The difference is that, unlike a try, the ball need not be placed down onto the playing surface. Rather, it has simply to be taken over the goal line — into the so-called End Zone. A touchdown, which is worth six points, is immediately followed by a kick from directly in front of the goal posts. This is equivalent to the conversion in rugby and is known as an Extra Point Attempt, Point After Touchdown (PAT for short); a PAT is worth one point. It may not seem much but it is very important as many games are decided by just one point.

Field Goal: This is exactly like a penalty kick at goal in rugby, though in American football a team doesn't need to be awarded a penalty to have a go. In fact, a team can take a field goal kick on any one of its four downs, but they usually wait until the fourth down, and even then, only when they're no more than 40 yards from their opponent's goal line. If the kick is successful, it's worth three points.

Safety: A safety is *given up* by a team when one of its players who has the ball is tackled *inside his own end zone*. In this case, the unlucky team gives up two points to the opposition.

The Playing Field The playing surface can be AstroTurf, Tartan Turf, (both man-made fibre) or grass. The field of play is 120 yards long and 53⅓ yards wide. The end zones take up 10 yards at each end of the field. In addition to the obvious gridiron markings, there are two lines of marks stretching the length of the field. These are called 'Hashmarks' and define a strip of ground in the middle of the field where all the downs begin.

Starting the Game The captains toss a coin and the winner decides *either* to kick off or to face the kick, *or* the direction in which to play. The action starts when the kicker boots the ball as far as possible down the field. The man who makes the catch runs as far as possible up the field until he is tackled. His team keeps possession of the ball and they set off on their first series of four downs.

The Squads Each 45-man squad has three teams of 11 men plus a few reserves. They are known as the Offense, the Defense and the Special Team. The offense tries to score points, the defense tries to stop the opposition from scoring and the special team comes on when attempting or facing a kick. So there is a great deal of coming and going as the different teams enter and leave the field.

The League System All 28 professional teams form the National Football League but for competition (and historical reasons) they are divided into two 14-team Conferences, the American Football Conference and the National Football Conference. Each Conference is divided into three Divisions, not first, second and third, as in the Football League, but Eastern, Central and Western Divisions. All the divisions are meant to be of the same standard, the object being to group local teams together.

The Road to the Super Bowl There is a 16-week regular season in which the teams play normal league football. At the end of this, the top two teams in each Conference go into a knockout competition to decide the 'World Championship'. One week after the whole season is over the best players in each Conference form teams who play in the Pro Bowl, held in Hawaii. To be selected for the Pro Bowl is a great honour, even though both teams ease off a bit and the tackling isn't quite as tough.

PLAYERS' NUMBERS

All NFL Players are numbered according to their position*
  1-19   Quarterbacks and Kickers
20-49   Running Backs and Defensive Backs
50-59   Centers and Linebackers
60-79   Defensive Linemen and Interior Offensive Linemen
80-89   Wide Receivers and Tight Ends
90-99   Defensive Linemen
*All players who had been in the National Football League prior to 1972 may use their old numbers.

OFFENSE

Quarterback: he directs the play by 'handing off' to a Running Back or throwing a forward pass.
Center, Guards and Tackles: The interior line — they pave the way for the Running Back or protect the Quarterback on passing plays.
Tight End: he has the dual role of blocking like an interior Lineman or catching medium range passes.
The Wide Receiver: The 'flyer' who catches the full range of passes.
The Half Back*: The lighter more elusive runner.
The Full Back*: The heavyweight power runner.
*Known as the Running Backs who 'rush' with the ball and catch short passes.

DEFENSE

Tackles and Ends: The defensive line — they tackle the Running Back or kill the play at source by 'sacking' the Quarterback.
Linebackers: They pursue the Running Back on rushing plays or, on obvious passing plays, drop back to reinforce the Defensive Backs.
Cornerbacks and Safeties: The Defensive Backs — primarily defend against the pass, they also advance to assist the Linebackers on rushing plays.

KEY TO DEPTH CHART

OFFENSE

WR — wide receiver
T — tackle
OLT — offensive left tackle
G — guard
OLG — offensive left guard
C — center
ORG — offensive right guard
ORT — offensive right tackle
TE — tight end
QB — quarterback
H-B — Half-back
RB — running back
F-B — Full-back

SPECIAL TEAMS

P — punter
K — kicker
H — holder
PR — punt returner
KR — kick returner
LSN — long snapper
LSN (P)— punting center
LSN (F)— field goal center

DEFENSE

DE — defensive end
DLE — defensive left end
DT — defensive tackle
DLT — defensive left tackle
NT — nose tackle
MG — middle guard
DRT — defensive right tackle
DRE — defensive right end
LB — linebacker
LOLB — left outside linebacker
LLB — left linebacker
LILB — left inside linebacker
MLB — middle linebacker
RILB — right inside linebacker
RLB — right linebacker
OLB — outside linebacker
ILB — inside linebacker
ROLB — right outside linebacker
CB — cornerback
LCB — left cornerback
RCB — right cornerback
S — safety
SS — strong safety
LS — left safety
FS — free safety
RS — right safety
WS — wide safety

AMERICAN FOOTBALL CONFERENCE

Buffalo Bills
Cincinnati Bengals
Cleveland Browns
Denver Broncos
Houston Oilers
Indianapolis Colts
Kansas City Chiefs
Los Angeles Raiders
Miami Dolphins
New England Patriots
New York Jets
Pittsburgh Steelers
San Diego Chargers
Seattle Seahawks

BUFFALO BILLS
AFC Eastern Division

Address: One Bills Drive, Orchard Park, New York 14127
Telephone: (716) 648-1800

CLUB OFFICIALS
President: Ralph C. Wilson, Jr.
Executive Vice President: David N. Olsen
General Manager and Vice President-Administration: Bill Polian
Assistant General Manager: Bill Munson
Treasurer: Jeff Littmann
Vice President-Head Coach: Marv Levy
Director of College Scouting: John Butler
Director of Pro Personnel: Bob Ferguson
Director of Media Relations: Dave Senko
Director of Public and Community Relations: Denny Lynch
Director of Marketing and Sales: Jerry Foran
Ticket Director: TBA
Director of Stadium Operations and Security: Ed Stillwell
Manager of Stadium Operations and Engineering: Steve Champlin
Trainers: Ed Abramoski, Bud Carpenter
Equipment Manager: Dave Hojnowski
Assistant Equipment Manager: Randy Ribbeck
Strength and Conditioning Coordinator: Rusty Jones

Stadium: Rich Stadium (Capacity 80,290)
Playing Surface: AstroTurf
Stadium Address: One Bills Drive, Orchard Park, N.Y. 14127
Colours: Royal Blue, Scarlet Red and White
Summer Training Camp: Fredonia State University,
   Fredonia, N.Y. 14063

BUFFALO BILLS 1987 SCHEDULE

PRE-SEASON

Aug.	15	at Atlanta	8:00
Aug.	22	at L.A. Raiders	6:00
Aug.	29	at Kansas City	7:30
Sep.	4	at Miami	8:00

REGULAR SEASON

Sep.	13	NEW YORK JETS	1:00
Sep.	20	HOUSTON	1:00
Sep.	27	at Dallas	12:00
Oct.	4	INDIANAPOLIS	1:00
Oct.	11	at New England	1:00
Oct.	18	NEW YORK GIANTS	4:00
Oct.	25	at Miami	1:00
Nov.	1	WASHINGTON	1:00
Nov.	8	DENVER	1:00
Nov.	15	at Cleveland	1:00
Nov.	22	at New York Jets	1:00
Nov.	29	MIAMI	1:00
Dec.	6	at Los Angeles Raiders	1:00
Dec.	13	at Indianapolis	1:00
Dec.	20	NEW ENGLAND	1:00
Dec.	27	at Philadelphia	1:00

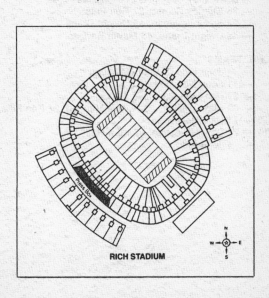

RICH STADIUM

BUFFALO BILLS
END OF SEASON DEPTH CHART

OFFENSE
WR	— 85 Chris Burkett, 86 Jimmy Teal, 82 Eric Richardson
OLT	— 72 Ken Jones, 65 Tim Vogler, 71 Dale Hellestrae
OLG	— 51 Jim Ritcher, 62 Mark Traynowicz
C	— 67 Kent Hull, 65 Tim Vogler
ORG	— 73 Will Wolford, 65 Tim Vogler
ORT	— 70 Joe Devlin, 71 Dale Hellestrae
TE	— 88 Pete Metzelaars, 87 Butch Rolle, 84 Don Kern
WR	— 83 Andre Reed, 85 Chris Burkett, 89 Steve Tasker
QB	— 12 Jim Kelly, 14 Frank Reich, 8 Stan Gelbaugh
F-B	— 49 Bruce King, 34 Gary Wilkins
RB	— 40 Robb Riddick, 28 Greg Bell, 33 Ronnie Harmon

DEFENSE
DLE	— 95 Sean McNanie, 79 Dean Prater
NT	— 76 Fred Smerlas, 74 Don Smith, 68 Kirt Ploeger
DRE	— 78 Bruce Smith, 75 Mike Hamby
ROLB	— 99 Hal Garner, 57 Lucius Sanford
ILB	— 54 Eugene Marve, 53 Tony Furjanic
ILB	— 50 Ray Bentley, 53 Tony Furjanic
LOLB	— 56 Darryl Talley, 99 Hal Garner
LC	— 36 Rodney Bellinger, 27 Ron Pitts
RC	— 26 Charles Romes, 27 Ron Pitts
FS	— 22 Steve Freeman, 45 Dwight Drane
SS	— 45 Dwight Drane, 43 Martin Bayless

SPECIAL TEAMS
P	— 4 John Kidd, 8 Stan Gelbaugh
K	— 11 Scott Norwood
PR	— 27 Ron Pitts, 89 Steve Tasker
KR	— 89 Steve Tasker, 33 Ronnie Harmon, 27 Ron Pitts
LSN(P)	— 71 Dale Hellestrae
LSN(F)	— 71 Dale Hellestrae, 67 Kent Hull
H	— 4 John Kidd

BUFFALO BILLS

INDIVIDUAL RUSHERS

	Att	Yards	Avg	Long	TD
Riddick, Robb	150	632	4.2	t41	4
Bell, Greg	90	377	4.2	42	4
Kelly, Jim	41	199	4.9	20	0
Harmon, Ronnie	54	172	3.2	38	0
Byrum, Carl	38	156	4.1	18	0
Moore, Ricky	33	104	3.2	14	1
Wilkins, Gary	3	18	6.0	11	0
King, Bruce	4	10	2.5	7	0
Kidd, John	1	0	0.0	0	0
Reich, Frank	1	0	0.0	0	0
Broughton, Walter	1	−6	−6.0	−6	0
Reed, Andre	3	−8	−2.7	4	0

INDIVIDUAL PASSING

	Att	Comp	Pct Comp	Yds	Avg Gain	TD	Pct TD	Long	Int	Pct Int	Rating Points
Kelly, Jim Buff.	480	285	59.4	3593	7.49	22	4.6	t84	17	3.5	83.3
Reich, Frank	19	9	47.4	104	5.47	0	0.0	37	2	10.5	24.8

INDIVIDUAL RECEIVERS

	No	Yards	Avg	Long	TD
Reed, Andre	53	739	13.9	t55	7
Metzelaars, Pete	49	485	9.9	t44	3
Riddick, Robb	49	468	9.6	t31	1
Burkett, Chris	34	778	22.9	t84	4
Moore, Ricky	23	184	8.0	27	0
Harmon, Ronnie	22	185	8.4	27	1
Butler, Jerry	15	302	20.1	53	2
Byrum, Carl	13	104	8.0	17	1
Bell, Greg	12	142	11.8	t40	2
Wilkins, Gary	8	74	9.3	26	0
Teal, Jimmy	6	60	10.0	20	1
Rolle, Butch	4	56	14.0	20	0
Broughton, Walter	3	71	23.7	57	0
Richardson, Eric	3	49	16.3	32	0

INDIVIDUAL INTERCEPTORS

	No	Yards	Avg	Long	TD
Romes, Charles	4	23	5.8	23	0
Burroughs, Derrick	2	49	24.5	41	0
Bellinger, Rodney	1	14	14.0	14	0
Smerlas, Fred	1	3	3.0	3	0
Bayless, Martin	1	0	0.0	0	0
Freeman, Steve	1	0	0.0	0	0

INDIVIDUAL KICKOFF RETURNERS

	No	Yards	Avg	Long	TD
Harmon, Ronnie	18	321	17.8	32	0
Tasker, Steve, Hou.-Buff.	12	213	17.8	24	0
Broughton, Walter	11	243	22.1	39	0
Riddick, Robb	8	200	25.0	49	0
Richardson, Eric	6	123	20.5	28	0
Bellinger, Rodney	2	32	16.0	16	0
Pitts, Ron	1	7	7.0	7	0

INDIVIDUAL PUNTERS

	No	Yards	Long	Avg	Total Punts	TB	Blk	Opp Ret	Ret Yds	In 20	Net Avg
Kidd, John	75	3031	57	40.4	75	9	0	32	260	14	34.5

INDIVIDUAL PUNT RETURNERS

	No	FC	Yards	Avg	Long	TD
Pitts, Ron	18	11	194	10.8	t49	1
Broughton, Walter	12	2	53	4.4	13	0
Hill, Rod	1	0	0	0.0	0	0
Richardson, Eric	1	0	0	0.0	0	0

INDIVIDUAL SCORERS

KICKERS	XP	XPA	FG	FGA	PTS
Norwood, Scott	32	34	17	27	83

NON-KICKERS	TD	TDR	TDP	TDM	PTS
Reed, Andre	7	0	7	0	42
Bell, Greg	6	4	2	0	36
Riddick, Robb	5	4	1	0	30
Burkett, Chris	4	0	4	0	24
Metzelaars, Pete	4	0	3	1	24
Butler, Jerry	2	0	2	0	12
Bellinger, Rodney	1	0	0	1	6
Byrum, Carl	1	0	1	0	6
Harmon, Ronnie	1	0	1	0	6
Moore, Ricky	1	1	0	0	6
Pitts, Ron	1	0	0	1	6
Teal, Jimmy	1	0	1	0	6

CINCINNATI BENGALS

AFC Central Division

Address: 200 Riverfront Stadium, Cincinnati, Ohio 45202
Telephone: (513) 621-3550

CLUB OFFICIALS
President: John Sawyer
General Manager: Paul E. Brown
Assistant General Manager: Michael Brown
Business Manager: Bill Connelly
Director of Public Relations: Allan Heim
Director of Player Personnel: Pete Brown
Accountant: Jay Reis
Ticket Manager: Paul Kelly
Consultant: John Murdough
Trainer: Marv Pollins
Equipment Manager: Tom Gray
Video Director: Al Davis

Stadium: Riverfront Stadium (Capacity 59,754)
Playing Surface: AstroTurf
Stadium Address: 200 Riverfront Stadium, Cincinnati, Ohio 45202
Colours: Black, Orange and White
Summer Training Camp: Wilmington College, Wilmington,
  Ohio 45177

CINCINNATI BENGALS 1987 SCHEDULE

PRE-SEASON

Aug.	15	at Tampa Bay	7:00
Aug.	22	at Detroit	8:00
Aug.	29	at Green Bay	7:00
Sep.	4	NEW ORLEANS	7:35

REGULAR SEASON

Sep.	13	at Indianapolis	12:00
Sep.	20	SAN FRANCISCO	1:00
Sep.	27	at Los Angeles Rams	1:00
Oct.	4	SAN DIEGO	1:00
Oct.	11	at Seattle	1:00
Oct.	18	CLEVELAND	1:00
Oct.	25	at Pittsburgh	1:00
Nov.	1	HOUSTON	1:00
Nov.	8	MIAMI	4:00
Nov.	15	at Atlanta	4:00
Nov.	22	PITTSBURGH	1:00
Nov.	29	at New York Jets	1:00
Dec.	6	KANSAS CITY	1:00
Dec.	13	at Cleveland	1:00
Dec.	20	NEW ORLEANS	1:00
Dec.	27	at Houston	12:00

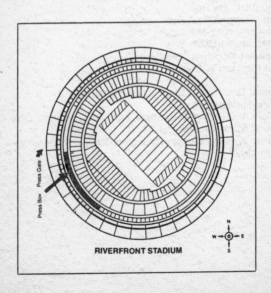

RIVERFRONT STADIUM

CINCINNATI BENGALS
END OF SEASON DEPTH CHART

OFFENSE

WR	— 80 Cris Collinsworth, 85 Tim McGee
OLT	— 78 Anthony Munoz, 63 Joe Walter
OLG	— 64 Bruce Kozerski, 75 Bruce Reimers, 74 Brian Blados
C	— 50 Dave Rimington, 64 Bruce Kozerski, 67 David Douglas
ORG	— 65 Max Montoya, 75 Bruce Reimers, 67 David Douglas
ORT	— 63 Joe Walter, 74 Brian Blados
TE	— 82 Rodney Holman, 84 Eric Kattus
WR	— 81 Eddie Brown, 86 Steve Kreider
QB	— 7 Boomer Esiason, 14 Ken Anderson, 11 Doug Gaynor
RB	— 21 James Brooks, 36 Stanford Jennings, 32 Stanley Wilson
F-B	— 32 Stanley Wilson, 28 Larry Kinnebrew, 30 Bill Johnson

DEFENSE

DLE	— 73 Eddie Edwards, 71 Mike Hammerstein
NT	— 69 Tim Krumrie, 71 Mike Hammerstein
DRE	— 79 Ross Browner, 70 Jim Skow
LOLB	— 90 Emanual King, 51 Leon White
LILB	— 91 Carl Zander, 56 Ron Simpkins, 55 Ed Brady
RILB	— 58 Joe Kelly, 53 Leo Barker
ROLB	— 57 Reggie Williams, 93 Kiki DeAyala
LCB	— 34 Louis Breeden, 20 Ray Horton
RCB	— 24 Lewis Billups, 20 Ray Horton
SS	— 33 David Fulcher, 27 Barney Bussey
FS	— 37 Robert Jackson, 26 Bobby Kemp

SPECIAL TEAMS

P	— 5 Jeff Hayes, 3 Jim Breech
K	— 3 Jim Breech
H	— 86 Steve Kreider, 14 Ken Anderson
KR	— 85 Tim McGee, 36 Stanford Jennings
PR	— 85 Tim McGee, 20 Ray Horton
LSN(P)	— 55 Ed Brady, 65 Max Montoya
LSN(F)	— 55 Ed Brady, 65 Max Montoya

CINCINNATI BENGALS

INDIVIDUAL RUSHERS

	Att	Yards	Avg	Long	TD
Brooks, James	205	1087	5.3	t56	5
Kinnebrew, Larry	131	519	4.0	39	8
Wilson, Stanley	68	379	5.6	t58	8
Johnson, Bill	39	226	5.8	34	0
Esiason, Boomer	44	146	3.3	23	1
Hayes, Jeff	3	92	30.7	t61	1
Jennings, Stanford	16	54	3.4	10	1
Brown, Eddie	8	32	4.0	17	0
McGee, Tim	4	10	2.5	8	0
Gaynor, Doug	1	4	4.0	4	0
Collinsworth, Cris	2	−16	−8.0	−6	0

INDIVIDUAL PASSING

	Att	Comp	Pct Comp	Yds	Avg Gain	TD	Pct TD	Long	Int	Pct Int	Rating Points
Esiason, Boomer	469	273	58.2	3959	8.44	24	5.1	57	17	3.6	87.7
Anderson, Ken	23	11	47.8	171	7.43	1	4.3	43	2	8.7	51.2
Brooks, James	1	0	0.0	0	0.00	0	0.0	0	0	0.0	39.6
Gaynor, Doug	3	3	100.0	30	10.00	0	0.0	16	0	0.0	108.3
Kreider, Steve	1	0	0.0	0	0.00	0	0.0	0	1	100.0	0.0

INDIVIDUAL RECEIVERS

	No	Yards	Avg	Long	TD
Collinsworth, Cris	62	1024	16.5	t46	10
Brown, Eddie	58	964	16.6	57	4
Brooks, James	54	686	12.7	54	4
Holman, Rodney	40	570	14.3	t34	2
McGee, Tim	16	276	17.3	51	1
Kinnebrew, Larry	13	136	10.5	31	1
Johnson, Bill	13	103	7.9	17	0
Kattus, Eric	11	99	9.0	28	1
Jennings, Stanford	6	86	14.3	34	0
Kreider, Steve	5	96	19.2	23	0
Wilson, Stanley	4	45	11.3	34	0
Martin, Mike	3	68	22.7	51	0
Munoz, Anthony	2	7	3.5	t5	2

INDIVIDUAL INTERCEPTORS

	No	Yards	Avg	Long	TD
Breeden, Louis	7	72	10.3	t36	1
Fulcher, David	4	20	5.0	15	0
Barker, Leo	2	7	3.5	7	0
Bussey, Barney	1	19	19.0	19	0
Zander, Carl	1	18	18.0	18	0
Kelly, Joe	1	6	6.0	6	0
Horton, Ray	1	4	4.0	4	0

INDIVIDUAL KICKOFF RETURNERS

	No	Yards	Avg	Long	TD
McGee, Tim	43	1007	23.4	94	0
Jennings, Stanford	12	257	21.4	41	0
Martin, Mike	4	83	20.8	21	0
Simpkins, Ron	2	24	12.0	15	0
Holman, Rodney	1	18	18.0	18	0
Simmons, John	1	0	0.0	0	0

INDIVIDUAL PUNTERS

	No	Yards	Long	Avg	Total Punts	TB	Blk	Opp Ret	Ret Yds	In 20	Net Avg
Hayes, Jeff	56	1965	52	35.1	58	3	2	19	182	11	29.7
Esiason, Boomer	1	31	31	31.0	1	0	0	0	0	1	31.0

INDIVIDUAL PUNT RETURNERS

	No	FC	Yards	Avg	Long	TD
Martin, Mike	13	6	96	7.4	14	0
Horton, Ray	11	3	111	10.1	25	0
McGee, Tim	3	4	21	7.0	9	0
Simmons, John	2	4	7	3.5	6	0

INDIVIDUAL SCORERS
KICKERS

	XP	XPA	FG	FGA	PTS
Breech, Jim	50	51	17	32	101

NON-KICKERS

	TD	TDR	TDP	TDM	PTS
Collinsworth, Cris	10	0	10	0	60
Brooks, James	9	5	4	0	54
Kinnebrew, Larry	9	8	1	0	54
Wilson, Stanley	8	8	0	0	48
Brown, Eddie	4	0	4	0	24
Holman, Rodney	2	0	2	0	12
Munoz, Anthony	2	0	2	0	12
Breeden, Louis	1	0	0	1	6
Edwards, Eddie	1	0	0	1	6
Esiason, Boomer	1	1	0	0	6
Hayes, Jeff	1	1	0	0	6
Jennings, Stanford	1	1	0	0	6
Kattus, Eric	1	0	1	0	6
McGee, Tim	1	0	1	0	6
White, Leon	0	0	0	0	*2

CLEVELAND BROWNS
AFC Central Division

Address: Tower B, Cleveland Stadium, Cleveland, Ohio 44114
Telephone: (216) 696-5555

CLUB OFFICIALS
President and Owner: Arthur B. Modell
Executive Vice President-Legal and Administrative: Jim Bailey
Executive Vice President-Football Operations: Ernie Accorsi
Vice President-Public Relations: Kevin Byrne
Vice President-Finance: Mike Poplar
Director of Player Personnel: Chip Falivene
Director of Player Relations: Ricky Feacher
Director of Marketing: David Modell
Director of Security: Ted Chappelle
Assistant Directors of Public Relations:
   Bob Eller, Francine Lubera
Area Scouts: Dom Anile, Tom Dimitroff, Tom Heckert, Tom Miner
Video Director: John Wuehrmann
Ticket Manager: Bill Breit
Head Trainer: Bill Tessendorf
Equipment Manager: Charley Cusick

Stadium: Cleveland Stadium (Capacity 80,098)
Playing Surface: Grass
Stadium Address: West 3rd Street, Cleveland, Ohio 44114
Colours: Seal Brown, Orange and White
Summer Training Camp: Lakeland Community College, Mentor,
   Ohio 44060

CLEVELAND BROWNS 1987 SCHEDULE

PRE-SEASON

Aug.	15	ST. LOUIS	7:30
Aug.	22	at New York Giants	8:00
Aug.	29	at Atlanta	8:00
Sep.	5	vs. Green Bay at Milwaukee	7:00

REGULAR SEASON

Sep.	13	at New Orleans	12:00
Sep.	20	PITTSBURGH	1:00
Sep.	28	DENVER	9:00
Oct.	4	at New England	1:00
Oct.	11	HOUSTON	1:00
Oct.	18	at Cincinnati	1:00
Oct.	26	LOS ANGELES RAMS	9:00
Nov.	1	at San Diego	1:00
Nov.	8	ATLANTA	1:00
Nov.	15	BUFFALO	1:00
Nov.	22	at Houston	12:00
Nov.	29	at San Francisco	5:00
Dec.	6	INDIANAPOLIS	1:00
Dec.	13	CINCINNATI	1:00
Dec.	20	at Los Angeles Raiders	1:00
Dec.	26	at Pittsburgh	12:30

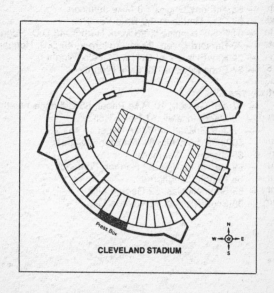

Press Box

CLEVELAND STADIUM

N W E S

CLEVELAND BROWNS
END OF SEASON DEPTH CHART

OFFENSE

WR	—	88 Reggie Langhorne, 85 Clarence Weathers, 80 Terry Greer
OLT	—	77 Rickey Bolden, 74 Paul Farren
OLG	—	74 Paul Farren, 70 Larry Williams, 62 George Lilja
C	—	61 Mike Baab, 62 George Lilja
ORG	—	69 Dan Fike, 62 George Lilja
ORT	—	63 Cody Risien, 74 Paul Farren
TE	—	82 Ozzie Newsome, 87 Travis Tucker, 81 Harry Holt
WR	—	84 Webster Slaughter, 86 Brian Brennan, 89 Gerald McNeil
QB	—	19 Bernie Kosar, 10 Mike Pagel, 7 Jeff Gossett
RB	—	33 Curtis Dickey, 28 Herman Fontenot
F-B	—	34 Kevin Mack, 39 Major Everett

DEFENSE

DLE	—	96 Reggie Camp, 91 Sam Clancy
NT	—	79 Bob Golic, 72 Dave Puzzuoli
DRE	—	78 Carl Hairston, 91 Sam Clancy, 90 Ralph Malone
LOLB	—	56 Chip Banks, 50 Brad Van Pelt
LILB	—	51 Eddie Johnson, 53 Anthony Griggs, 58 Scott Nicolas
RILB	—	53 Anthony Griggs, 59 Mike Johnson
ROLB	—	57 Clay Matthews, 50 Brad Van Pelt
LCB	—	31 Frank Minnifield, 23 Mark Harper, 48 D.D. Hoggard
RCB	—	29 Hanford Dixon, 23 Mark Harper, 48 D.D. Hoggard
SS	—	24 Ray Ellis, 27 Al Gross, 22 Felix Wright
FS	—	37 Chris Rockins, 22 Felix Wright

SPECIAL TEAMS

P	—	7 Jeff Gossett, 10 Mike Pagel, 85 Clarence Weathers
K	—	3 Mark Moseley, 81 Harry Holt
H	—	7 Jeff Gossett, 10 Mike Pagel
PR	—	89 Gerald McNeil, 84 Webster Slaughter, 85 Clarence Weathers
KR	—	89 Gerald McNeil, 28 Herman Fontenot, 88 Reggie Langhorne
LSN(P)	—	58 Scott Nicolas, 62 George Lilja
LSN(K)	—	58 Scott Nicolas, 62 George Lilja

CLEVELAND BROWNS

INDIVIDUAL RUSHERS

	Att	Yards	Avg	Long	TD
Mack, Kevin	174	665	3.8	20	10
Dickey, Curtis	135	523	3.9	47	6
Byner, Earnest	94	277	2.9	37	2
Fontenot, Herman	25	105	4.2	16	1
Everett, Major	12	43	3.6	8	0
Kosar, Bernie	24	19	0.8	17	0
Holt, Harry	1	16	16.0	t16	1
McNeil, Gerald	1	12	12.0	12	0
Slaughter, Webster	1	1	1.0	1	0
Pagel, Mike	2	0	0.0	0	0
Langhorne, Reggie	1	-11	-11.0	-11	0

INDIVIDUAL PASSING

	Att	Comp	Pct Comp	Yds	Avg Gain	TD	Pct TD	Long	Int	Pct Int	Rating Points
Kosar, Bernie	531	310	58.4	3854	7.26	17	3.2	t72	10	1.9	83.8
Brennan, Brian	1	1	100.0	35	35.00	0	0.0	35	0	0.0	118.8
Fontenot, Herman	1	1	100.0	46	46.00	1	100.0	t46	0	0.0	158.3
Gossett, Jeff	2	1	50.0	30	15.00	0	0.0	30	1	50.0	56.3
Pagel, Mike	3	2	66.7	53	17.67	0	0.0	45	0	0.0	109.7

INDIVIDUAL RECEIVERS

	No	Yards	Avg	Long	TD
Brennan, Brian	55	838	15.2	t57	6
Fontenot, Herman	47	559	11.9	t72	1
Slaughter, Webster	40	577	14.4	t47	4
Langhorne, Reggie	39	678	17.4	66	1
Newsome, Ozzie	39	417	10.7	31	3
Byner, Earnest	37	328	8.9	40	2
Mack, Kevin	28	292	10.4	44	0
Dickey, Curtis	10	78	7.8	12	0
Weathers, Clarence	9	100	11.1	16	0
Holt, Harry	4	61	15.3	34	1
Greer, Terry	3	51	17.0	22	0
Tucker, Travis	2	29	14.5	16	0
McNeil, Gerald	1	9	9.0	9	0
Kosar, Bernie	1	1	1.0	1	0

INDIVIDUAL INTERCEPTORS

	No	Yards	Avg	Long	TD
Dixon, Hanford	5	35	7.0	19	0
Wright, Felix	3	33	11.0	33	0
Minnifield, Frank	3	20	6.7	20	0
Rockins, Chris	2	41	20.5	24	0
Ellis, Ray	2	12	6.0	7	0

	No	Yards	Avg	Long	TD
Matthews, Clay	2	12	6.0	8	0
Harper, Mark	1	31	31.0	31	0

INDIVIDUAL KICKOFF RETURNERS

	No	Yards	Avg	Long	TD
McNeil, Gerald	47	997	21.2	t100	1
Fontenot, Herman	7	99	14.1	19	0
Langhorne, Reggie	4	57	14.3	20	0
Nicolas, Scott	3	28	9.3	13	0
Puzzuoli, Dave	1	32	32.0	32	0

INDIVIDUAL PUNTERS

	No	Yards	Long	Avg	Total Punts	TB	Blk	Opp Ret	Ret Yds	In 20	Net Avg
Gossett, Jeff	83	3423	61	41.2	83	10	0	44	268	21	35.6

INDIVIDUAL PUNT RETURNERS

	No	FC	Yards	Avg	Long	TD
McNeil, Gerald	40	10	348	8.7	t84	1
Slaughter, Webster	1	0	2	2.0	2	0

INDIVIDUAL SCORERS

KICKERS	XP	XPA	FG	FGA	PTS
Bahr, Matt	30	30	20	26	90
Moseley, Mark, Wash.-Clev.	25	28	12	19	61

NON-KICKERS	TD	TDR	TDP	TDM	PTS
Mack, Kevin	10	10	0	0	60
Brennan, Brian	7	0	6	1	42
Dickey, Curtis	6	6	0	0	36
Slaughter, Webster	5	0	4	1	30
Byner, Earnest	4	2	2	0	24
Newsome, Ozzie	3	0	3	0	18
Fontenot, Herman	2	1	1	0	12
Holt, Harry	2	1	1	0	12
McNeil, Gerald	2	0	0	2	12
Gross, Al	1	0	0	1	6
Langhorne, Reggie	1	0	1	0	6
Minnifield, Frank	1	0	0	1	6
Wright, Felix	1	0	0	1	6

DENVER BRONCOS
AFC Western Division

Address: 5700 Logan Street, Denver, Colorado 80216
Telephone: (303) 296-1982

CLUB OFFICIALS
President-Chief Executive Officer: Patrick D. Bowlen
Vice President-Head Coach: Dan Reeves
General Manager: John Beake
Chief Financial Officer and Treasurer: Robert M. Hurley
Director of Administration: Sandy Waters
Director of Player Personnel: Reed Johnson
Director of Pro Personnel: Carroll Hardy
Director of Media Relations: Jim Saccomano
Ticket Manager: Gail Stuckey
Marketing Director: Bill Harpole
Video Director: Rusty Nail
Director of Player and Community Relations: Charlie Lee
Equipment Manager: Dan Bill
Trainer: Steve Antonopulos

Stadium: Denver Mile High Stadium (Capacity 76,274)
Playing Surface: Grass (PAT)
Stadium Address: 1900 West Eliot, Denver, Colorado 80204
Colours: Orange, Royal Blue and White
Summer Training Camp: University of Northern Colorado,
Greeley, Colorado 80639

DENVER BRONCOS 1987 SCHEDULE

PRE-SEASON

Aug.	9	vs. L.A. Rams at Wembley, London	6:00
Aug.	15	vs. Green Bay at Tempe, Ariz.	7:00
Aug.	24	MIAMI..	6:00
Aug.	29	at Los Angeles Rams	7:00
Sep.	3	MINNESOTA	6:00

REGULAR SEASON

Sep.	13	SEATTLE..	2:00
Sep.	20	Green Bay at Milwaukee........................	12:00
Sep.	28	at Cleveland	9:00
Oct.	4	HOUSTON	2:00
Oct.	12	LOS ANGELES RAIDERS......................	7:00
Oct.	18	at Kansas City	3:00
Oct.	25	at Minnesota	12:00
Nov.	1	DETROIT..	2:00
Nov.	8	at Buffalo..	1:00
Nov.	16	CHICAGO	7:00
Nov.	22	at Los Angeles Raiders.........................	1:00
Nov.	29	at San Diego	1:00
Dec.	6	NEW ENGLAND	2:00
Dec.	13	at Seattle..	5:00
Dec.	19	KANSAS CITY	2:00
Dec.	27	SAN DIEGO...	2:00

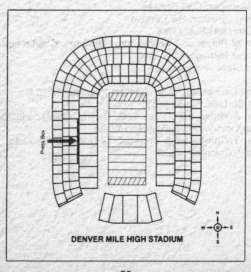

DENVER MILE HIGH STADIUM

DENVER BRONCOS
END OF SEASON DEPTH CHART

OFFENSE
```
WR    — 82 Vance Johnson, 80 Mark Jackson
OLT   — 70 Dave Studdard, 74 Dan Remsberg
OLG   — 54 Keith Bishop, 63 Mark Cooper, 62 Mike Freeman
C     — 64 Billy Bryan, 54 Keith Bishop, 62 Mike Freeman
ORG   — 63 Mark Cooper, 62 Mike Freeman
ORT   — 76 Ken Lanier, 74 Dan Remsberg
TE    — 89 Orson Mobley, 85 Joey Hackett, 87 Bobby Micho
WR    — 81 Steve Watson, 84 Clint Sampson, 30 Steve Sewell
QB    —  7 John Elway, 8 Gary Kubiak
RB    — 23 Sammy Winder, 35 Ken Bell, 30 Steve Sewell
RB    — 47 Gerald Willhite, 33 Gene Lang
```

DEFENSE
```
DLE   — 75 Rulon Jones, 90 Freddie Gilbert
NT    — 71 Greg Kragen, 69 Tony Colorito
DRE   — 61 Andre Townsend, 73 Simon Fletcher
LOLB  — 50 Jim Ryan, 59 Darren Comeaux
LILB  — 77 Karl Mecklenburg, 55 Rick Dennison
RILB  — 98 Ricky Hunley, 55 Rick Dennison
ROLB  — 57 Tom Jackson, 52 Ken Woodard
LCB   — 20 Louis Wright, 45 Steve Wilson
RCB   — 31 Mike Harden, 36 Mark Haynes
SS    — 49 Dennis Smith, 48 Randy Robbins
FS    — 43 Steve Foley, 22 Tony Lilly
```

SPECIAL TEAMS
```
K     —  3 Rich Karlis
P     —  2 Mike Horan
H     —  8 Gary Kubiak, 2 Mike Horan
KR    — 33 Gene Lang, 35 Ken Bell, 80 Mark Jackson
PR    — 47 Gerald Willhite, 82 Vance Johnson
LSN   — 54 Keith Bishop, 64 Billy Bryan
```

DENVER BRONCOS

INDIVIDUAL RUSHERS

	Att	Yards	Avg	Long	TD
Winder, Sammy	240	789	3.3	31	9
Willhite, Gerald	85	365	4.3	42	5
Elway, John	52	257	4.9	24	1
Sewell, Steve	23	123	5.3	15	1
Lang, Gene	29	94	3.2	14	1
Kubiak, Gary	6	22	3.7	10	0
Bell, Ken	9	17	1.9	12	0
Johnson, Vance	5	15	3.0	6	0
Jackson, Mark	2	6	3.0	5	0
Boddie, Tony	1	2	2.0	2	0
Horan, Mike	1	0	0.0	0	0
Mobley, Orson	1	-1	-1.0	-1	0
Norman, Chris	1	-11	-11.0	-11	0

INDIVIDUAL PASSING

	Att	Comp	Pct Comp	Yds	Avg Gain	TD	Pct TD	Long	Int	Pct Int	Rating Points
Elway, John	504	280	55.6	3485	6.91	19	3.8	53	13	2.6	79.0
Kubiak, Gary	38	23	60.5	249	6.55	1	2.6	26	3	7.9	55.7
Johnson, Vance	1	0	0.0	0	0.00	0	0.0	0	0	0.0	39.6
Norman, Chris	1	1	100.0	43	43.00	1	100.0	t43	0	0.0	158.3
Sewell, Steve	1	1	100.0	23	23.00	1	100.0	t23	0	0.0	158.3
Willhite, Gerald	41	1	25.0	11	2.75	0	0.0	11	0	0.0	39.6

INDIVIDUAL RECEIVERS

	No	Yards	Avg	Long	TD
Willhite, Gerald	64	529	8.3	31	3
Watson, Steve	45	699	15.5	46	3
Jackson, Mark	38	738	19.4	53	1
Johnson, Vance	31	363	11.7	t34	2
Winder, Sammy	26	171	6.6	t20	5
Sewell, Steve	23	294	12.8	40	1
Mobley, Orson	22	332	15.1	32	1
Sampson, Clinton	21	259	12.3	43	0
Kay, Clarence	15	195	13.0	34	1
Lang, Gene	13	105	8.1	26	2
Hackett, Joey	3	48	16.0	19	0
Bell, Ken	2	10	5.0	7	0
Wilson, Steve	1	43	43.0	t43	1
Elway, John	1	23	23.0	t23	1
Studdard, Dave	1	2	2.0	t2	1

INDIVIDUAL INTERCEPTORS

	No	Yards	Avg	Long	TD
Harden, Mike	6	179	29.8	52	2
Wright, Louis	3	56	18.7	56	0
Lilly, Tony	3	22	7.3	15	0

Foley, Steve	2	39	19.5	24	0
Hunley, Ricky	1	22	22.0	22	0
Dennison, Rick	1	5	5.0	5	0
Smith, Dennis	1	0	0.0	0	0
Wilson, Steve	1	−5	−5.0	−5	0

INDIVIDUAL KICKOFF RETURNERS

	No	Yards	Avg	Long	TD
Bell, Ken	23	531	23.1	42	0
Lang, Gene	21	480	22.9	42	0
Willhite, Gerald	3	35	11.7	23	0
Johnson, Vance	2	21	10.5	21	0
Hunley, Ricky	2	11	5.5	6	0
Jackson, Mark	1	16	16.0	16	0
Ryan, Jim	1	0	0.0	0	0

INDIVIDUAL PUNTERS

	No	Yards	Long	Avg	Total Punts	TB	Blk	Opp Ret	Ret Yds	In 20	Net Avg
Weil, Jack	34	1344	55	39.5	34	3	0	20	169	5	32.8
Norman, Chris	30	1168	57	38.9	31	4	1	9	94	2	32.1
Horan, Mike	21	864	50	41.1	21	2	0	11	99	8	34.5

INDIVIDUAL PUNT RETURNERS

	No	FC	Yards	Avg	Long	TD
Willhite, Gerald	42	8	468	11.1	t70	1
Johnson, Vance	3	0	36	12.0	19	0
Jackson, Mark	2	0	7	3.5	6	0
Harden, Mike	1	0	41	41.0	t41	1

INDIVIDUAL SCORERS

KICKERS	XP	XPA	FG	FGA	PTS
Karlis, Rich	44	45	20	28	104

NON-KICKERS	TD	TDR	TDP	TDM	PTS
Winder, Sammy	14	9	5	0	84
Willhite, Gerald	9	5	3	1	54
Harden, Mike	3	0	0	3	18
Lang, Gene	3	1	2	0	18
Watson, Steve	3	0	3	0	18
Elway, John	2	1	1	0	12
Johnson, Vance	2	0	2	0	12
Sewell, Steve	2	1	1	0	12
Jackson, Mark	1	0	1	0	6
Kay, Clarence	1	0	1	0	6
Mobley, Orson	1	0	1	0	6
Studdard, Dave	1	0	1	0	6
Townsend, Andre	1	0	0	1	6
Wilson, Steve	1	0	1	0	6
Woodard, Ken	1	0	0	1	6
Jones, Rulon	0	0	0	0	*2

HOUSTON OILERS
AFC Central Division

Address: PO Box 1516, Houston, Texas 77001
Telephone: (713) 797-9111

CLUB OFFICIALS
President: K.S. 'Bud' Adams, Jr.
Executive Vice President-General Manager: Ladd K. Herzeg
Vice President-Player Personnel: Mike Holovak
Director of Administration: Rick Nichols
Director of Media Relations: Chip Namias
Director of Public Relations: Gregg Stengel
Ticket Manager: Mike Mullis
Head Trainer: Brad Brown
Assistant Trainer: Don Moseley
Equipment Manager: Gordon Batty

Stadium: Astrodome (Capacity 50,599)
Playing Surface: AstroTurf
Stadium Address: Loop 610, Kirby and Fannin Streets, Houston,
Texas 77054
Colours: Columbia Blue, Scarlet and White
Summer Training Camp: Angelo State University, San Angelo,
Texas 76901

HOUSTON OILERS 1987 SCHEDULE

PRE-SEASON

Aug.	13	KANSAS CITY	7:00
Aug.	22	at New Orleans	7:00
Aug.	29	at Indianapolis	7:30
Sep.	5	at Dallas	8:00

REGULAR SEASON

Sep.	13	LOS ANGELES RAMS	12:00
Sep.	20	at Buffalo	1:00
Sep.	27	LOS ANGELES RAIDERS	12:00
Oct.	4	at Denver	2:00
Oct.	11	at Cleveland	1:00
Oct.	18	NEW ENGLAND	12:00
Oct.	25	ATLANTA	12:00
Nov.	1	at Cincinnati	1:00
Nov.	8	at San Francisco	1:00
Nov.	15	at Pittsburgh	1:00
Nov.	22	CLEVELAND	12:00
Nov.	29	at Indianapolis	1:00
Dec.	6	SAN DIEGO	12:00
Dec.	13	at New Orleans	12:00
Dec.	20	PITTSBURGH	12:00
Dec.	27	CINCINNATI	12:00

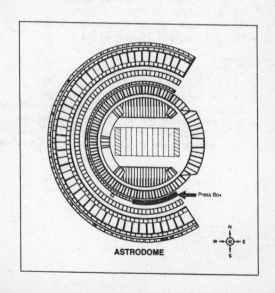

ASTRODOME

HOUSTON OILERS
END OF SEASON DEPTH CHART

OFFENSE

WR — 85 Drew Hill, 82 Willie Drewrey, 86 Mike Aklu
OLT — 74 Bruce Matthews, 78 Don Maggs, 76 Eric Moran
OLG — 78 Don Maggs, 52 Jay Pennison, 76 Eric Moran
C   — 52 Jay Pennison, 74 Bruce Matthews, 55 Jim Romane
ORG — 72 Kent Hill, 76 Eric Morgan, 69 Doug Williams
ORT — 70 Dean Steinkuhler, 78 Don Maggs, 76 Eric Moran
TE — 87 Jamie Williams, 88 Chris Dressel
WR — 81 Ernest Givins, 83 Tim Smith, 86 Mike Aklu
QB — 1 Warren Moon, 10 Oliver Luck, 12 John Witkowski
RB — 20 Allen Pinkett, 32 Stan Edwards
F-B — 38 Chuck Banks, 39 Hubert Oliver

DEFENSE

LE   — 79 Ray Childress, 75 Jesse Baker, 98 Lynn Madson
NT   — 68 Mike Golic, 67 Karl Morgan, 69 Doug Williams
RE   — 71 Richard Byrd, 95 William Fuller, 75 Jesse Baker
LLB — 93 Robert Lyles, 51 Eric Fairs
LILB — 59 John Grimsley, 53 Avon Riley, 50 Kirk Dodge
RILB — 56 Robert Abraham, 53 Avon Riley, 50 Kirk Dodge
RLB — 91 Johnny Meads, 51 Eric Fairs
LCB — 24 Steve Brown, 26 Audrey McMillan
RCB — 29 Patrick Allen, 23 Richard Johnson
SS   — 25 Keith Bostic, 31 Jeff Donaldson, 28 Allen Lyday
FS   — 31 Jeff Donaldson, 28 Allen Lyday

SPECIAL TEAMS

K   — 7 Tony Zendejas, 11 Lee Johnson
P   — 11 Lee Johnson, 83 Tim Smith
H   — 11 Lee Johnson, 12 John Witkowski
PR   — 82 Willie Drewrey, 81 Ernest Givins, 20 Allen Pinkett
KR   — 82 Willie Drewrey, 20 Allen Pinkett, 86 Mike Aklu
LSN(P) — 74 Bruce Matthews, 52 Jay Pennison, 55 Jim Romane
LSN(F) — 74 Bruce matthews, 52 Jay Pennison, 55 Jim Romane

HOUSTON OILERS

INDIVIDUAL RUSHERS

	Att	Yards	Avg	Long	TD
Rozier, Mike	199	662	3.3	t19	4
Pinkett, Allen	77	225	2.9	14	2
Wallace, Ray	52	218	4.2	19	3
Moon, Warren	42	157	3.7	19	2
Givins, Earnest	9	148	16.4	t43	1
Banks, Chuck	29	80	2.8	9	0
Woolfolk, Butch	23	57	2.5	15	0
Luck, Oliver	2	12	6.0	8	0
Edwards, Stan	1	3	3.0	3	0
Oliver, Hubert	1	1	1.0	1	0

INDIVIDUAL PASSING

	Att	Comp	Pct Comp	Yds	Avg Gain	TD	Pct TD	Long	Int	Pct Int	Rating Points
Moon, Warren	488	256	52.5	3489	7.15	13	2.7	t81	26	5.3	62.3
Luck, Oliver	60	31	51.7	341	5.68	1	1.7	27	5	8.3	39.7
Givins, Earnest	2	0	0.0	0	0.00	0	0.0	0	0	0.0	39.6
Rozier, Mike	1	1	100.0	13	13.00	0	0.0	13	0	0.0	118.8

INDIVIDUAL RECEIVERS

	No	Yards	Avg	Long	TD
Hill, Drew	65	1112	17.1	t81	5
Givins, Earnest	61	1062	17.4	60	3
Pinkett, Allen	35	248	7.1	20	1
Woolfolk, Butch	28	314	11.2	30	2
Rozier, Mike	24	180	7.5	23	0
Williams, Jamie	22	227	10.3	33	1
Drewrey, Willie	18	299	16.6	31	0
Wallace, Ray	17	177	10.4	t35	2
Banks, Chuck	7	71	10.1	17	0
Smith, Tim	4	72	18.0	25	0
Akiu, Mike	4	67	16.8	27	0
Oliver, Hubert	1	-2	-2.0	-2	0

INDIVIDUAL INTERCEPTORS

	No	Yards	Avg	Long	TD
Lyday, Allen	3	24	8.0	24	0
Allen, Patrick	3	20	6.7	18	0
Brown, Steve	2	34	17.0	38	0
Eason, Bo	2	16	8.0	11	0
Johnson, Richard	2	6	3.0	6	0
Lyles, Robert	2	0	0.0	0	0
Bostic, Keith	1	0	0.0	0	0
Donaldson, Jeff	1	0	0.0	0	0

INDIVIDUAL KICKOFF RETURNERS

	No	Yards	Avg	Long	TD
Drewrey, Willie	25	500	20.0	32	0
Pinkett, Allen	26	519	20.0	48	0
Woolfolk, Butch	2	38	19.0	21	0
Riley, Avon	2	17	8.5	10	0
Madsen, Lynn	1	0	0.0	0	0

INDIVIDUAL PUNTERS

	No	Yards	Long	Avg	Total Punts	TB	Blk	Opp Ret	Ret Yds	In 20	Net Avg
Johnson, Lee	88	3623	66	41.2	88	9	0	40	303	26	35.7
Zendejas, Tony	1	36	36	36.0	1	0	0	0	0	1	36.0

INDIVIDUAL PUNT RETURNERS

	No	FC	Yards	Avg	Long	TD
Drewrey, Willie	34	13	262	7.7	25	0
Givins, Earnest	8	0	80	10.0	17	0
Pinkett, Allen	1	2	-1	-1.0	-1	0

INDIVIDUAL SCORERS

KICKERS	XP	XPA	FG	FGA	PTS
Zendejas, Tony	28	29	22	27	94

NON-KICKERS	TD	TDR	TDP	TDM	PTS
Hill, Drew	5	0	5	0	30
Wallace, Ray	5	3	2	0	30
Givins, Earnest	4	1	3	0	24
Rozier, Mike	4	4	0	0	24
Pinkett, Allen	3	2	1	0	18
Moon, Warren	2	2	0	0	12
Woolfolk, Butch	2	0	2	0	12
Donaldson, Jeff	1	0	0	1	6
Lyles, Robert	1	0	0	1	6
Moriarty, Larry	1	1	0	0	6
Munchak, Mike	1	0	0	1	6
Williams, Jamie	1	0	1	0	6

INDIANAPOLIS COLTS
AFC Eastern Division

Address: PO Box 24100, Indianapolis, Indiana 46224-0100
Telephone: (317) 297-2658

CLUB OFFICIALS
President-Treasurer: Robert Irsay
Vice President-General Manager: James Irsay
Vice President-General Counsel: Michael G. Chernoff
Assistant General Manager: Bob Terpening
Director of Player Personnel: Jack Bushofsky
Director of Pro Personnel: Clyde Powers
Controller: Kurt Humphrey
Director of Operations: Pete Ward
Director of Public Relations: Craig Kelley
Ticket Manager: Larry Hall
Public Relations Assistant: Anne Phillips
Purchasing Administrator: David Filar
Equipment Manager: Jon Scott
Assistant Equipment Manager: Chris Matlock
Video Director: Marty Heckscher
Assistant Video Director: John Starliper
Head Trainer: Hunter Smith
Assistant Trainer: Dave Hammer

Stadium: Hoosier Dome (Capacity 60,127)
Playing Surface: AstroTurf
Stadium Address: 100 South Capitol Avenue, Indianapolis,
Indiana 46225
Colours: Royal Blue, White and Silver
Summer Training Camp: Anderson College, Anderson,
Indiana 46011

INDIANAPOLIS COLTS 1987 SCHEDULE

PRE-SEASON

Aug.	15	at Detroit	8:00
Aug.	22	at Minnesota	7:00
Aug.	29	HOUSTON	7:30
Sep.	5	TAMPA BAY	7:30

REGULAR SEASON

Sep.	13	CINCINNATI	12:00
Sep.	20	MIAMI	12:00
Sep.	27	at St. Louis	12:00
Oct.	4	at Buffalo	1:00
Oct.	11	NEW YORK JETS	12:00
Oct.	18	at Pittsburgh	1:00
Oct.	25	NEW ENGLAND	1:00
Nov.	1	at New York Jets	1:00
Nov.	8	SAN DIEGO	1:00
Nov.	15	at Miami	1:00
Nov.	22	at New England	1:00
Nov.	29	HOUSTON	1:00
Dec.	6	at Cleveland	1:00
Dec.	13	BUFFALO	1:00
Dec.	20	at San Diego	1:00
Dec.	27	TAMPA BAY	1:00

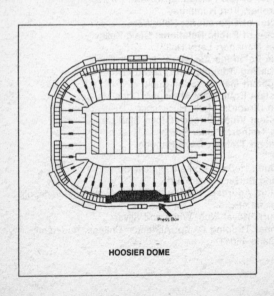

HOOSIER DOME

INDIANAPOLIS COLTS
END OF SEASON DEPTH CHART

OFFENSE

WR	—	85 Matt Bouza, 86 Walter Murray
OLT	—	75 Chris Hinton, 71 Kevin Call, 74 Bob Brotzki
OLG	—	63 Mark Kirchner, 67 Roger Caron
C	—	53 Ray Donaldson, 63 Mark Kirchner
ORG	—	66 Ron Solt, 63 Mark Kirchner, 67 Roger Caron
ORT	—	71 Kevin Call, 72 Karl Baldischwiler, 74 Bob Brotzki
TE	—	81 Pat Beach, 84 Mark Boyer, 83 Tim Sherwin
WR	—	80 Bill Brooks, 87 James Harbour
QB	—	7 Gary Hogeboom, 10 Jack Trudeau, 5 Blair Kiel
F-B	—	32 Randy McMillan, 44 Owen Gill
H-B	—	34 George Wonsley, 20 Albert Bentley

DEFENSE

DLE	—	99 Donnell Thompson, 79 Harvey Armstrong
NT	—	94 Scott Kellar, 68 Willie Broughton
DRE	—	78 Jon Hand, 79 Harvey Armstrong, 90 John Haines
LOLB	—	98 Johnie Cooks, 59 Orlando Lowry
LILB	—	93 Cliff Odom, 57 Dave Ahrens
RILB	—	57 Dave Ahrens, 92 Jeff Leiding, 58 Glen Redd
ROLB	—	50 Duane Bickett, 59 Orlando Lowry
LCB	—	31 Leonard Coleman, 21 John Holt, 23 Kenny Daniel
RCB	—	38 Eugene Daniel, 21 John Holt, 23 Kenny Daniel
SS	—	25 Nesby Glasgow, 40 Pat Ballage
FS	—	29 Dwight Hicks, 35 Tate Randle, 23 Kenny Daniel

SPECIAL TEAMS

P	—	3 Rohn Stark, 5 Blair Kiel, 4 Dean Biasucci
K	—	4 Dean Biasucci, 57 Dave Ahrens
H	—	3 Rohn Stark, 5 Blair Kiel
PR	—	80 Bill Brooks, 38 Eugene Daniel
KR	—	20 Albert Bentley, 44 Owen Gill, 23 Kenny Daniel
LSN(P)	—	81 Pat Beach, 72 Karl Baldischwiler
LSN(K)	—	53 Ray Donaldson, 72 Karl Baldischwiler

INDIANAPOLIS COLTS

INDIVIDUAL RUSHERS

	Att	Yards	Avg	Long	TD
McMillan, Randy	189	609	3.2	28	3
Bentley, Albert	73	351	4.8	t70	3
Gill, Owen	53	228	4.3	18	1
Wonsley, George	60	214	3.6	46	1
Trudeau, Jack	13	21	1.6	8	1
Hogeboom, Gary	10	20	2.0	6	1
Kiel, Blair	3	20	6.7	9	0
Bouza, Matt	1	12	12.0	12	0
Capers, Wayne	1	11	11.0	11	0
Brooks, Bill	4	5	1.3	12	0

INDIVIDUAL PASSING

	Att	Comp	Pct Comp	Yds	Avg Gain	TD	Pct TD	Long	Int	Pct Int	Rating Points
Trudeau, Jack	417	204	48.9	2225	5.34	8	1.9	t84	18	4.3	53.5
Kiel, Blair	25	11	44.0	236	9.44	2	8.0	50	0	0.0	104.8
Hogeboom, Gary	144	85	59.0	1154	8.01	6	4.2	60	6	4.2	81.2
Bentley, Albert	0	0	—	0	—	0	—	0	0	—	0.0

INDIVIDUAL RECEIVERS

	No	Yards	Avg	Long	TD
Bouza, Matt	71	830	11.7	33	5
Brooks, Bill	65	1131	17.4	t84	8
McMillan, Randy	34	289	8.5	45	0
Beach, Pat	25	265	10.6	26	1
Bentley, Albert	25	230	9.2	38	0
Boyer, Mark	22	237	10.8	38	1
Wonsley, George	16	175	10.9	60	0
Gill, Owen	16	137	8.6	15	0
Capers, Wayne	9	118	13.1	27	0
LaFleur, Greg	7	56	8.0	11	0
Harbour, James	4	46	11.5	28	0
Sherwin, Tim	3	26	8.7	15	1
Murray, Walter	2	34	17.0	24	0
Martin, Robbie	1	41	41.0	41	0

INDIVIDUAL INTERCEPTORS

	No	Yards	Avg	Long	TD
Coleman, Leonard	4	36	9.0	31	0
Daniel, Eugene	3	11	3.7	5	0
Hicks, Dwight	2	16	8.0	16	0
Bickett, Duane	2	10	5.0	10	0

	No	Yards	Avg	Long	TD
Holt, John	1	80	80.0	80	0
Hand, Jon	1	8	8.0	8	0
Armstrong, Harvey	1	4	4.0	4	0
Cooks, Johnie	1	1	1.0	1	0
Daniel, Kenny	1	0	0.0	0	0

INDIVIDUAL KICKOFF RETURNERS

	No	Yards	Avg	Long	TD
Bentley, Albert	32	687	21.5	37	0
Martin, Robbie	21	385	18.3	27	0
Brooks, Bill	8	143	17.9	24	0
Daniel, Kenny	5	109	21.8	30	0
Gill, Owen	5	73	14.6	28	0
Wonsley, George	2	31	15.5	20	0
Williams, Oliver	1	15	15.0	15	0

INDIVIDUAL PUNTERS

	No	Yards	Long	Avg	Total Punts	TB	Blk	Opp Ret	Ret Yds	In 20	Net Avg
Stark, Rohn	76	3432	63	45.2	76	5	0	48	502	22	37.2
Kiel, Blair	5	190	43	38.0	5	0	0	4	31	0	31.8

INDIVIDUAL PUNT RETURNERS

	No	FC	Yards	Avg	Long	TD
Brooks, Bill	18	7	141	7.8	18	0
Martin, Robbie	17	5	109	6.4	25	0
Jackson, Victor	0	1	0	—	0	0

INDIVIDUAL SCORERS

KICKERS	XP	XPA	FG	FGA	PTS
Biasucci, Dean	26	27	13	25	65

NON-KICKERS	TD	TDR	TDP	TDM	PTS
Brooks, Bill	8	0	8	0	48
Bouza, Matt	5	0	5	0	30
Bentley, Albert	3	3	0	0	18
McMillan, Randy	3	3	0	0	18
Beach, Pat	1	0	1	0	6
Boyer, Mark	1	0	1	0	6
Daniel, Eugene	1	0	0	1	6
Gill, Owen	1	1	0	0	6
Hogeboom, Gary	1	1	0	0	6
Sherwin, Tim	1	0	1	0	6
Trudeau, Jack	1	1	0	0	6
Wonsley, George	1	1	0	0	6
Leiding, Jeff	0	0	0	0	*2

KANSAS CITY CHIEFS
AFC Western Division

Address: One Arrowhead Drive, Kansas City, Missouri 64129
Telephone: (816) 924-9300

CLUB OFFICIALS
Owner: Lamar Hunt
President: Jack Steadman
Vice President-General Manager: Jim Schaaf
Assistant to General Manager: Dennis Thum
Vice President-Administration: Don Steadman
Treasurer: Bob Tamasi
Secretary: Jim Seigfreid
College Personnel Director: Les Miller
Director of Public Relations and Community Relations:
  Gary Heise
Community Relations Manager: Brenda Boatright
Director of Sales and Promotions: Mitch Wheeler
Director of Marketing: Ken Blume
Manager of Ticket Operations: Phil Youtsey
Stadium Operations: Bob Wachter
Trainer: Dave Kendall
Equipment Coordinator: Jon Phillips
Video Coordinator: Mike Dennis

Stadium: Arrowhead Stadium (Capacity: 78,067)
Playing Surface: AstroTurf-8
Stadium Address: One Arrowhead Drive, Kansas City,
  Missouri 64129
Colours: Red, Gold and White
Summer Training Camp: William Jewell College, Liberty,
  Missouri 64068

KANSAS CITY CHIEFS 1987 SCHEDULE

PRE-SEASON

Aug.	8	vs. San Francisco (Hall of Fame Game).	12:00
Aug.	13	at Houston	7:00
Aug.	22	ATLANTA	7:30
Aug.	29	BUFFALO	7:30
Sep.	6	vs. St. Louis at Memphis, Tenn.	1:30

REGULAR SEASON

Sep.	13	SAN DIEGO	12:00
Sep.	20	at Seattle	1:00
Sep.	27	MINNESOTA	12:00
Oct.	4	at Los Angeles Raiders	1:00
Oct.	11	at Miami	1:00
Oct.	18	DENVER	3:00
Oct.	25	at San Diego	1:00
Nov.	1	at Chicago	12:00
Nov.	8	PITTSBURGH	12:00
Nov.	15	NEW YORK JETS	12:00
Nov.	22	GREEN BAY	12:00
Nov.	26	at Detroit	12:30
Dec.	6	at Cincinnati	1:00
Dec.	13	LOS ANGELES RAIDERS	3:00
Dec.	19	at Denver	2:00
Dec.	27	SEATTLE	12:00

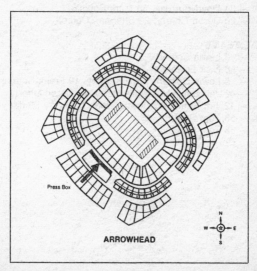

Press Box

ARROWHEAD

KANSAS CITY CHIEFS
END OF SEASON DEPTH CHART

OFFENSE

WR	— 89 Henry Marshall, 86 Emile Harry, 88 Carlos Carson
OLT	— 75 Irv Eatman, 76 John Alt, 73 Brian Jozwiak
OLG	— 71 Brad Budde, 73 Brian Jozwiak, 77 Rich Baldinger
C	— 51 Rick Donnalley, 58 Tom Baugh
ORG	— 61 Mark Adickes, 73 Brian Jozwiak, 77 Rich Balinger
ORT	— 72 David Lutz, 77 Rich Baldinger, 76 John Alt
TE	— 87 Walt Arnold, 85 Jonathan Hayes, 84 Paul Coffman
WR	— 83 Stephone Paige, 89 Henry Marshall, 88 Carlos Carson
QB	— 9 Bill Kenney, 14 Todd Blackledge, 10 Frank Seurer
RB	— 40 Boyce Green, 44 Herman Heard, 42 Jeff Smith
F-B	— 43 Mike Pruitt, 32 Larry Moriarty, 40 Boyce Green

DEFENSE

DLE	— 67 Art Still, 98 Leonard Griffin, 93 Eric Holle
NT	— 63 Bill Mass, 93 Eric Holle, 74 Pete Koch
DRE	— 74 Pete Koch, 70 Kit Lathrop, 98 Leonard Griffin
LOLB	— 55 Louis Cooper, 57 Whitney Paul
LILB	— 56 Dino Hackett, 96 Aaron Pearson
RILB	— 59 Gary Spani, 97 Scott Radecic
ROLB	— 54 Tim Cofield, 57 Whitney Paul, 96 Aaron Pearson
LCB	— 29 Albert Lewis, 22 Sherman Cocroft
RCB	— 31 Kevin Ross, 24 J.C. Pearson
SS	— 34 Lloyd Burruss, 30 Mark Robison
FS	— 20 Deron Cherry, 22 Sherman Cocroft

SPECIAL TEAMS

P	— 5 Lewis Colbert
K	— 8 Nick Lowery
H	— 5 Lewis Colbert, 9 Bill Kenney, 10 Frank Seurer
PR	— 42 Jeff Smith, 86 Emile Harry, 20 Deron Cherry
KR	— 42 Jeff Smith, 40 Boyce Green, 32 Larry Moriarty
LSN(P)	— 58 Tom Baugh
LSN(F)	— 58 Tom Baugh

KANSAS CITY CHIEFS

INDIVIDUAL RUSHERS

	Att	Yards	Avg	Long	TD
Pruitt, Mike	139	448	3.2	16	2
Green, Boyce	90	314	3.5	27	3
Heard, Herman	71	295	4.2	40	2
Moriarty, Larry, Hou.-K.C.	90	252	2.8	11	1
Smith, Jeff	54	238	4.4	t32	3
Blackledge, Todd	23	60	2.6	14	0
Kenney, Bill	18	0	0.0	9	0
Paige, Stephone	2	−2	−1.0	12	0

INDIVIDUAL PASSING

	Att	Comp	Pct Comp	Yds	Avg Gain	TD	Pct TD	Long	Int	Pct Int	Rating Points
Kenney, Bill	308	161	52.3	1922	6.24	13	4.2	53	11	3.6	70.8
Blackledge, Todd	211	96	45.5	1200	5.69	10	4.7	t70	6	2.8	67.6
Green, Boyce	1	0	0.0	0	0.00	0	0.0	0	1	100.0	0.0
Marshall, Henry	1	0	0.0	0	0.00	0	0.0	0	0	0.0	39.6

INDIVIDUAL RECEIVERS

	No	Yards	Avg	Long	TD
Paige, Stephone	52	829	15.9	51	11
Marshall, Henry	46	652	14.2	31	1
Smith, Jeff	33	230	7.0	18	3
Carson, Carlos	21	497	23.7	t70	4
Arnold, Walt	20	169	8.5	27	1
Green, Boyce	19	137	7.2	17	0
Heard, Herman	17	83	4.9	13	0
Coffman, Paul	12	75	6.3	10	2
Harry, Emile	9	211	23.4	53	1
Moriarty, Larry, Hou.-K.C.	9	67	7.4	19	0
Hayes, Jonathan	8	69	8.6	16	0
Pruitt, Mike	8	56	7.0	13	0
Hancock, Anthony	4	63	15.8	25	0
Kenney, Bill	1	0	0.0	0	0

INDIVIDUAL INTERCEPTORS

	No	Yards	Avg	Long	TD
Cherry, Deron	9	150	16.7	49	0
Burruss, Lloyd	5	193	38.6	t72	3
Ross, Kevin	4	66	16.5	35	0
Lewis, Albert	4	18	4.5	13	0
Hill, Greg	3	64	21.3	t26	1
Cocroft, Sherman	3	32	10.7	13	0
Spani, Gary	1	24	24.0	24	0
Radecic, Scott	1	20	20.0	20	0
Hackett, Dino	1	0	0.0	0	0

INDIVIDUAL KICKOFF RETURNERS

	No	Yards	Avg	Long	TD
Smith, Jeff	29	557	19.2	29	0
Green, Boyce	10	254	25.4	t97	1
Harry, Emile	6	115	19.2	26	0
Carson, Carlos	5	88	17.6	29	0
Moriarty, Larry	4	80	20.0	23	0
Cocroft, Sherman	1	23	23.0	23	0
Pearson, Aaron	1	0	0.0	0	0

INDIVIDUAL PUNTERS

	No	Yards	Long	Avg	Total Punts	TB	Blk	Opp Ret	Ret Yds	In 20	Net Avg
Colbert, Lewis	99	4033	56	40.7	99	6	0	52	572	23	33.7

INDIVIDUAL PUNT RETURNERS

	No	FC	Yards	Avg	Long	TD
Smith, Jeff	29	11	245	8.4	48	0
Harry, Emile	6	7	20	3.3	7	0

INDIVIDUAL SCORERS

KICKERS

	XP	XPA	FG	FGA	PTS
Lowery, Nick	43	43	19	26	100

NON-KICKERS

	TD	TDR	TDP	TDM	PTS
Paige, Stephone	11	0	11	0	66
Smith, Jeff	6	3	3	0	36
Burruss, Lloyd	4	0	0	4	24
Carson, Carlos	4	0	4	0	24
Green, Boyce	4	3	0	1	24
Arnold, Walt	2	0	1	1	12
Cherry, Deron	2	0	0	2	12
Coffman, Paul	2	0	2	0	12
Heard, Herman	2	2	0	0	12
Pruitt, Mike	2	2	0	0	12
Harry, Emile	1	0	1	0	6
Hill, Greg	1	0	0	1	6
Marshall, Henry	1	0	1	0	6
Ross, Kevin	1	0	0	1	6

LOS ANGELES RAIDERS
AFC Western Division

Address: 332 Center Street, El Segundo, California 90245
Telephone: (213) 322-3451

CLUB OFFICIALS
Managing General Partner: Al Davis
Executive Assistant: Al LoCasale
Player Personnel: Ron Wolf
Business Manager: Ken LaRue
Senior Administrators: Irv Kaze, Mike Ornstein, John Herrera
Finance: Michael Reinfeldt
Pro Football Scout: George Karras
Community Relations: Gil Hernandez, Calvin Peterson
Publications: Steve Hartman
Ticket Operations: Peter Eiges
Trainers: George Anderson, H. Rod Martin
Equipment Manager: Richard Romanski

Stadium: Los Angeles Memorial Coliseum (Capacity 92,516)
Playing Surface: Grass
Stadium Address: 3911 South Figueroa Street, Los Angeles,
  California 90037
Colours: Silver and Black
Summer Training Camp: Radisson Hotel, Oxnard,
  California 93030

LOS ANGELES RAIDERS 1987 SCHEDULE

PRE-SEASON

Aug.	15	SAN FRANCISCO	7:00
Aug.	22	BUFFALO	6:00
Aug.	30	at Dallas	7:00
Sep.	5	CHICAGO	1:00

REGULAR SEASON

Sep.	13	at Green Bay	3:00
Sep.	20	DETROIT	1:00
Sep.	27	at Houston	12:00
Oct.	4	KANSAS CITY	1:00
Oct.	12	at Denver	7:00
Oct.	18	SAN DIEGO	1:00
Oct.	25	SEATTLE	1:00
Nov.	1	at New England	1:00
Nov.	8	at Minnesota	12:00
Nov.	15	at San Diego	5:00
Nov.	22	DENVER	1:00
Nov.	30	at Seattle	6:00
Dec.	6	BUFFALO	1:00
Dec.	13	at Kansas City	3:00
Dec.	20	CLEVELAND	1:00
Dec.	27	CHICAGO	1:00

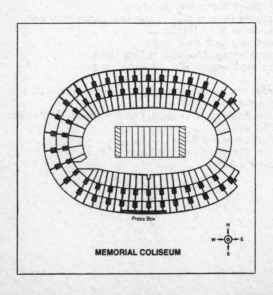

Press Box

MEMORIAL COLISEUM

LOS ANGELES RAIDERS
END OF SEASON DEPTH CHART

OFFENSE

WR   — 88 Rod Barksdale, 84 Jessie Hester, 83 Tim Moffett
OLT   — 79 Bruce Davis, 77 Chris Riehm
OLG   — 77 Chris Riehm, 73 Charley Hannah
C   — 72 Don Mosebar, 51 Bill Lewis
ORG   — 65 Mickey Marvin, 51 Bill Lewis
ORT   — 74 Shelby Jordan, Henry Lawrence
TE   — 46 Todd Christensen, 81 Andy Parker,
        39 Steve Strachan
WR   — 85 Dokie Williams, 83 Tim Moffett, 89 Mark Pattison
QB   — 16 Jim Plunkett, 6 Marc Wilson, 12 Rusty Hilger
RB   — 27 Frank Hawkins, 39 Steve Strachan
RB   — 32 Marcus Allen, 34 Napoleon McCallum,
        42 Vance Mueller

DEFENSE

DLE   — 75 Howie Long, 93 Greg Townsend
MG   — 71 Bill Pickel, 98 Mitch Willis
DRE   — 99 Sean Jones, 93 Greg Townsend
LLB   — 57 Jerry Robinson, 52 Linden King
ILB   — 55 Matt Millen, 59 Jamie Kimmel
ILB   — 54 Reggie McKenzie, 59 Jamie Kimmel
RLB   — 53 Rod Martin, 56 Jeff Barnes
LCB   — 43 Sam Seale, 45 James Davis
RCB   — 22 Mike Haynes, 45 James Davis
SS   — 30 Stacey Toran, 23 Odis McKinney, 41 Fulton Walker
FS   — 26 Vann McElroy, 44 Stefon Adams,
        23 Odis McKinney

SPECIAL TEAMS

P   — 8 Ray Guy, 10 Chris Bahr
K   — 10 Chris Bahr, 8 Ray Guy
H   — 6 Marc Wilson, 12 Rusty Hilger, 26 Van McElroy
PR   — 41 Fulton Walker, 34 Napoleon McCallum,
        83 Tim Moffett
KR   — 44 Stefon Adams, 41 Fulton Walker, 42 Vance Mueller
LSN(P)   — 59 Jamie Kimmel, 81 Andy Parker,
        46 Todd Christensen
LSN(F)   — 59 Jamie Kimmel, 73 Charley Hannah

LOS ANGELES RAIDERS

INDIVIDUAL RUSHERS

	Att	Yards	Avg	Long	TD
Allen, Marcus	208	759	3.6	t28	5
McCallum, Napoleon	142	536	3.8	18	1
Hawkins, Frank	58	245	4.2	15	0
Strachan, Steve	18	53	2.9	10	0
Hilger, Rusty	6	48	8.0	16	0
Plunkett, Jim	12	47	3.9	11	0
Wilson, Marc	14	45	3.2	13	0
Mueller, Vance	13	30	2.3	8	0
Williams, Dokie	3	27	9.0	19	0
Guy, Ray	1	0	0.0	0	0

INDIVIDUAL PASSING

	Att	Comp	Pct Comp	Yds	Avg Gain	TD	Pct TD	Long	Int	Pct Int	Rating Points
Plunkett, Jim	252	133	52.8	1986	7.88	14	5.6	t81	9	3.6	82.5
Wilson, Marc	240	129	53.8	1721	7.17	12	5.0	t57	15	6.3	67.4
Hilger, Rusty	38	19	50.0	266	7.00	1	2.6	54	1	2.6	70.7

INDIVIDUAL RECEIVERS

	No	Yards	Avg	Long	TD
Christensen, Todd	95	1153	12.1	35	8
Allen, Marcus	46	453	9.8	36	2
Williams, Dokie	43	843	19.6	53	8
Hawkins, Frank	25	166	6.6	16	0
Hester, Jessie	23	632	27.5	t81	6
Barksdale, Rod	18	434	24.1	t57	2
McCallum, Napoleon	13	103	7.9	22	0
Moffett, Tim	6	77	12.8	17	0
Mueller, Vance	6	54	9.0	20	0
Junkin, Trey	2	38	19.0	19	0
Pattison, Mark	2	12	6.0	6	0
Parker, Andy	2	8	4.0	6	1

INDIVIDUAL INTERCEPTORS

	No	Yards	Avg	Long	TD
McElroy, Vann	7	105	15.0	28	0
Robinson, Jerry	4	42	10.5	t32	1
Seale, Sam	4	2	0.5	2	0
Haynes, Mike	2	28	14.0	22	0
Toran, Stacey	2	28	14.0	19	0
Barnes, Jeff	2	7	3.5	7	0
Hayes, Lester	2	7	3.5	7	0
Adams, Stefon	1	32	32.0	32	0
Martin, Rod	1	15	15.0	15	0
McKenzie, Reggie	1	9	9.0	9	0

INDIVIDUAL KICKOFF RETURNERS

	No	Yards	Avg	Long	TD
Adams, Stefon	27	573	21.2	51	0
Walker, Fulton	23	368	16.0	27	0
McCallum, Napoleon	8	183	22.9	59	0
Millen, Matt	3	40	13.3	19	0
Mueller, Vance	2	73	36.5	46	0
Hawkins, Frank	1	15	15.0	15	0

INDIVIDUAL PUNTERS

	No	Yards	Long	Avg	Total Punts	TB	Blk	Opp Ret	Ret Yds	In 20	Net Avg
Guy, Ray	90	3620	64	40.2	90	11	0	42	357	20	33.8

INDIVIDUAL PUNT RETURNERS

	No	FC	Yards	Avg	Long	TD
Walker, Fulton	49	15	440	9.0	t70	1
McCallum, Napoleon	7	1	44	6.3	13	0

INDIVIDUAL SCORERS

KICKERS

	XP	XPA	FG	FGA	PTS
Bahr, Chris	36	36	21	28	99

NON-KICKERS

	TD	TDR	TDP	TDM	PTS
Christensen, Todd	8	0	8	0	48
Williams, Dokie	8	0	8	0	48
Allen, Marcus	7	5	2	0	42
Hester, Jessie	6	0	6	0	36
Barksdale, Rod	2	0	2	0	12
Robinson, Jerry	2	0	0	2	12
Hayes, Lester	1	0	0	1	6
McCallum, Napoleon	1	1	0	0	6
Parker, Andy	1	0	1	0	6
Walker, Fulton	1	0	0	1	6
Townsend, Greg	0	0	0	0	2

MIAMI DOLPHINS
AFC Eastern Division

Address: 4770 Biscayne Boulevard, Suite 1440, Miami,
Florida 33137
Telephone: (305) 576-1000

CLUB OFFICIALS
President: Joseph Robbie
Executive Vice President-General Manager: J. Michael Robbie
Vice President-Head Coach: Don Shula
Director of Pro Scouting: Charley Winner
Director of Player Personnel: Chuck Connor
Director of Publicity: Eddie White
Ticket Director: Kevin Fitzgerald
Controller: Howard Rieman
Travelling Secretary: Bryan Wiedmeier
Trainer: Bob Lundy
Equipment Manager: Bob Monica

Stadium: Joe Robbie Stadium (Capacity: 75,500)
Playing Surface: Grass
Stadium Address: N.W. 27th Avenue & N.W. 199th Street,
Miami, Florida 33125
Colours: Aqua, Coral and White
Summer Training Camp: St. Thomas University,
16400-D N.W. 32nd Avenue, Miami, Florida 33054

MIAMI DOLPHINS 1987 SCHEDULE

PRE-SEASON

Aug.	16	CHICAGO	8:00
Aug.	24	at Denver	6:00
Aug.	29	at Philadelphia	7:30
Sep.	4	BUFFALO	8:00

REGULAR SEASON

Sep.	13	at New England	1:00
Sep.	20	at Indianapolis	12:00
Sep.	27	NEW YORK GIANTS	1:00
Oct.	4	at Seattle	1:00
Oct.	11	KANSAS CITY	1:00
Oct.	18	at New York Jets	1:00
Oct.	25	BUFFALO	1:00
Nov.	1	PITTSBURGH	1:00
Nov.	8	at Cincinnati	4:00
Nov.	15	INDIANAPOLIS	1:00
Nov.	22	at Dallas	7:00
Nov.	29	at Buffalo	1:00
Dec.	7	NEW YORK JETS	9:00
Dec.	13	at Philadelphia	1:00
Dec.	20	WASHINGTON	8:00
Dec.	28	NEW ENGLAND	9:00

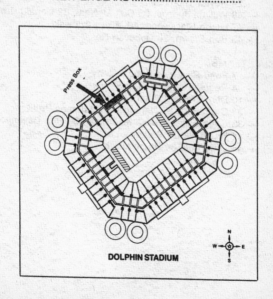

DOLPHIN STADIUM

MIAMI DOLPHINS
END OF SEASON DEPTH CHART

OFFENSE

WR   — 85 Mark Duper, 89 Nat Moore
OLT — 65 Jeff Dellenbach, 76 Tom Toth
OLG — 61 Roy Foster, 66 Larry Lee
C   — 57 Dwight Stephenson, 66 Larry Lee
ORG — 72 Ronnie Lee, 66 Larry Lee
ORT — 68 Greg Koch, 65 Jeff Dellenbach, 76 Tom Toth
TE   — 84 Bruce Hardy, 87 Dan Johnson
WR   — 83 Mark Clayton, 82 James Pruitt, 11 Jim Jensen
QB   — 13 Dan Marino, 10 Don Strock, 11 Jim Jensen
RB   — 27 Lorenzo Hampton, 22 Tony Nathan, 33 Craig Ellis
F-B — 34 Woody Bennett, 30 Ron Davenport

DEFENSE

DLE — 95 T.J. Turner, 70 Brian Sochia
NT   — 73 Bob Baumhower, 71 Mike Charles, 70 Brian Sochia
DRE — 99 George Little, 75 Doug Betters
LOLB — 59 Bob Brúdzinski, 91 Fred Robinson
LILB — 94 Larry Kolic, 50 Jackie Shipp
RILB — 56 John Offerdahl, 90 Andy Hendel, 51 Mark Brown
ROLB — 51 Mark Brown, 53 David Frye
LCB — 24 Reyna Thompson
RCB — 49 William Judson, 28 Don McNeal, 32 Donald Brown
SS   — 47 Glenn Blackwood, 40 Mike Kozlowski
FS   — 43 Bud Brown, 26 Donovan Rose

SPECIAL TEAMS

K   — 7 Fuad Reveiz, 4 Reggie Roby
P   — 4 Reggie Roby, 10 Don Strock
H   — 10 Don Strock, 11 Jim Jensen
PR   — 33 Craig Ellis, 89 Nat Moore, 82 James Pruitt
KR   — 33 Craig Ellis, 40 Mike Kozlowski, 30 Ron Davenport
LSN(P) — 84 Bruce Hardy, 66 Larry Lee
LSN(F) — 66 Larry Lee, 84 Bruce Hardy

MIAMI DOLPHINS

INDIVIDUAL RUSHERS

	Att	Yards	Avg	Long	TD
Hampton, Lorenzo	186	830	4.5	t54	9
Davenport, Ron	75	314	4.2	35	0
Nathan, Tony	27	203	7.5	20	0
Bennett, Woody	36	162	4.5	16	0
Clayton, Mark	2	33	16.5	22	0
Carter, Joe	4	18	4.5	9	0
Ellis, Craig	3	6	2.0	2	0
Strock, Don	1	0	0.0	0	0
Marino, Dan	12	-3	-0.3	13	0
Roby, Reggie	2	-8	-4.0	0	0
Duper, Mark	1	-10	-10.0	-10	0

INDIVIDUAL PASSING

	Att	Comp	Pct Comp	Yds	Avg Gain	TD	Pct TD	Long	Int	Pct Int	Rating Points
Marino, Dan	623	378	60.7	4746	7.62	44	7.1	t85	23	3.7	92.5
Strock, Don	20	14	70.0	152	7.60	2	10.0	21	0	0.0	125.4
Jensen, Jim	2	0	0.0	0	0.00	0	0.0	0	0	0.0	39.6

INDIVIDUAL RECEIVERS

	No	Yards	Avg	Long	TD
Duper, Mark	67	1313	19.6	t85	11
Hampton, Lorenzo	61	446	7.3	19	3
Clayton, Mark	60	1150	19.2	t68	10
Hardy, Bruce	54	430	8.0	t18	5
Nathan, Tony	48	457	9.5	t23	2
Moore, Nat	38	431	11.3	t38	7
Davenport, Ron	20	177	8.9	27	1
Johnson, Dan	19	170	8.9	20	4
Pruitt, James	15	235	15.7	27	2
Jensen, Jim	5	50	10.0	t20	1
Bennett, Woody	4	33	8.3	13	0
Carter, Joe	1	6	6.0	6	0

INDIVIDUAL INTERCEPTORS

	No	Yards	Avg	Long	TD
Rose, Don	2	63	31.5	36	0
McNeal, Don	2	46	23.0	29	0
Blackwood, Glenn	2	10	5.0	7	0
Judson, William	2	0	0.0	0	0
Blackwood, Lyle	1	14	14.0	14	0
Offerdahl, John	1	14	14.0	14	0
Brown, Bud	1	3	3.0	3	0
Charles, Mike	1	2	2.0	2	0
Kozlowski, Mike	1	0	0.0	0	0

INDIVIDUAL KICKOFF RETURNERS

	No	Yards	Avg	Long	TD
Ellis, Craig	25	541	21.6	41	0
Davenport, Ron	16	285	17.8	37	0
Hampton, Lorenzo	9	182	20.2	25	0
Carter, Joe	9	133	14.8	22	0
Hardy, Bruce	3	39	13.0	16	0
Lee, Larry	1	5	5.0	5	0
Johnson, Dan	1	0	0.0	0	0
Toth, Tom	1	0	0.0	0	0

INDIVIDUAL PUNTERS

	No	Yards	Long	Avg	Total Punts	TB	Blk	Opp Ret	Ret Yds	In 20	Net Avg
Roby, Reggie	56	2476	73	44.2	56	9	0	23	200	13	37.4

INDIVIDUAL PUNT RETURNERS

	No	FC	Yards	Avg	Long	TD
Ellis, Craig	24	1	149	6.2	17	0
Pruitt, James	11	1	150	13.6	t71	1
Blackwood, Glenn	1	0	0	0.0	0	0
Blackwood, Lyle	1	0	0	0.0	0	0
Clayton, Mark	1	0	0	0.0	0	0
Thompson, Reyna	1	0	0	0.0	0	0
Moore, Nat	1	6	-2	-2.0	0	0
Kozlowski, Mike	0	3	0	—	0	0

INDIVIDUAL SCORERS

KICKERS	XP	XPA	FG	FGA	PTS
Reveiz, Fuad	52	55	14	22	94

NON-KICKERS	TD	TDR	TDP	TDM	PTS
Hampton, Lorenzo	12	9	3	0	72
Duper, Mark	11	0	11	0	66
Clayton, Mark	10	0	10	0	60
Moore, Nat	7	0	7	0	42
Hardy, Bruce	5	0	5	0	30
Johnson, Dan	4	0	4	0	24
Pruitt, James	3	0	2	1	18
Nathan, Tony	2	0	2	0	12
Davenport, Ron	1	0	1	0	6
Jensen, Jim	1	0	1	0	6

NEW ENGLAND PATRIOTS
AFC Eastern Division

Address: Sullivan Stadium, Route 1, Foxboro, Massachusetts 02035
Telephone: (617) 543-7911

CLUB OFFICIALS
President: William H. Sullivan, Jr.
Executive Vice President: Charles W. Sullivan
Vice President: Francis J. (Bucko) Kilroy
General Manager: Patrick J. Sullivan
Director of Player Development: Dick Steinberg
Director of Pro Scouting: Bill McPeak
Director of College Scouting: Joe Mendes
Executive Director of Player Personnel: Darryl Stingley
Personnel Scouts: George Blackburn, Larry Cook, Charles Garcia, Pat Naughton, Bob Teahan
Director of Public Relations and Sales: Dave Wintergrass
Director of Publicity: Jim Greenidge
Assistant Publicity Director: Jimmy Oldham
Box Office Manager: Ken Sternfeld
Trainer: Ron O'Neil
Equipment Manager: George Luongo
Video Manager: Ken Deininger

Stadium: Sullivan Stadium (Capacity: 61,000)
Playing Surface: SuperTurf
Stadium Address: Route 1, Foxboro, Massachusetts 02035
Colours: Red, White and Blue
Summer Training Camp: Bryant College, Smithfield, Rhode Island 02917

NEW ENGLAND PATRIOTS 1987 SCHEDULE

PRE-SEASON

Aug.	16	NEW YORK GIANTS	1:30
Aug.	23	PHILADELPHIA	7:00
Aug.	29	at Minnesota	2:00
Sep.	4	vs. Atlanta at Jacksonville, Fla.	8:00

REGULAR SEASON

Sep.	13	MIAMI	1:00
Sep.	21	at New York Jets	9:00
Sep.	27	at Washington	1:00
Oct.	4	CLEVELAND	1:00
Oct.	11	BUFFALO	1:00
Oct.	18	at Houston	12:00
Oct.	25	at Indianapolis	1:00
Nov.	1	LOS ANGELES RAIDERS	1:00
Nov.	8	at New York Giants	8:00
Nov.	15	DALLAS	1:00
Nov.	22	INDIANAPOLIS	1:00
Nov.	29	PHILADELPHIA	1:00
Dec.	6	at Denver	2:00
Dec.	13	NEW YORK JETS	1:00
Dec.	20	at Buffalo	1:00
Dec.	28	at Miami	9:00

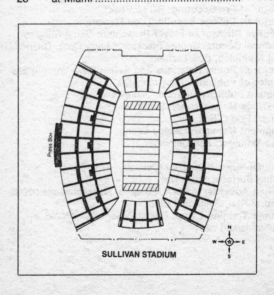

SULLIVAN STADIUM

NEW ENGLAND PATRIOTS
END OF SEASON DEPTH CHART

OFFENSE

WR	— 86 Stanley Morgan, 83 Cedric Jones
OLT	— 76 Brian Holloway, 68 Darryl Haley
OLG	— 64 Trevor Matich, 66 Paul Fairchild, 75 Guy Morriss
C	— 58 Pete Brock, 64 Trevor Matich, 62 Bill Bain
ORG	— 61 Ron Wooten, 75 Guy Morriss
ORT	— 68 Darryl Haley, 64 Trevor Matich, 62 Bill Bain
TE	— 48 Greg Baty, 27 Greg Hawthorne, 88 Willie Scott
WR	— 80 Irving Fryar, 81 Stephen Starring, 82 Derwin Williams
QB	— 11 Tony Eason, 14 Steve Grogan, 12 Tom Ramsey
RB	— 33 Tony Collins, 21 Reggie Dupard
F-B	— 32 Craig James, 30 Mosi Tatupu

DEFENSE

DLE	— 96 Brent Williams, 98 Dennis Owens
NT	— 90 Toby Williams, 98 Dennis Owens, 97 Milford Hodge
DRE	— 60 Garin Veris, 98 Dennis Owens
LOLB	— 56 Andre Tippett, 50 Lawrence McGrew, 94 Mel Black
LILB	— 52 Johnny Rembert, 95 Ed Reynolds, 59 Steve Doig
RILB	— 50 Lawrence McGrew, 95 Ed Reynolds
ROLB	— 55 Don Blackmon, 95 Ed Reynolds, 94 Mel Black
LCB	— 42 Ronnie Lippett, 23 Rod McSwain, 43 Ernest Gibson
RCB	— 26 Raymond Clayborn, 23 Rod McSwain, 22 Eugene Profit
SS	— 38 Roland James, 28 Jim Bowman
FS	— 31 Fred Marion, 28 Jim Bowman

SPECIAL TEAMS

K	— 1 Tony Franklin, 14 Steve Grogan
P	— 3 Rich Camarillo, 32 Craig James
H	— 11 Tony Eason, 12 Tom Ramsey
PR	— 80 Irving Fryar, 81 Stephen Starring, 86 Stanley Morgan
KR	— 81 Stephen Starring, 80 Irving Fryar, 21 Reggie Dupard
LSN(P)	— 75 Guy Morriss, 64 Trevor Matich, 61 Ron Wooten
LSN(F)	— 75 Guy Morriss, 64 Trevor Matich, 61 Ron Wooten

NEW ENGLAND PATRIOTS

INDIVIDUAL RUSHERS

	Att	Yards	Avg	Long	TD
James, Craig	154	427	2.8	16	4
Collins, Tony	156	412	2.6	17	3
Tatupu, Mosi	71	172	2.4	13	1
Eason, Tony	35	170	4.9	26	0
Fryar, Irving	4	80	20.0	31	0
Weathers, Robert	21	58	2.8	t16	1
Dupard, Reggie	15	39	2.6	11	0
Grogan, Steve	9	23	2.6	10	1
Hawthorne, Greg	1	5	5.0	5	0
Starring, Stephen	1	0	0.0	0	0
Ramsey, Tom	1	-6	-6.0	-6	0
Jones, Cedric	1	-7	-7.0	-7	0

INDIVIDUAL PASSING

	Att	Comp	Pct Comp	Yds	Avg Gain	TD	Pct TD	Long	Int	Pct Int	Rating Points
Eason, Tony	448	276	61.6	3328	7.43	19	4.2	49	10	2.2	89.2
Grogan, Steve	102	62	60.8	976	9.57	9	8.8	t69	2	2.0	113.8
James, Craig	4	1	25.0	10	2.50	1	25.0	t10	1	25.0	39.6
Ramsey, Tom	3	1	33.3	7	2.33	0	0.0	7	0	0.0	42.4

INDIVIDUAL RECEIVERS

	No	Yards	Avg	Long	TD
Morgan, Stanley	84	1491	17.8	t44	10
Collins, Tony	77	684	8.9	49	5
Fryar, Irving	43	737	17.1	t69	6
Baty, Greg	37	331	8.9	22	2
Hawthorne, Greg	24	192	8.0	17	0
James, Craig	18	129	7.2	17	0
Starring, Stephen	16	295	18.4	47	2
Tatupu, Mosi	15	145	9.7	25	0
Jones, Cedric	14	222	15.9	28	1
Scott, Willie	8	41	5.1	t8	3
Williams, Derwin	2	35	17.5	26	0
Weathers, Robert	1	14	14.0	14	0
Holloway, Brian	1	5	5.0	5	0

INDIVIDUAL INTERCEPTORS

	No	Yards	Avg	Long	TD
Lippett, Ronnie	8	76	9.5	43	0
Clayborn, Ray	3	4	1.3	4	0
Marion, Fred	2	56	28.0	t37	1
McGrew, Larry	2	44	22.0	27	0
James, Roland	2	39	19.5	21	0
Nelson, Steve	2	21	10.5	17	0
Rembert, Johnny	1	37	37.0	37	0

McSwain, Rod	1	3	3.0	3	0
Tippett, Andre	0	32	—	32	0

INDIVIDUAL KICKOFF RETURNERS

	No	Yards	Avg	Long	TD
Starring, Stephen	36	802	22.3	52	0
Fryar, Irving	10	192	19.2	33	0
Jones, Cedric	4	63	15.8	20	0
Dupard, Reggie	3	50	16.7	21	0
Rembert, Johnny	3	27	9.0	14	0
Hawthorne, Greg	2	13	6.5	13	0

INDIVIDUAL PUNTERS

	No	Yards	Long	Avg	Total Punts	TB	Blk	Opp Ret	Ret Yds	In 20	Net Avg
Camarillo, Rich	89	3746	64	42.1	92	7	3	60	565	16	33.1

INDIVIDUAL PUNT RETURNERS

	No	FC	Yards	Avg	Long	TD
Fryar, Irving	35	10	366	10.5	t59	1
Starring, Stephen	6	0	18	3.0	12	0
Marion, Fred	1	1	12	12.0	12	0
James, Roland	0	1	0	—	0	0

INDIVIDUAL SCORERS

KICKERS	XP	XPA	FG	FGA	PTS
Franklin, Tony	44	45	32	41	140

NON-KICKERS	TD	TDR	TDP	TDM	PTS
Morgan, Stanley	10	0	10	0	60
Collins, Tony	8	3	5	0	48
Fryar, Irving	7	0	6	1	42
James, Craig	4	4	0	0	24
Scott, Willie	3	0	3	0	18
Baty, Greg	2	0	2	0	12
Starring, Stephen	2	0	2	0	12
Tatupu, Mosi	2	1	0	1	12
Grogan, Steve	1	1	0	0	6
Jones, Cedric	1	0	1	0	6
Marion, Fred	1	0	0	1	6
McSwain, Rod	1	0	0	1	6
Rembert, Johnny	1	0	0	1	6
Weathers, Robert	1	1	0	0	6
Williams, Brent	1	0	0	1	6

NEW YORK JETS
AFC Eastern Division

Address: 598 Madison Avenue, New York, N.Y. 10022
Telephone: (212) 421-6600

CLUB OFFICIALS
Chairman of the Board: Leon Hess
President-Chief Operating Officer: Jim Kensil
Corporate Treasurer-Secretary and Administrative Manager: Steve Gutman
Director of Player Personnel: Mike Hickey
Pro Personnel Director: Jim Royer
Talent Scouts: Joe Collins, Don Grammer, Sid Hall, Marv Sunderland
Director of Public Relations: Frank Ramos
Assistant Director of Public Relations: Ron Cohen
Director of Operations: Mike Kensil
Ticket Manager: Bob Parente
Video Director: Jim Pons
Trainer: Bob Reese
Assistant Trainers: Pepper Burruss, Joe Patten
Equipment Manager: Bill Hampton

Stadium: Giants Stadium (Capacity 76,891)
Playing Surface: AstroTurf
Stadium Address: East Rutherford, New Jersey 07073
Colours: Kelly Green and White
Summer Training Camp: 1000 Fulton Avenue, Hempstead, N.Y. 11550
Telephone: (516) 538-6600

NEW YORK JETS 1987 SCHEDULE

PRE-SEASON

Aug.	15	PHILADELPHIA	8:00
Aug.	22	at Tampa Bay	7:00
Aug.	29	at New York Giants	9:00
Sep.	4	at San Diego	7:00

REGULAR SEASON

Sep.	13	at Buffalo	1:00
Sep.	21	NEW ENGLAND	9:00
Sep.	27	at Pittsburgh	4:00
Oct.	4	DALLAS	4:00
Oct.	11	at Indianapolis	12:00
Oct.	18	MIAMI	1:00
Oct.	25	at Washington	1:00
Nov.	1	INDIANAPOLIS	1:00
Nov.	9	SEATTLE	9:00
Nov.	15	at Kansas City	12:00
Nov.	22	BUFFALO	1:00
Nov.	29	CINCINNATI	1:00
Dec.	7	at Miami	9:00
Dec.	13	at New England	1:00
Dec.	20	PHILADELPHIA	1:00
Dec.	27	at New York Giants	1:00

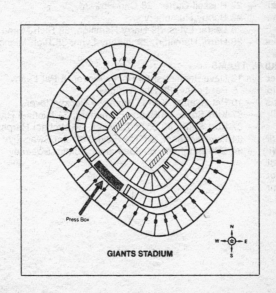

Press Box

GIANTS STADIUM

NEW YORK JETS
END OF SEASON DEPTH CHART

OFFENSE

WR	— 88 Al Toon, 87 Kurt Sohn, 84 Michael Harper
OLT	— 53 Jim Sweeney, 79 Mike Haight, 72 Gordon King
OLG	— 64 Guy Bingham, 63 Ted Banker, 79 Mike Haight
C	— 65 Joe Fields, 64 Guy Bingham, 63 Ted Banker
ORG	— 60 Dan Alexander, 64 Guy Bingham, 79 Mike Haight
ORT	— 72 Gordon King, 79 Mike Haight, 53 Jim Sweeney
TE	— 82 Mickey Shuler, 89 Rocky Klever, 81 Billy Griggs
WR	— 85 Wesley Walker, 87 Kurt Sohn, 83 JoJo Townsell
QB	— 7 Ken O'Brien, 10 Pat Ryan, 89 Rocky Kelver
RB	— 24 Freeman McNeil, 30 Nuu Faaola, 34 Johnny Hector
F-B	— 49 Tony Paige, 31 Marion Barber, 34 Johnny Hector

DEFENSE

DLE	— 93 Marty Lyons, 76 Ben Rudolph, 98 Jerome Foster
NT	— 95 Tom Baldwin, 74 Derland Moore, 78 Barry Bennett
DRE	— 78 Barry Bennett, 76 Ben Rudolph, 98 Jerome Foster
LOLB	— 50 Bob Crable, 55 Charles Jackson, 58 Matt Monger
LILB	— 59 Kyle Clifton, 54 Troy Benson, 58 Matt Monger
RILB	— 57 Kevin McArthur, 58 Matt Monger, 54 Troy Benson
ROLB	— 94 Rusty Guilbeau, 58 Matt Monger, 54 Troy Benson
LCB	— 47 Jerry Holmes, 48 Bobby Humphery, 28 Carl Howard
RCB	— 27 Russell Carter, 28 Carl Howard, 48 Bobby Humphery
SS	— 26 Lester Lyles, 39 Harry Hamilton, 36 Rich Miano
FS	— 39 Harry Hamilton, 29 Johnny Lynn, 36 Rich Miano

SPECIAL TEAMS

P	— 13 Dave Jennings, 89 Rocky Klever, 5 Pat Leahy
K	— 5 Pat Leahy, 89 Rocky Klever
H	— 10 Pat Ryan, 7 Ken O'Brien, 89 Rocky Klever
KR	— 87 Kurt Sohn, 48 Bobby Humphery, 84 Michael Harper
PR	— 87 Kurt Sohn, 83 JoJo Townsell, 84 Michael Harper
LSN(P)	— 64 Guy Bingham, 65 Joe Fields, 53 Jim Sweeney
LSN(F)	— 64 Guy Bingham, 65 Joe Fields, 53 Jim Sweeney

NEW YORK JETS

INDIVIDUAL RUSHERS

	Att	Yards	Avg	Long	TD
McNeil, Freeman	214	856	4.0	40	5
Hector, Johnny	164	605	3.7	41	8
Paige, Tony	47	109	2.3	9	2
Bligen, Dennis	20	65	3.3	10	1
O'Brien, Ken	17	46	2.7	11	0
Ryan, Pat	8	28	3.5	18	0
Barber, Marion	11	27	2.5	8	0
Faaola, Nuu	3	5	1.7	2	0
Townsell, JoJo	1	2	2.0	2	0
Jennings, Dave	1	0	0.0	0	0
Toon, Al	2	−3	−1.5	2	0
Sohn, Kurt	2	−11	−5.5	−3	0

INDIVIDUAL PASSING

	Att	Comp	Pct Comp	Yds	Avg Gain	TD	Pct TD	Long	Int	Pct Int	Rating Points
O'Brien, Ken	482	300	62.2	3690	7.66	25	5.2	t83	20	4.1	85.8
Ryan, Pat	55	34	61.8	342	6.22	2	3.6	36	1	1.8	84.1

INDIVIDUAL RECEIVERS

	No	Yards	Avg	Long	TD
Toon, Al	85	1176	13.8	t62	8
Shuler, Mickey	69	675	9.8	t36	4
Walker, Wesley	49	1016	20.7	t83	12
McNeil, Freeman	49	410	8.4	26	1
Hector, Johnny	33	302	9.2	23	0
Paige, Tony	18	121	6.7	18	0
Klever, Rocky	15	150	10.0	21	0
Sohn, Kurt	8	129	16.1	t24	2
Barber, Marion	5	36	7.2	16	0
Bligen, Dennis	2	6	3.0	4	0
Townsell, JoJo	1	11	11.0	11	0

INDIVIDUAL INTERCEPTORS

	No	Yards	Avg	Long	TD
Holmes, Jerry	6	29	4.8	28	0
Lyles, Lester	5	36	7.2	22	0
Lynn, Johnny	5	36	7.2	26	0
Clifton, Kyle	2	8	4.0	7	0
Hamilton, Harry	1	29	29.0	29	0
Crable, Bob	1	26	26.0	26	0

INDIVIDUAL KICKOFF RETURNERS

	No	Yards	Avg	Long	TD
Humphery, Bobby	28	655	23.4	t96	1
Townsell, JoJo	13	322	24.8	t93	1
Sohn, Kurt	7	124	17.7	36	0
Harper, Michael	7	71	10.1	19	0
Rudolph, Ben	3	17	5.7	10	0
Baldwin, Tom	2	3	1.5	4	0
Shuler, Mickey	2	−3	−1.5	0	0
Lynn, Johnny	1	0	0.0	0	0

INDIVIDUAL PUNTERS

	No	Yards	Long	Avg	Total Punts	TB	Blk	Opp Ret	Ret Yds	In 20	Net Avg
Jennings, Dave	85	3353	55	39.4	85	6	0	36	165	27	36.1

INDIVIDUAL PUNT RETURNERS

	No	FC	Yards	Avg	Long	TD
Sohn, Kurt	35	8	289	8.3	27	0
Townsell, JoJo	4	1	52	13.0	28	0

INDIVIDUAL SCORERS

KICKERS

	XP	XPA	FG	FGA	PTS
Leahy, Pat	44	44	16	19	92

NON-KICKERS

	TD	TDR	TDP	TDM	PTS
Walker, Wesley	12	0	12	0	72
Hector, Johnny	8	8	0	0	48
Toon, Al	8	0	8	0	48
McNeil, Freeman	6	5	1	0	36
Shuler, Mickey	4	0	4	0	24
Paige, Tony	2	2	0	0	12
Sohn, Kurt	2	0	2	0	12
Humphery, Bobby	1	0	0	1	*8
Bligen, Dennis	1	1	0	0	6
Townsell, JoJo	1	0	0	1	6

PITTSBURGH STEELERS
AFC Central Division

Address: Three Rivers Stadium, 300 Stadium Circle, Pittsburgh, Pennsylvania 15212
Telephone: (412) 323-1200

CLUB OFFICIALS
Chairman of the Board: Arthur J. Rooney, Sr.
President: Daniel M. Rooney
Vice President: John R. McGinley
Vice President: Arthur J. Rooney, Jr.
Treasurer: Dennis P. Thimons
Business Manager: Joe Gordon
Chief Negotiator: James A. Boston
Office Manager- Stadium: Dan Ferens
Publicity Director: Dan Edwards
Assistant Publicity Director: Pat Hanlon
Director of Player Personnel: Dick Haley
Director of Pro Scouting: Tom Modrak
Talent Scout-West Coast: Bob Schmitz
Talent Scout-East: Tom Donahoe
Talent Scout-Midwest: Jesse Kaye
Director of Ticket Sales: Geraldine R. Glenn
Computer Director-Accounting: Jim Ellenberger
Trainers: Ralph Berlin, Francis Feld
Equipment Manager: Anthony Parisi

Stadium: Three Rivers Stadium (Capacity 59,000)
Playing Surface: AstroTurf
Stadium Address: 300 Stadium Circle, Pittsburgh, Pennsylvania 15212
Colours: Black and Gold
Summer Training Camp: St. Vincent College, Latrobe, Pennsylvania 15650

PITTSBURGH STEELERS 1987 SCHEDULE

PRE-SEASON

Aug.	14	at Washington	8:00
Aug.	22	at Chicago	6:00
Aug.	29	at New Orleans	7:00
Sep.	5	NEW YORK GIANTS	9:00

REGULAR SEASON

Sep.	13	SAN FRANCISCO	1:00
Sep.	20	at Cleveland	1:00
Sep.	27	NEW YORK JETS	4:00
Oct.	4	at Atlanta	1:00
Oct.	11	at Los Angeles Rams	1:00
Oct.	18	INDIANAPOLIS	1:00
Oct.	25	CINCINNATI	1:00
Nov.	1	at Miami	1:00
Nov.	8	at Kansas City	12:00
Nov.	15	HOUSTON	1:00
Nov.	22	at Cincinnati	1:00
Nov.	29	NEW ORLEANS	1:00
Dec.	6	SEATTLE	1:00
Dec.	13	at San Diego	1:00
Dec.	20	at Houston	12:00
Dec.	26	CLEVELAND	12:30

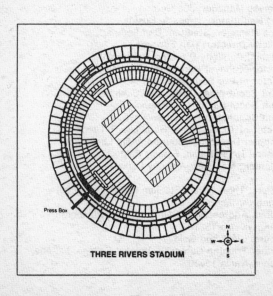

Press Box

N
W — E
S

THREE RIVERS STADIUM

PITTSBURGH STEELERS
END OF SEASON DEPTH CHART

OFFENSE
WR   — 82 John Stallworth, 85 Calvin Sweeney
OLT   — 65 Ray Pinney, 66 Mark Behning, 63 Pete Rostosky
OLG   — 73 Craig Wolfley, 63 Pete Rostosky
C   — 52 Mike Webster, 51 Dan Turk
ORG   — 74 Terry Long, 63 Pete Rostosky
ORT   — 62 Tunch Ilkin, 66 Mark Behning
TE   — 86 Preston Gothard, 80 Warren Seitz
WR   — 83 Louis Lipps, 87 Weegie Thompson
QB   — 16 Mark Malone, 6 Bubby Brister
RB   — 34 Walter Abercrombie, 24 Rich Erenberg,
          45 Chuck Sanders
F-B   — 43 Earnest Jackson, 40 Dan Reeder, 30 Frank Pollard,
          35 Gordon Brown

DEFENSE
DLE   — 93 Keith Willis, 92 Keith Gary, 99 Darryl Sims
NT   — 67 Gary Dunn, 98 Gerald Williams, 64 Edmund Nelson
DRE   — 64 Edmund Nelson, 92 Keith Gray, 99 Darryl Sims
LOLB — 57 Mike Merriweather, 96 Anthony Henton
LILB — 50 David Little, 55 Dennis Winston, 90 Larry Station
RILB — 56 Robin Cole, 91 Gregg Carr, 90 Larry Station
ROLB — 53 Bryan Hinkle, 96 Anthony Henton, 91 Gregg Carr
LCB   — 26 John Swain, 41 Chris Sheffield
RCB   — 28 Lupe Sanchez, 33 Harvey Clayton
SS   — 31 Donnie Shell, 42 Dave Edwards, 28 Lupe Sanchez
FS   — 21 Eric Williams, 22 Rick Woods

SPECIAL TEAMS
P   — 18 Harry Newsome
LSN(P) — 51 Dan Turk, 65 Ray Pinney
K   — 1 Gary Anderson
LSN(F) — 52 Mike Webster, 51 Dan Turk, 65 Ray Pinney
H   — 18 Harry Nesome, 6 Bubby Brister
PR   — 22 Rick Woods, 28 Lupe Sanchez, 83 Louis Lipps
KR   — 28 Lupe Sanchez, 45 Chuck Sanders, 40 Dan Reeder

PITTSBURGH STEELERS

INDIVIDUAL RUSHERS

	Att	Yards	Avg	Long	TD
Jackson, Earnest	216	910	4.2	31	5
Abercrombie, Walter	214	877	4.1	t38	6
Erenberg, Rich	42	170	4.0	17	1
Malone, Mark	31	107	3.5	45	5
Pollard, Frank	24	86	3.6	12	0
Hughes, David	14	32	2.3	8	0
Reeder, Dan	6	20	3.3	6	0
Sanders, Chuck	4	12	3.0	13	0
Brister, Bubby	6	10	1.7	9	1
Seitz, Warren	3	2	0.7	2	0
Lipps, Louis	4	−3	−0.8	8	0

INDIVIDUAL PASSING

	Att	Comp	Pct Comp	Yds	Avg Gain	TD	Pct TD	Long	Int	Pct Int	Rating Points
Malone, Mark, Pitt	425	216	50.8	2444	5.75	15	3.5	48	18	4.2	62.5
Brister, Bubby	60	21	35.0	291	4.85	0	0.0	58	2	3.3	37.6
Newsome, Harry	2	1	50.0	12	6.00	1	50.0	t12	0	0.0	108.3

INDIVIDUAL RECEIVERS

	No	Yards	Avg	Long	TD
Abercrombie, Walter	47	395	8.4	27	2
Lipps, Louis	38	590	15.5	48	3
Stallworth, John	34	466	13.7	t40	1
Erenberg, Rich	27	217	8.0	19	3
Sweeney, Calvin	21	337	16.0	58	1
Gothard, Preston	21	246	11.7	34	1
Thompson, Weegie	17	191	11.2	20	5
Jackson, Earnest	17	169	9.9	28	0
Hughes, David	10	98	9.8	22	0
Sanders, Chuck	2	19	9.5	10	0
Pollard, Frank	2	15	7.5	10	0
Reeder, Dan	2	4	2.0	3	0

INDIVIDUAL INTERCEPTORS

	No	Yards	Avg	Long	TD
Sanchez, Lupe	3	71	23.7	t67	1
Williams, Eric	3	44	14.7	25	0
Shell, Donnie	3	29	9.7	17	0
Woods, Rick	3	26	8.7	23	0
Clayton, Harvey	3	18	6.0	14	0
Hinkle, Bryan	3	7	2.3	6	0
Merriweather, Mike	2	14	7.0	11	0
Swain, John	0	9	—	9	0

INDIVIDUAL KICKOFF RETURNERS

	No	Yards	Avg	Long	TD
Sanchez, Lupe	25	591	23.6	64	0
Sanders, Chuck	8	148	18.5	29	0
Reeder, Dan	4	52	13.0	17	0
Seitz, Warren	2	25	12.5	14	0
Hughes, David	2	16	8.0	16	0
Merriweather, Mike	1	27	27.0	27	0
Woods, Rick	1	17	17.0	17	0
Rostosky, Pete	1	3	3.0	3	0
Sweeney, Calvin	1	0	0.0	0	0

INDIVIDUAL PUNTERS

	No	Yards	Long	Avg	Total Punts	TB	Blk	Opp Ret	Ret Yds	In 20	Net Avg
Newsome, Harry	86	3447	64	40.1	89	11	3	34	364	18	32.2

INDIVIDUAL PUNT RETURNERS

	No	FC	Yards	Avg	Long	TD
Woods, Rick	33	12	294	8.9	41	0
Lipps, Louis	3	1	16	5.3	10	0

INDIVIDUAL SCORERS

KICKERS

	XP	XPA	FG	FGA	PTS
Anderson, Gary	32	32	21	32	95

NON-KICKERS

	TD	TDR	TDP	TDM	PTS
Abercrombie, Walter	8	6	2	0	48
Jackson, Earnest	5	5	0	0	30
Malone, Mark	5	5	0	0	30
Thompson, Weegie	5	0	5	0	30
Erenberg, Rich	4	1	3	0	24
Lipps, Louis	3	0	3	0	18
Brister, Bubby	1	1	0	0	6
Gothard, Preston	1	0	1	0	6
Sanchez, Lupe	1	0	0	1	6
Stallworth, John	1	0	1	0	6
Sweeney, Calvin	1	0	1	0	6
Edwards, David	0	0	0	0	*2

SAN DIEGO CHARGERS
AFC Western Division

Address: San Diego Jack Murphy Stadium, PO Box 20666,
San Diego, California 92120
Telephone: (619) 280-2111

CLUB OFFICIALS
Chairman of the Board-President: Alex G. Spanos
Director of Football Operations: Steve Ortmayer
Assistant Director of Football Operations: John Sanders
Director of Administration: Jack Teele
Pro Scouting: Rudy Feldman
Director of Player Personnel: Chet Franklin
Director of Public Relations: Rick Smith
Business Manager: Pat Curran
Director of Marketing: Rich Israel
Director of Ticket Operations: Joe Scott
Assistant Director of Public Relations: Bill Johnston
Chief Financial Officer: Jerry Murphy
Head Trainer: Mark Howard
Equipment Manager: Sid Brooks

Stadium: San Diego Jack Murphy Stadium (Capacity 60,750)
Playing Surface: Grass
Stadium Address: 9449 Friars Road, San Diego, California 92108
Colours: Blue, White, and Gold
Summer Training Camp: University of California-San Diego
Third College La Jolla, California 92037

SAN DIEGO CHARGERS 1987 SCHEDULE

PRE-SEASON

Aug.	15	DALLAS	6:00
Aug.	23	LOS ANGELES RAMS	5:00
Aug.	27	at San Francisco	6:00
Sep.	4	NEW YORK JETS	7:00

REGULAR SEASON

Sep.	13	at Kansas City	12:00
Sep.	20	ST. LOUIS	1:00
Sep.	27	SEATTLE	1:00
Oct.	4	at Cincinnati	1:00
Oct.	11	at Tampa Bay	1:00
Oct.	18	at Los Angeles Raiders	1:00
Oct.	25	KANSAS CITY	1:00
Nov.	1	CLEVELAND	1:00
Nov.	8	at Indianapolis	1:00
Nov.	15	LOS ANGELES RAIDERS	5:00
Nov.	22	at Seattle	1:00
Nov.	29	DENVER	1:00
Dec.	6	at Houston	12:00
Dec.	13	PITTSBURGH	1:00
Dec.	20	INDIANAPOLIS	1:00
Dec.	27	at Denver	2:00

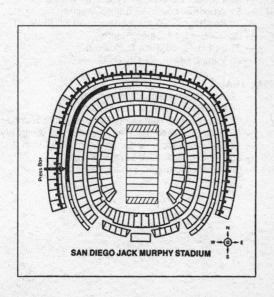

SAN DIEGO JACK MURPHY STADIUM

SAN DIEGO CHARGERS
END OF SEASON DEPTH CHART

OFFENSE

WR	— 18 Charlie Joiner, 83 Trumaine Johnson, 81 Timmie Ware
OLT	— 74 Jim Lachey, 61 Ken Dallafior
OLG	— 77 Sam Claphan, 72 Jeff Walker
C	— 62 Don Macek, 63 Jim Leonard
ORG	— 60 Dennis McKnight, 75 Curt DiGiacomo
ORT	— 68 Gary Kowaiski, 61 Ken Dallafior
TE	— 80 Kellen Winslow, 88 Pete Holohan
WR	— 89 Wes Chandler, 83 Trumaine Johnson, 81 Timmie Ware
QB	— 14 Dan Fouts, 9 Mark Herrmann, 12 Tom Flick
F-B	— 43 Tim Spencer, 42 Curtis Adams
RB	— 40 Gary Anderson, 42 Curtis Adams

DEFENSE

DLE	— 99 Lee Williams, 90 Mack Moore
NT	— 98 Terry Unrein, 96 Blaise Winter
DRE	— 93 Earl Wilson, 92 Dee Hardison
LOLB	— 54 Billy Ray Smith, 59 Andy Hawkins
LILB	— 50 Gary Plummer, 55 Derrie Nelson
RILB	— 57 Thomas Benson, 56 Ty Allert
ROLB	— 51 Woodrow Lowe, 52 Angelo Snipes
LCB	— 24 Ken Taylor, 20 Wayne Davis, 30 Kevin Wyatt
RCB	— 22 Gill Byrd, 27 Daniel Hunter
SS	— 37 Jeff Dale, 33 John L. Sullivan
FS	— 25 Vencie Glenn, 22 Gill Byrd

SPECIAL TEAMS

P	— 2 Ralf Mojsiejenko, 89 Wes Chandler
K	— 6 Rolf Benirschke, 2 Ralf Mojsiejenko
H	— 12 Tom Flick, 2 Ralf Mojsiejenko, 88 Pete Holohan
PR	— 40 Gary Anderson, 89 Wes Chandler, 30 Kevin Wyatt
KR	— 40 Gary Anderson, 42 Curtis Adams, 30 Kevin Wyatt
LSN(P)	— 63 Jim Leonard, 60 Dennis McKnight
LSN(F)	— 60 Dennis McKnight, 63 Jim Leonard

SAN DIEGO CHARGERS

INDIVIDUAL RUSHERS

	Att	Yards	Avg	Long	TD
Anderson, Gary	127	442	3.5	17	1
Adams, Curtis	118	366	3.1	22	4
Spencer, Tim	99	350	3.5	23	6
James, Lionel	51	224	4.4	24	0
McGee, Buford	63	187	3.0	20	7
Herrmann, Mark	2	6	3.0	6	0
Flick, Tom	6	5	0.8	7	1
Mathison, Bruce	1	−1	−1.0	−1	0
Fouts, Dan	4	−3	−0.8	0	0

INDIVIDUAL PASSING

	Att	Comp	Pct Comp	Yds	Avg Gain	TD	Pct TD	Long	Int	Pct Int	Rating Points
Fouts, Dan	430	252	58.6	3031	7.05	16	3.7	t65	22	5.1	71.4
Herrmann, Mark	97	51	52.6	627	6.46	2	2.1	28	3	3.1	66.8
Flick, Tom	73	33	45.2	361	4.95	2	2.7	26	8	11.0	29.9
Anderson, Gary	1	1	100.0	4	4.00	1	100.0	t4	0	0.0	122.9
Holohan, Pete	2	1	50.0	21	10.50	0	0.0	21	0	0.0	87.5
McGee, Buford	1	1	100.0	1	1.00	0	0.0	1	0	0.0	79.2

INDIVIDUAL RECEIVERS

	No	Yards	Avg	Long	TD
Anderson, Gary	80	871	10.9	t65	8
Winslow, Kellen	64	728	11.4	t28	5
Chandler, Wes	56	874	15.6	40	4
Joiner, Charlie	34	440	12.9	33	2
Johnson, Trumaine	30	399	13.3	30	1
Holohan, Pete	29	356	12.3	34	1
James, Lionel	23	173	7.5	18	0
McGee, Buford	10	105	10.5	18	0
Spencer, Tim	6	48	8.0	15	0
Adams, Curtis	4	26	6.5	10	0
Sievers, Eric	2	14	7.0	9	0
Ware, Timmie	1	11	11.0	11	0

INDIVIDUAL INTERCEPTORS

	No	Yards	Avg	Long	TD
Byrd, Gill	5	45	9.0	18	0
Dale, Jeffery	4	153	38.3	50	0
Glenn, Vencie	2	31	15.5	31	0
O'Neal, Leslie	2	22	11.0	17	1
Brown, Donald	1	23	23.0	23	0
Taylor, Ken	1	0	0.0	0	0

INDIVIDUAL KICKOFF RETURNERS

	No	Yards	Avg	Long	TD
Anderson, Gary	24	482	20.1	35	0
James, Lionel	18	315	17.5	31	0
Adams, Curtis	5	100	20.0	25	0
Spencer, Tim	5	81	16.2	21	0
Wyatt, Kevin	5	74	14.8	23	0
Johnson, Trumaine	3	48	16.0	21	0
Winslow, Kellen	2	11	5.5	8	0
McGee, Buford	1	15	15.0	15	0
Chandler, Wes	1	11	11.0	11	0
Plummer, Gary	1	0	0.0	0	0

INDIVIDUAL PUNTERS

	No	Yards	Long	Avg	Total Punts	TB	Blk	Opp Ret	Ret Yds	In 20	Net Avg
Mojsiejenko, Ralf	72	3026	62	42.0	74	11	2	42	368	15	32.9
Chandler, Wes	5	167	38	33.4	5	0	0	1	2	0	33.0

INDIVIDUAL PUNT RETURNERS

	No	FC	Yards	Avg	Long	TD
Anderson, Gary	25	10	227	9.1	30	0
James, Lionel	9	6	94	10.4	21	0
Chandler, Wes	3	0	13	4.3	10	0

INDIVIDUAL SCORERS

KICKERS	XP	XPA	FG	FGA	PTS
Benirschke, Rolf	39	41	16	25	87

NON-KICKERS	TD	TDR	TDP	TDM	PTS
Anderson, Gary	9	1	8	0	54
McGee, Buford	7	7	0	0	42
Spencer, Tim	6	6	0	0	36
Winslow, Kellen	5	0	5	0	30
Adams, Curtis	4	4	0	0	24
Chandler, Wes	4	0	4	0	24
Joiner, Charlie	2	0	2	0	12
Flick, Tom	1	1	0	0	6
Holohan, Pete	1	0	1	0	6
Johnson, Trumaine	1	0	1	0	6
O'Neal, Leslie	1	0	0	1	6

SEATTLE SEAHAWKS
AFC Western Division

Address: 11220 N.E. 53rd Street, Kirkland,
   Washington 98033
Telephone: (206) 827-9777

CLUB OFFICIALS
President-General Manager: Mike McCormack
Assistant General Manager: Chuck Allen
Player Personnel Director: Mike Allman
Public Relations Director: Gary Wright
Assistant Public Relations Director: Dave Neubert
Adminstrative Assistant: Sandy Gregory
Sales and Marketing Coordinator: Lowell Perry
Sales and Marketing Assistant: Reggie McKenzie
Business Manager: Mickey Loomis
Data Processing Director: Tom Monroe
Ticket Manager: James Nagaoka
Trainer: Jim Whitesel
Equipment Manager: Walt Loeffler

Stadium: Kingdome (Capacity 64,984)
Playing Surface: AstroTurf
Stadium Address: 201 South King Street, Seattle,
   Washington 98104
Colours: Blue, Green and Silver
Summer Training Camp: 11220 N.E. 53rd Street,
   Kirkland, Washington 98033

SEATTLE SEAHAWKS 1987 SCHEDULE

PRE-SEASON
Aug.	13	at Los Angeles Rams	7:30
Aug.	22	at St. Louis	7:00
Aug.	28	DETROIT	7:30
Sep.	4	SAN FRANCISCO	5:00

REGULAR SEASON
Sep.	13	at Denver	2:00
Sep.	20	KANSAS CITY	1:00
Sep.	27	at San Diego	1:00
Oct.	4	MIAMI	1:00
Oct.	11	CINCINNATI	1:00
Oct.	18	at Detroit	1:00
Oct.	25	at Los Angeles Raiders	1:00
Nov.	1	MINNESOTA	1:00
Nov.	9	at New York Jets	9:00
Nov.	15	GREEN BAY	1:00
Nov.	22	SAN DIEGO	1:00
Nov.	30	LOS ANGELES RAIDERS	6:00
Dec.	6	at Pittsburgh	1:00
Dec.	13	DENVER	5:00
Dec.	20	at Chicago	12:00
Dec.	27	at Kansas City	12:00

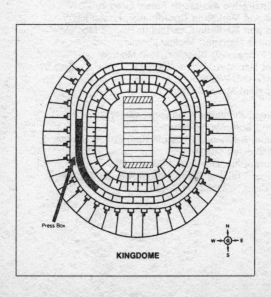

Press Box

KINGDOME

SEATTLE SEAHAWKS
END OF SEASON DEPTH CHART

OFFENSE

WR	— 81 Daryl Turner, 83 Ray Butler
OLT	— 70 Ron Mattes, 74 Curt Singer
OLG	— 65 Edwin Bailey, 76 Jon Borchardt
C	— 52 Will Grant, 62 Kani Kauahi, 60 Glenn Hyde
ORG	— 71 Bryan Millard, 76 Jon Borchardt
ORT	— 75 Mike Wilson, 74 Curt Singer
TE	— 86 Mike Tice, 85 Gordon Hudson
WR	— 80 Steve Largent, 82 Paul Skansi, 89 Byron Walker
QB	— 17 Dave Krieg, 7 Gale Gilbert
RB	— 28 Curt Warner, 43 Randall Morris, 30 Bobby Joe Edmonds
F-B	— 32 John L. Williams, 37 Eric Lane

DEFENSE

DLE	— 79 Jacob Green, 61 Alonzo Mitz
NT	— 72 Joe Nash, 68 Randy Edwards
DRE	— 77 Jeff Bryant, 61 Alonzo Mitz
LOLB	— 58 Bruce Scholtz, 54 John Kaiser
LILB	— 50 Fredd Young, 51 Sam Merriman
RILB	— 53 Keith Butler, 51 Sam Merriman
ROLB	— 56 Greg Gains, 55 Michael Jackson
LCB	— 20 Terry Taylor, 26 Kerry Justin
RCB	— 22 Dave Brown, 23 Patrick Hunter
SS	— 21 Paul Moyer, 27 Greggory Johnson, 47 Eddie Anderson
FS	— 41 Eugene Robinson, 27 Greggory Johnson

SPECIAL TEAMS

K	— 9 Norm Johnson
P	— 2 Vince Gamache
KR	— 30 Bobby Joe Edmonds, 43 Randall Morris, 82 Paul Skansi
PR	— 30 Bobby Joe Edmonds, 82 Paul Skansi
LSN(F)	— 62 Kani Kauahi, 60 Glenn Hyde
LSN(P)	— 60 Glenn Hyde, 62 Kani Kauahi
H	— 7 Gale Gilbert, 80 Steve Largent

SEATTLE SEAHAWKS

INDIVIDUAL RUSHERS

	Att	Yards	Avg	Long	TD
Warner, Curt	319	1481	4.6	t60	13
Williams, John L.	129	538	4.2	36	0
Morris, Randall	19	149	7.8	t49	1
Krieg, Dave	35	122	3.5	19	1
Lane, Eric	6	11	1.8	4	0
Gilbert, Gale	3	8	2.7	12	0
Franklin, Byron	1	2	2.0	2	0
Edmonds, Bobby Joe	1	-11	-11.0	-11	0

INDIVIDUAL PASSING

	Att	Comp	Pct Comp	Yds	Avg Gain	TD	Pct TD	Long	Int	Pct Int	Rating Points
Krieg, Dave	375	225	60.0	2921	7.79	21	5.6	t72	11	2.9	91.0
Gilbert, Gale	76	42	55.3	485	6.38	3	3.9	t38	3	3.9	71.4
Largent, Steve	1	1	100.0	18	18.00	0	0.0	18	0	0.0	118.8
Morris, Randall	1	0	0.0	0	0.00	0	0.0	0	0	0.0	39.6

INDIVIDUAL RECEIVERS

	No	Yards	Avg	Long	TD
Largent, Steve	70	1070	15.3	t38	9
Warner, Curt	41	342	8.3	26	0
Franklin, Byron	33	547	16.6	49	2
Williams, John L.	33	219	6.6	23	0
Skansi, Paul	22	271	12.3	30	0
Butler, Raymond	19	351	18.5	t67	4
Turner, Daryl	18	334	18.6	t72	7
Tice, Mike	15	150	10.0	25	0
Hudson, Gordon	13	131	10.1	30	1
Lane, Eric	3	6	2.0	4	0
Bailey, Edwin	1	3	3.0	3	0

INDIVIDUAL INTERCEPTORS

	No	Yards	Avg	Long	TD
Brown, Dave	5	58	11.6	24	1
Justin, Kerry	4	29	7.3	18	0
Robinson, Eugene	3	39	13.0	25	0
Moyer, Paul	3	38	12.7	20	0
Easley, Ken	2	34	17.0	24	0
Scholtz, Bruce	2	10	5.0	10	0
Taylor, Terry	2	0	0.0	0	0
Gaines, Greg	1	8	8.0	8	0

INDIVIDUAL KICKOFF RETURNERS

	No	Yards	Avg	Long	TD
Edmonds, Bobby Joe	34	764	22.5	46	0
Morris, Randall	23	465	20.2	38	0
Scholtz, Bruce	3	39	13.0	16	0
Skansi, Paul	1	21	21.0	21	0
Tice, Mike	1	17	17.0	17	0
Edwards, Randy	1	13	13.0	13	0
Lane, Eric	1	3	3.0	3	0

INDIVIDUAL PUNTERS

	No	Yards	Long	Avg	Total Punts	TB	Blk	Opp Ret	Ret Yds	In 20	Net Avg
Gamache, Vince	79	3048	55	38.6	79	7	0	38	298	10	33.0

INDIVIDUAL PUNT RETURNERS

	No	FC	Yards	Avg	Long	TD
Edmonds, Bobby Joe	34	14	419	12.3	t75	1
Skansi, Paul	5	0	38	7.6	14	0

INDIVIDUAL SCORERS

KICKERS	XP	XPA	FG	FGA	PTS
Johnson, Norm	42	42	22	35	108

NON-KICKERS	TD	TDR	TDP	TDM	PTS
Warner, Curt	13	13	0	0	78
Largent, Steve	9	0	9	0	54
Turner, Daryl	7	0	7	0	42
Butler, Raymond	4	0	4	0	24
Franklin, Byron	2	0	2	0	12
Lane, Eric	2	0	1	1	12
Brown, Dave	1	0	0	1	6
Edmonds, Bobby Joe	1	0	0	1	6
Hudson, Gordon	1	0	1	0	6
Krieg, Dave	1	1	0	0	6
Morris, Randall	1	1	0	0	6
Moyer, Paul	1	0	0	1	6

NFL SUPPORTERS CLUB

THE CLUB THAT PLAYS ALL YEAR ROUND

You can watch it on the telly from September through to Jan.
But the next six months are empty for the eager football fan.
Now there is a simple remedy to make the summers shorter.
For just fifteen pounds you can become an NFL Supporter.

Yes, the new NFL Supporters Club brings you the facts and inside information direct from the NFL teams. PLUS travel offers and exciting club privileges.

MEMBERS RECEIVE:

1. "Line Call" The regular exclusive Club Newsletter with all the inside news and views direct from the NFL.
2. Exclusive club Privilege Card, entitling you to shop, club and restaurant discounts.
3. Enamel club lapel pin.
4. NFL Sticker.
5. NFL Poster.
6. Exclusive members note pad.
7. Unique travel offers and opportunities.
8. Supporters Club Party Night priority invitations.
9. Special NFL merchandise offers.

To become a member just fill in the form below and post it to:
NFL Supporters Club, Cape House, 60A Priory Road, Tonbridge, KENT TN9 2BL.
Telephone: 0732-360426.

Name..
Address..
.... Post code.................
Team supported or lapel badge preference ....
I enclose cheque/postal order for £15 ☐ please tick box.
Or charge to my credit card £15 VISA/ACCESS/DINERS/AMERICAN EXPRESS
My card number is ☐☐☐☐☐☐☐☐☐☐☐☐☐☐☐☐
Expiry date .... Signed...

ATTENTION ALL JUNIOR NFL FANS

SEND NOW FOR YOUR JUNIOR FUN PACK FOR JUST £5.95 inc VAT & P&P

You will receive:
1. NFL Junior Supporters Club Certificate.
2. NFL button badge.
3. NFL poster.
4. PVC team sticker sheet.
5. Helmet bubble gum.
6. Super Bowl poster/mag.
7. Special offer vouchers for NFL merchandise (worth £10.00)

Please fill in order form below.
Please allow 28 days delivery. Money back guarantee.

Name..
Street...
Town... County.......................................
Post code.. Age...
Favourite NFL Team...
Parent/Guardian's Signature..
(Just to say OK)

Cheques or Postal Orders to:
NFL Supporters Club and send to Cape House, 60A Priory Road, Tonbridge, Kent TN9 2BL.

DON'T SIT ON DEFENSE – JOIN NOW!
It's an OFFENSE not to!

NFL SUPPORTERS CLUB

NATIONAL FOOTBALL CONFERENCE

Atlanta Falcons
Chicago Bears
Dallas Cowboys
Detroit Lions
Green Bay Packers
Los Angeles Rams
Minnesota Vikings
New Orleans Saints
New York Giants
Philadelphia Eagles
St. Louis Cardinals
San Francisco 49ers
Tampa Bay Buccaneers
Washington Redskins

ATLANTA FALCONS
NFC Western Division

Address: Suwanee Road at 1-85, Suwanee, Georgia 30174
Telephone: (404) 945-1111

CLUB OFFICIALS
Chairman of the Board: Rankin M. Smith, Sr.
President: Rankin Smith, Jr.
Executive Vice President: Taylor Smith
Vice President & Chief Financial Officer: Jim Hay
Director of College Player Personnel: Ken Herock
Director of Pro Personnel: Bill Jobko
Scouts: Elbert Dubenion, Bill Groman, Joe Mack, Tom Miner
Director of Marketing: Tommy Nobis
Marketing/Community Affairs: Carol Breeding
Director of Public Relations: Charlie Taylor
Assistant Director of Public Relations: Frank Kleha
Ticket Manager: Jack Ragsdale
Assistant Ticket Manager: Luci Bailey
Director of Video Operations: Tom Atcheson
Assistant Director of Video Operations: Danny Mock
Head Trainer: Jerry Rhea
Assistant Trainer: Billy Brooks
Equipment Manager: Whitey Zimmerman
Assistant Equipment Manager: Horace Daniel

Stadium: Atlanta-Fulton County Stadium (Capacity 59,643)
Playing Surface: Grass
Stadium Address: 521 Capitol Avenue S.W., Atlanta,
   Georgia 30312
Colours: Red, Black, White and Silver
Summer Training Camp: Suwanee Road at 1-85, Suwanee,
   Georgia 30174

ATLANTA FALCONS 1987 SCHEDULE

PRE-SEASON

Aug.	15	BUFFALO	8:00
Aug.	22	at Kansas City	7:30
Aug.	29	CLEVELAND	8:00
Sep.	4	vs. New England at Jacksonville, Fla.	8:00

REGULAR SEASON

Sep.	13	at Tampa Bay	1:00
Sep.	20	WASHINGTON	1:00
Sep.	27	at New Orleans	12:00
Oct.	4	PITTSBURGH	1:00
Oct.	11	at San Francisco	1:00
Oct.	18	LOS ANGELES RAMS	1:00
Oct.	25	at Houston	12:00
Nov.	1	NEW ORLEANS	1:00
Nov.	8	at Cleveland	1:00
Nov.	15	CINCINNATI	4:00
Nov.	22	at Minnesota	12:00
Nov.	29	ST. LOUIS	1:00
Dec.	6	at Dallas	1:00
Dec.	13	at Los Angeles Rams	1:00
Dec.	20	SAN FRANCISCO	1:00
Dec.	27	DETROIT	1:00

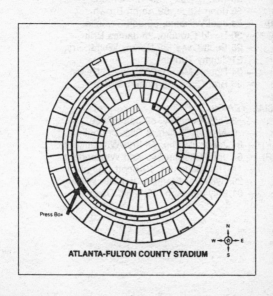

Press Box

N W—E S

ATLANTA-FULTON COUNTY STADIUM

ATLANTA FALCONS
END OF SEASON DEPTH CHART

OFFENSE

WR	— 86 Floyd Dixon, 82 Stacey Bailey, 83 Aubrey Matthews
OLT	— 78 Mike Kenn, 71 Glen Howe, 66 Billy Hinson
OLG	— 64 Joe Pellegrini, 73 Jamie Dukes
C	— 55 Wayne Radloff, 57 Jeff Van Note, 64 Joe Pellegrini
ORG	— 79 Bill Fralic, 73 Jamie Dukes
ORT	— 71 Glen Howe
TE	— 88 Arthur Cox, 87 Ron Middleton
WR	— 89 Charlie Brown, 81 Billy Johnson, 83 Aubrey Matthews
QB	— 14 Turk Schonert, 10 Scott Campbell
RB	— 42 Gerald Riggs, 31 William Andrews, 39 Cliff Austin, 35 Keith Williams
TE	— 45 Ken Whisenhunt, 87 Ron Middleton

DEFENSE

DLE	— 76 Mike Gann, 74 Mike Pitts, 68 Dennis Harrison
NT	— 75 Tony Casillas, 72 Andrew Provence
DRE	— 77 Rick Bryan, 68 Dennis Harrison, 72 Andrew Provence
LOLB	— 51 Reggie Wilkes, 56 Joe Costello
LILB	— 50 Buddy Curry, 99 Tim Green
RILB	— 59 John Rade, 52 Aaron Brown
ROLB	— 54 Joel Williams, 56 Joe Costello
LCB	— 30 David Croudip, 26 James Britt
RCB	— 25 Scott Case, 22 Dennis Woodberry, 21 Jimmy Turner
SS	— 34 Robert Moore, 20 Wendell Cason
WS	— 28 Bret Clark, 34 Robert Moore

SPECIAL TEAMS

P	— 3 Rick Donnelly, 59 John Rade
K	— 6 Ali Haji-Sheikh, 3 Rick Donnelly
LSN(P)	— 64 Joe Pellegrini, 45 Ken Whisenhunt
LSN(F)	— 64 Joe Pellegrini, 45 Ken Whisenhunt
H	— 14 Turk Schonert, 10 Scott Campbell
KR	— 29 Sylvester Stamps, 35 Keith Williams
PR	— 81 Billy Johnson, 86 Floyd Dixon

ATLANTA FALCONS

INDIVIDUAL RUSHERS

	Att	Yards	Avg	Long	TD
Riggs, Gerald	343	1327	3.9	31	9
Archer, David	52	298	5.7	22	0
Austin, Cliff	62	280	4.5	22	1
Stamps, Sylvester	30	220	7.3	48	0
Andrews, William	52	214	4.1	13	1
Dixon, Floyd	11	67	6.1	23	0
Johnson, Billy	6	25	4.2	10	0
Whisenhunt, Ken	1	20	20.0	20	0
Williams, Keith	3	18	6.0	8	0
Matthews, Aubrey	1	12	12.0	12	0
Schonert, Turk	11	12	1.1	7	1
Clark, Bret	2	8	4.0	6	0
Campbell, Scott	1	7	7.0	7	0
Jones, Joey	1	7	7.0	7	0
Bailey, Stacey	1	6	6.0	6	0
Baker, Tony	1	3	3.0	3	0

INDIVIDUAL PASSING

	Att	Comp	Pct Comp	Yds	Avg Gain	TD	Pct TD	Long	Int	Pct Int	Rating Points
Archer, David	294	150	51.0	2007	6.83	10	3.4	65	9	3.1	71.6
Schonert, Turk	154	95	61.7	1032	6.70	4	2.6	41	8	5.2	68.4
Campbell, Scott, Pitt.-Atl.	7	1	14.3	7	1.00	0	0.0	7	0	0.0	39.6
Riggs, Gerald	1	0	0.0	0	0.00	0	0.0	0	0	0.0	39.6

INDIVIDUAL RECEIVERS

	No	Yards	Avg	Long	TD
Brown, Charlie	63	918	14.6	42	4
Dixon, Floyd	42	617	14.7	65	2
Cox, Arthur	24	301	12.5	49	1
Riggs, Gerald	24	136	5.7	11	0
Stamps, Sylvester	20	221	11.1	t39	1
Whisenhunt, Ken	20	184	9.2	t23	3
Williams, Keith	12	164	13.7	t32	1
Allen, Anthony	10	156	15.6	32	2
Jones, Joey	7	141	20.1	41	0
Johnson, Billy	6	57	9.5	27	0
Middleton, Ron	6	31	5.2	8	0
Andrews, William	5	35	7.0	14	0
Bailey, Stacey	3	39	13.0	21	0
Austin, Cliff	3	21	7.0	9	0
Matthews, Aubrey	1	25	25.0	25	0

INDIVIDUAL INTERCEPTORS

Clark, Bret	5	94	18.8	34	0
Case, Scott	4	41	10.3	41	0
Croudip, David	2	35	17.5	29	0
Williams, Joel	2	18	9.0	t14	1
Woodberry, Dennis	2	14	7.0	9	0
Wilkes, Reggie	2	11	5.5	10	0

	No	Yards	Avg	Long	TD
Butler, Bobby	1	33	33.0	t33	1
Curry, Buddy	1	32	32.0	32	0
Cason, Wendell	1	10	10.0	10	0
Rade, John	1	6	6.0	6	0
Moore, Robert	1	0	0.0	0	0

INDIVIDUAL KICKOFF RETURNERS

	No	Yards	Avg	Long	TD
Stamps, Sylvester	24	514	21.4	35	0
Williams, Keith	14	255	18.2	32	0
Austin, Cliff	7	120	17.1	25	0
Andrews, William	4	71	17.8	22	0
Matthews, Aubrey	3	42	14.0	20	0
Croudip, David	1	20	20.0	20	0
Dixon, Floyd	1	13	13.0	13	0

INDIVIDUAL PUNTERS

	No	Yards	Long	Avg	Total Punts	TB	Blk	Opp Ret	Ret Yds	In 20	Net Avg
Donnelly, Rick	78	3421	71	43.9	79	9	1	47	477	19	35.0

INDIVIDUAL PUNT RETURNERS

	No	FC	Yards	Avg	Long	TD
Dixon, Floyd	26	3	151	5.8	16	0
Johnson, Billy	8	8	87	10.9	30	0
Jones, Joey	7	1	36	5.1	14	0
Allen, Anthony	2	0	10	5.0	9	0
Stamps, Sylvester	1	0	8	8.0	8	0

INDIVIDUAL SCORERS
KICKERS

	XP	XPA	FG	FGA	PTS
Luckhurst, Mick	21	21	14	24	63
Haji-Sheikh, Ali	7	8	9	12	34
Donnelly, Rick	1	1	0	0	1

NON-KICKERS

	TD	TDR	TDP	TDM	PTS
Riggs, Gerald	9	9	0	0	54
Brown, Charlie	4	0	4	0	24
Whisenhunt, Ken	3	0	3	0	18
Allen, Anthony	2	0	2	0	12
Dixon, Floyd	2	0	2	0	12
Andrews, William	1	1	0	0	6
Austin, Cliff	1	1	0	0	6
Britt, James	1	0	0	1	6
Butler, Bobby	1	0	0	1	6
Cox, Arthur	1	0	1	0	6
Pitts, Mike	1	0	0	1	6
Schonert, Turk	1	1	0	0	6
Stamps, Sylvester	1	0	1	0	6
Williams, Joel	1	0	0	1	6
Williams, Keith	1	0	1	0	6
Gann, Mike	0	0	0	0	*2

CHICAGO BEARS
NFC Central Division

Corporate Headquarters: Halas Hall, 250 North Washington,
Lake Forest, Illinois 60045
Telephone: (312) 295-6600

CLUB OFFICIALS
Chairman of the Board: Edward W. McCaskey
President and Chief Executive Officer: Michael B. McCaskey
Vice President: Charles A. Brizzolara
Secretary: Virginia H. McCaskey
Vice President-Player Personnel: Bill Tobin
Director of Administration: Bill McGrane
Director of Community Involvement: Pat McCaskey
Director of Finance: Ted Phillips
Director of Public Relations: Ken Valdiserri
Public Relations Assistant: Bryan Harlan
Ticket Manager: Gary Christenson
Trainer: Fred Caito
Assistant Trainer: Brian McCaskey
Strength Coordinator: Clyde Emrich
Equipment Manager: Ray Earley
Assistant Equipment Manager: Gary Haeger
Scouts: Jim Parmer, Rod Graves, Don King

Stadium: Soldier Field (Capacity 66,030)
Playing Surface: AstroTurf
Stadium Address: 425 McFetridge Place, Chicago, Illinois 60605
Colours: Navy Blue, Orange and White
Summer Training Camp: Wisconsin-Platteville, Platteville,
Wisconsin 53818

CHICAGO BEARS 1987 SCHEDULE

PRE-SEASON

Aug.	16	at Miami	8:00
Aug.	22	PITTSBURGH	6:00
Aug.	31	ST. LOUIS	7:00
Sep.	5	at Los Angeles Raiders	1:00

REGULAR SEASON

Sep.	14	NEW YORK GIANTS	8:00
Sep.	20	TAMPA BAY	12:00
Sep.	27	at Detroit	1:00
Oct.	4	at Philadelphia	1:00
Oct.	11	MINNESOTA	12:00
Oct.	18	NEW ORLEANS	12:00
Oct.	25	at Tampa Bay	1:00
Nov.	1	KANSAS CITY	12:00
Nov.	8	at Green Bay	12:00
Nov.	16	at Denver	7:00
Nov.	22	DETROIT	12:00
Nov.	29	GREEN BAY	12:00
Dec.	6	at Minnesota	7:00
Dec.	14	at San Francisco	6:00
Dec.	20	SEATTLE	12:00
Dec.	27	at Los Angeles Raiders	1:00

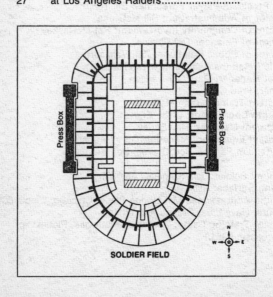

SOLDIER FIELD

CHICAGO BEARS
END OF SEASON DEPTH CHART

OFFENSE
WR   — 83 Willie Gualt, 89 Keith Ortego, 81 Lew Barnes
OLT   — 74 Jim Covert, 68 Paul Blair, 79 Kurt Becker
OLG   — 62 Mark Bortz, 79 Kurt Becker, 75 Stefan Humphries
C   — 63 Jay Hilgenberg, 52 Larry Rubens
ORG   — 57 Tom Thayer, 79 Kurt Becker, 75 Stefan Humphries
ORT   — 78 Keith Van Horne, 68 Paul Blair, 79 Kurt Becker
TE   — 87 Emery Moorehead, 80 Tim Wrightman,
        49 Riley Walton
WR   — 89 Keith Ortego, 29 Dennis Gentry,
        85 Dennis McKinnon
RB   — 34 Walter Payton, 20 Thomas Sanders,
        35 Neal Anderson
RB   — 26 Matt Suhey, 33 Calvin Thomas
QB   — 2 Doug Flutie, 18 Mike Tomczak, 4 Steve Fuller,
        9 Jim McMahon

DEFENSE
DLE   — 99 Dan Hampton, 73 Mike Hartenstine, 90 Al Harris
DLT   — 76 Steve McMichael, 70 Henry Waechter
DRT   — 72 William Perry, 70 Henry Waechter
DRE   — 95 Richard Dent, 73 Mike Hartenstine, 90 Al Harris,
        53 Dan Rains
LLB   — 55 Otis Wilson, 59 Ron Rivera, 54 Brian Cabral
MLB   — 50 Mike Singletary, 59 Ron Rivera, 51 Jim Morrissey
        53 Dan Rains
RLB   — 58 Wilber Marshall, 90 Al Harris, 54 Brian Cabral
LCB   — 27 Mike Richardson, 24 Vestee Jackson
RCB   — 24 Vestee Jackson, 48 Reggie Phillips, 21 Les Frazier
SS   — 22 Dave Duerson, 25 Todd Bell
FS   — 45 Gary Fencik, 23 Shaun Gayle

SPECIAL TEAMS
K   — 6 Kevin Butler
P   — 8 Maury Buford
PR   — 81 Lew Barnes, 89 Keith Ortego
KR   — 29 Dennis Gentry, 20 Thomas Sanders
LSN(F) — 63 Jay Hilgenberg, 52 Larry Rubens
LSN(P) — 52 Larry Rubens, 63 Jay Hilgenberg
H   — 4 Steve Fuller, 18 Mike Tomczak

CHICAGO BEARS

INDIVIDUAL RUSHERS

	Att	Yards	Avg	Long	TD
Payton, Walter	321	1333	4.2	41	8
Suhey, Matt	84	270	3.2	17	2
Sanders, Thomas	27	224	8.3	t75	5
Thomas, Calvin	56	224	4.0	23	0
McMahon, Jim	22	152	6.9	23	1
Anderson, Neal	35	146	4.2	23	0
Tomczak, Mike	23	117	5.1	16	3
Gentry, Dennis	11	103	9.4	29	1
Gault, Willie	8	79	9.9	33	0
Flutie, Doug	9	36	4.0	19	1
Fuller, Steve	8	30	3.8	10	0
Perry, William	1	-1	-1.0	-1	0
Buford, Maury	1	-13	-13.0	-13	0

INDIVIDUAL PASSING

	Att	Comp	Pct Comp	Yds	Avg Gain	TD	Pct TD	Long	Int	Pct Int	Rating Points
Flutie, Doug	46	23	50.0	361	7.85	3	6.5	t58	2	5.3	80.1
McMahon, Jim Chi	150	77	51.3	995	6.63	5	3.3	t58	8	5.3	61.4
Fuller, Steve	64	34	53.1	451	7.05	2	3.1	t50	4	6.3	60.1
Tomczak, Mike	151	74	49.0	1105	7.32	2	1.3	85	10	6.6	50.2
Payton, Walter	4	0	0.0	0	0.00	0	0.0	0	1	25.0	0.0

INDIVIDUAL RECEIVERS

	No	Yards	Avg	Long	TD
Gault, Willie	42	818	19.5	t53	5
Payton, Walter	37	382	10.3	57	3
Moorehead, Emery	26	390	15.0	85	1
Suhey, Matt	24	235	9.8	58	0
Ortego, Keith	23	430	18.7	t58	2
Wrightman, Tim	22	241	11.0	29	0
Gentry, Dennis	19	238	12.5	41	0
Anderson, Neal	4	80	20.0	t58	1
Barnes, Lew	4	54	13.5	14	0
Thomas, Calvin	4	18	4.5	18	0
Sanders, Thomas	2	18	9.0	18	0
Bortz, Mark	1	8	8.0	8	0

INDIVIDUAL INTERCEPTORS

	No	Yards	Avg	Long	TD
Richardson, Mike	7	69	9.9	32	0
Duerson, Dave	6	139	23.2	38	0
Marshall, Wilber	5	68	13.6	t58	1
Fencik, Gary	3	37	12.3	24	0
Jackson, Vestee	3	0	0.0	0	0
Wilson, Otis	2	31	15.5	21	0
Gayle, Shaun	1	13	13.0	13	0
Phillips, Reggie	1	6	6.0	6	0
McMichael, Steve	1	5	5.0	5	0
Singletary, Mike	1	3	3.0	3	0
Bell, Todd	1	-1	-1.0	-1	0

INDIVIDUAL KICKOFF RETURNERS

	No	Yards	Avg	Long	TD
Gentry, Dennis	20	576	28.8	t91	1
Sanders, Thomas	22	399	18.1	44	0
Anderson, Neal	4	26	6.5	13	0
Barnes, Lew	3	94	31.3	t85	1
Gault, Willie	1	20	20.0	20	0

INDIVIDUAL PUNTERS

	No	Yards	Long	Avg	Total Punts	TB	Blk	Opp Ret	Ret Yds	In 20	Net Avg
Buford, Maury	69	2850	59	41.3	70	8	1	23	110	20	36.9

INDIVIDUAL PUNT RETURNERS

	No	FC	Yards	Avg	Long	TD
Barnes, Lew	57	9	482	8.5	35	0

INDIVIDUAL SCORERS

KICKERS

	XP	XPA	FG	FGA	PTS
Butler, Kevin	36	37	28	41	120

NON-KICKERS

	TD	TDR	TDP	TDM	PTS
Payton, Walter	11	8	3	0	66
Gault, Willie	5	0	5	0	30
Sanders, Thomas	5	5	0	0	30
Gentry, Dennis	3	1	0	2	18
Tomczak, Mike	3	3	0	0	18
Marshall, Wilber	2	0	0	2	12
Ortego, Keith	2	0	2	0	12
Suhey, Matt	2	2	0	0	12
Anderson, Neal	1	0	1	0	6
Barnes, Lew	1	0	0	1	6
Flutie, Doug	1	1	0	0	6
McMahon, Jim	1	1	0	0	6
Moorehead, Emery	1	0	1	0	6
Hampton, Dan	0	0	0	0	*2
McMichael, Steve	0	0	0	0	*2

DALLAS COWBOYS
NFC Eastern Division

Address: Cowboys Center, One Cowboys Parkway, Irving,
   Texas 75063
Telephone: (214) 556-9900

CLUB OFFICIALS
General Partner: H. R. Bright
President-General Manager: Texas E. Schramm
Vice President-Personnel Development: Gil Brandt
Vice President-Treasurer: Don Wilson
Vice President-Administration: Joe Bailey
Vice President-Pro Personnel: Bob Ackles
Director of Public Relations: Doug Todd
Media Relations-Marketing: Greg Aiello
Business Manager: Dan Werner
Director of Counselling Services: Larry Wansley
Ticket Manager: Steve Orsini
Trainers: Don Cochren, Ken Locker
Equipment Manager: William T. (Buck) Buchanan
Cheerleaders Director: Suzanne Mitchell

Stadium: Texas Stadium (Capacity 63,855)
Playing Surface: Texas Turf
Stadium Address: Irving, Texas 75062
Colours: Royal Blue, Metallic Silver Blue and White
Summer Training Camp: California Lutheran University,
   Thousand Oaks, California 91360

DALLAS COWBOYS 1987 SCHEDULE

PRE-SEASON

Aug.	15	at San Diego	6:00
Aug.	22	at San Francisco	6:00
Aug.	30	LOS ANGELES RAIDERS	7:00
Sep.	5	HOUSTON	8:00

REGULAR SEASON

Sep.	13	at St. Louis	12:00
Sep.	20	at New York Giants	4:00
Sep.	27	BUFFALO	12:00
Oct.	4	at New York Jets	4:00
Oct.	11	PHILADELPHIA	12:00
Oct.	19	WASHINGTON	8:00
Oct.	25	at Philadelphia	1:00
Nov.	2	NEW YORK GIANTS	8:00
Nov.	8	at Detroit	1:00
Nov.	15	at New England	1:00
Nov.	22	MIAMI	7:00
Nov.	26	MINNESOTA	3:00
Dec.	6	ATLANTA	12:00
Dec.	13	at Washington	1:00
Dec.	21	at Los Angeles Rams	6:00
Dec.	27	ST. LOUIS	12:00

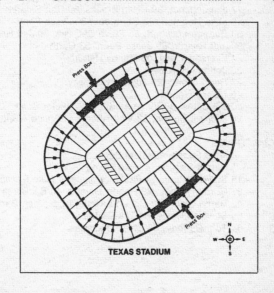

TEXAS STADIUM

DALLAS COWBOYS
END OF SEASON DEPTH CHART

OFFENSE

WR — 80 Tony Hill, 87 Gordon Banks, 82 Mike Renfro
OLT — 71 Mark Tuinei, 70 Howard Richards,
        62 Brian Baldinger
OLG — 63 Glen Titensor, 61 Nate Newton
C — 64 Tom Rafferty, 62 Brian Baldinger, 71 Mark Tuinei
ORG — 68 Crawford Ker, 61 Nate Newton
ORT — 75 Phil Pozderac, 70 Howard Richards,
        62 Brian Baldinger
TE — 84 Doug Crosbie, 85 Thornton Chandler,
        30 Timmy Newsome
WR — 86 Mike Sherrard, 82 Mike Renfro, 81 Karl Powe
QB — 11 Danny White, 16 Steve Pelluer, 10 Reggie Collier,
        14 Paul McDonald
RB — 33 Tony Dorsett, 42 Darryl Clack, 29 Robert Lavette
F-B — 34 Herschel Walker, 30 Timmy Newsome,
        46 Todd Fowler

DEFENSE

DLE — 72 Ed Jones, 99 Kevin Brooks, 60 Don Smerek
DLT — 78 John Dutton, 60 Don Smerek, 99 Kevin Brooks
DRT — 54 Randy White, 60 Don Smerek, 99 Kevin Brooks
DRE — 77 Jim Jeffcoat, 99 Kevin Brooks, 60 Don Smerek
LLB — 58 Mike Hegman, 53 Garth Jax, 59 Jesse Penn
MLB — 56 Eugene Lockhart, 55 Steve DeOssie, 50 Jeff Rohrer
RLB — 50 Jeff Rohrer, 59 Jesse Penn, 53 Garth Jax
LCB — 24 Everson Walls, 45 Manny Hendrix,
        23 Johnny Holloway
RCB — 27 Ron Fellows, 23 Johnny Holloway,
        45 Manny Hendrix
SS — 40 Bill Bates, 36 Vince Albritton, 22 Victor Scott
FS — 26 Michael Downs, 22 Victor Scott, 36 Vince Albritton

SPECIAL TEAMS

P — 4 Mike Saxon, 1 Rafael Septien
K — 1 Rafael Septien, 4 Mike Saxon
H — 16 Steve Pelluer, 14 Paul McDonald, 4 Mike Saxon
PR — 87 Gordon Banks, 29 Robert Lavette, 40 Bill Bates
KR — 42 Darryl Clack, 29 Robert Lavette, 87 Gordon Banks
LSN(P) — 55 Steve DeOssie, 64 Tom Rafferty
LSN(F) — 64 Tom Rafferty, 55 Steve DeOssie

DALLAS COWBOYS

INDIVIDUAL RUSHERS

	Att	Yards	Avg	Long	TD
Dorsett, Tony	184	748	4.1	33	5
Walker, Herschel	151	737	4.9	t84	12
Pelluer, Steve	41	255	6.2	21	1
Newsome, Tim	34	110	3.2	13	2
Collier, Reggie	6	53	8.8	21	0
Clack, Darryl	4	19	4.8	8	0
White, Danny	8	16	2.0	10	1
Sherrard, Mike	2	11	5.5	8	0
Cosbie, Doug	1	9	9.0	9	0
Lavette, Robert	10	6	0.6	5	0
Fowler, Todd	6	5	0.8	2	0

INDIVIDUAL PASSING

	Att	Comp	Pct Comp	Yds	Avg Gain	TD	Pct TD	Long	Int	Pct Int	Rating Points
Pelluer, Steve	378	215	56.9	2727	7.21	8	2.1	t84	17	4.5	67.9
White Danny	153	95	62.1	1157	7.56	12	7.8	63	5	3.3	97.9
Collier, Reggie	15	8	53.3	96	6.40	1	6.7	27	2	13.3	55.8
Renfro, Mike	1	1	100.0	23	23.00	0	0.0	23	0	0.0	118.8

INDIVIDUAL RECEIVERS

	No	Yards	Avg	Long	TD
Walker, Herschel	76	837	11.0	t84	2
Hill, Tony	49	770	15.7	63	3
Newsome, Tim	48	421	8.8	30	3
Sherrard, Mike	41	744	18.1	t68	5
Cosbie, Doug	28	312	11.1	t22	1
Dorsett, Tony	25	267	10.7	t36	1
Renfro, Mike	22	325	14.8	t30	3
Banks, Gordon	17	202	11.9	23	0
Chandler, Thornton	6	57	9.5	15	2
Lavette, Robert	5	31	6.2	9	1
Fowler, Todd	1	19	19.0	19	0
Clack, Darryl	1	18	18.0	18	0

INDIVIDUAL INTERCEPTORS

	No	Yards	Avg	Long	TD
Downs, Michael	6	54	9.0	31	0
Fellows, Ron	5	46	9.2	t34	1
Walls, Everson	3	46	15.3	24	0
Scott, Victor	1	31	31.0	31	0
Lockhart, Eugene	1	5	5.0	5	0
Holloway, Johnny	1	1	1.0	1	0

INDIVIDUAL KICKOFF RETURNERS

	No	Yards	Avg	Long	TD
Lavette, Robert	36	699	19.4	37	0
Clack, Darryl	19	421	22.2	51	0
Newsome, Tim	2	32	16.0	18	0
Banks, Gordon	1	56	56.0	56	0
Tuinei, Mark	1	0	0.0	0	0

INDIVIDUAL PUNTERS

	No	Yards	Long	Avg	Total Punts	TB	Blk	Opp Ret	Ret Yds	In 20	Net Avg
Saxon, Mike	86	3498	58	40.7	87	10	1	41	301	28	34.4

INDIVIDUAL PUNT RETURNERS

	No	FC	Yards	Avg	Long	TD
Banks, Gordon	27	14	160	5.9	20	0
Lavette, Robert	18	3	92	5.1	28	0
Holloway, Johnny	1	0	0	0.0	0	0

INDIVIDUAL SCORERS

KICKERS	XP	XPA	FG	FGA	PTS
Septien, Rafael	43	43	15	21	88

NON-KICKERS	TD	TDR	TDP	TDM	PTS
Walker, Herschel	14	12	2	0	84
Dorsett, Tony	6	5	1	0	36
Newsome, Tim	5	2	3	0	30
Sherrard, Mike	5	0	5	0	30
Hill, Tony	3	0	3	0	18
Renfro, Mike	3	0	3	0	18
Chandler, Thornton	2	0	2	0	12
Cosbie, Doug	1	0	1	0	6
Fellows, Ron	1	0	0	1	6
Lavette, Robert	1	0	1	0	6
Pelluer, Steve	1	1	0	0	6
White, Danny	1	1	0	0	6

DETROIT LIONS
NFC Central Division

Address: Pontiac Silverdome, 1200 Featherstone Road,
   Box 4200, Pontiac, Michigan 48057
Telephone: (313) 335-4131

CLUB OFFICIALS
Owner-President: William Clay Ford
Executive Vice President-General Manager: Russell Thomas
Director of Football Operations-Head Coach: Darryl Rogers
Director of Player Personnel: Joe Bushofsky
Controller: Charles Schmidt
In-House Counsel: Jerome R. Vainisi
Scouts: Dirk Dierking, Ron Hughes, Jim Owens,
   Jerry Neri, John Trump
Director of Public Relations: TBA
Assistant Director of Public Relations: Bill Keenist
Public and Community Relations: Tim Pendell
Ticket Manager: Fred Otto
Trainer: Kent Falb
Strength and Conditioning: Don Clemons
Equipment Manager: Dan Jaroshewich

Stadium: Pontiac Silverdome (Capacity 80,638)
Playing Surface: AstroTurf
Stadium Address: 1200 Featherstone Road, Pontiac,
   Michigan 48057
Colours: Honolulu Blue and Silver
Summer Training Camp: Oakland University, Rochester,
   Michigan 48063

DETROIT LIONS 1987 SCHEDULE

PRE-SEASON

Aug.	15	INDIANAPOLIS	8:00
Aug.	22	CINCINNATI	8:00
Aug.	28	at Seattle	7:30
Sep.	3	at Philadelphia	7:30

REGULAR SEASON

Sep.	13	at Minnesota	12:00
Sep.	20	at Los Angeles Raiders	1:00
Sep.	27	CHICAGO	1:00
Oct.	4	TAMPA BAY	1:00
Oct.	11	at Green Bay	12:00
Oct.	18	SEATTLE	1:00
Oct.	25	GREEN BAY	1:00
Nov.	1	at Denver	2:00
Nov.	8	DALLAS	1:00
Nov.	15	at Washington	1:00
Nov.	22	at Chicago	12:00
Nov.	26	KANSAS CITY	12:30
Dec.	6	LOS ANGELES RAMS	1:00
Dec.	13	at Tampa Bay	4:00
Dec.	20	MINNESOTA	1:00
Dec.	27	at Atlanta	1:00

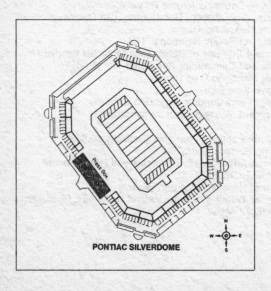

PONTIAC SILVERDOME

DETROIT LIONS
END OF SEASON DEPTH CHART

OFFENSE

WR	— 39 Leonard Thompson, 89 Jeff Chadwick
OLT	— 75 Lomas Brown, 61 Scott Barrows, 64 Eric Sanders
OLG	— 73 Harvey Salem, 61 Scott Barrows, 64 Eric Sanders
C	— 52 Steve Mott, 61 Scott Barrows
ORG	— 70 Keith Dorney, 61 Scott Barrows, 64 Eric Sanders
ORT	— 71 Rich Strenger, 70 Keith Dorney, 64 Eric Sanders
TE	— 81 Jimmie Giles, 87 David Lewis, 84 Rob Rubick
WR	— 80 Carl Bland, 82 Pete Mandley
QB	— 16 Chuck Long, 12 Joe Ferguson, 17 Eric Hipple
RB	— 32 Garry James, 24 Alvin Moore, 36 Herman Hunter
F-B	— 30 James Jones, 38 Scott Williams

DEFENSE

DLE	— 77 Keith Ferguson, 62 Curtis Green, 66 Leon Evans
NT	— 76 Eric Williams, 62 Curtis Green, 68 Steve Baack
DRE	— 79 William Gay, 62 Curtis Green, 66 Leon Evans
LOLB	— 92 Angelo King, 54 James Johnson, 96 Paul Butcher
LILB	— 51 Shelton Robinson, 58 James Harrell, 96 Paul Butcher
RILB	— 57 Vernon Maxwell, 58 James Harrell, 92 Angelo King
ROLB	— 55 Michael Cofer, 92 Angelo King, 54 James Johnson
LCB	— 40 Duane Galloway, 43 Donnie Elder, 47 Rod Hill
RCB	— 29 Bruce McNorton, 43 Donnie Elder, 47 Rod Hill
SS	— 21 Demetrious Johnson, 33 William Graham, 34 James Griffin
FS	— 31 Devon Mitchell, 34 James Griffin, 33 William Graham

SPECIAL TEAMS

PK	— 3 Eddie Murray, 6 Jim Arnold
P	— 6 Jim Arnold, 3 Eddie Murray
H	— 17 Eric Hipple, 6 Jim Arnold
LSN	— 64 Eric Sanders, 61 Scott Barrows
PR	— 82 Pete Mandley, 80 Carl Bland, 43 Donnie Elder
KOR	— 36 Herman Hunter, 82 Pete Mandley, 43 Donnie Elder

DETROIT LIONS

INDIVIDUAL RUSHERS

	Att	Yards	Avg	Long	TD
Jones, James	252	903	3.6	39	8
James, Garry	159	688	4.3	t60	3
Moore, Alvin	19	73	3.8	18	0
Hipple, Eric	16	46	2.9	13	0
Ferguson, Joe	5	25	5.0	14	0
Hunter, Herman	3	22	7.3	18	0
Williams, Scott	13	22	1.7	5	2
Long, Chuck	2	0	0.0	0	0
Black, Mike	1	−8	−8.0	−8	0

INDIVIDUAL PASSING

	Att	Comp	Pct Comp	Yds	Avg Gain	TD	Pct TD	Long	Int	Pct Int	Rating Points
Hipple, Eric	305	192	63.0	1919	6.29	9	3.0	46	11	3.6	75.6
Long, Chuck	155	73	47.1	941	6.07	7	4.5	73	7	4.5	62.0
Ferguson, Joe	155	73	47.1	941	6.07	7	4.5	73	7	4.5	62.9

INDIVIDUAL RECEIVERS

	No	Yards	Avg	Long	TD
Jones, James	54	334	6.2	21	1
Chadwick, Jeff	53	995	18.8	73	5
Bland, Carl	44	511	11.6	34	2
Giles, Jimmie, T.B.-Det.	37	376	10.2	30	4
James, Garry	34	219	6.4	26	0
Thompson, Leonard	25	320	12.8	t36	5
Hunter, Herman	25	218	8.7	t18	1
Lewis, David	10	88	8.8	16	1
Moore, Alvin	8	47	5.9	8	0
Mandley, Pete	7	106	15.1	51	0
Rubick, Rob	5	62	12.4	27	0
Williams, Scott	2	9	4.5	6	0

INDIVIDUAL INTERCEPTORS

	No	Yards	Avg	Long	TD
Mitchell, Devon	5	41	8.2	17	0
Galloway, Duane	4	58	14.5	36	0
McNorton, Bruce	4	10	2.5	10	0
Griffin, James	2	34	17.0	21	0
Johnson, Demetrious	2	18	9.0	18	0
Williams, Jimmy	2	12	6.0	11	0
Bostic, John	1	8	8.0	8	0
Ferguson, Keith	1	7	7.0	7	0
Williams, Eric	1	2	2.0	2	0

INDIVIDUAL KICKOFF RETURNERS

	No	Yards	Avg	Long	TD
Hunter, Herman	49	1007	20.6	54	0
Elder, Donnie, Pitt.-Det.	22	435	19.8	36	0
Bland, Carl	6	114	19.0	24	0
Smith, Oscar	5	81	16.2	30	0
Graham, William	3	72	24.0	27	0
Mandley, Pete	2	37	18.5	37	0
Evans, Leon	1	0	0.0	0	0

INDIVIDUAL PUNTERS

	No	Yards	Long	Avg	Total Punts	TB	Blk	Opp Ret	Ret Yds	In 20	Net Avg
Black, Mike	46	1819	57	39.5	47	5	1	21	250	11	31.3
Arnold, Jim	36	1533	60	42.6	37	4	1	18	267	7	32.1
Murray, Ed	1	37	37	37.0	1	1	0	0	0	0	17.0

INDIVIDUAL PUNT RETURNERS

	No	FC	Yards	Avg	Long	TD
Mandley, Pete	43	9	420	9.8	t81	1

INDIVIDUAL SCORERS

KICKERS

	XP	XPA	FG	FGA	PTS
Murray, Ed	31	32	18	25	85

NON-KICKERS

	TD	TDR	TDP	TDM	PTS
Jones, James	9	8	1	0	54
Chadwick, Jeff	5	0	5	0	30
Thompson, Leonard	5	0	5	0	30
Giles, Jimmie, T.B.-Det.	4	0	4	0	24
James, Garry	3	3	0	0	18
Bland, Carl	2	0	2	0	12
Williams, Scott	2	2	0	0	12
Hunter, Herman	1	0	1	0	6
Lewis, David	1	0	1	0	6
Mandley, Pete	1	0	0	1	6

GREEN BAY PACKERS
NFC Central Division

Address: 1265 Lombardi Avenue, Green Bay,
  Wisconsin 54307-0628
Telephone: (414) 494-2351

CLUB OFFICIALS
Chairman of the Board: Dominic Olejniczak
President, CEO: Robert Parins
Vice President: Tony Canadeo
Secretary: Peter M. Platten III
Treasurer: Phil Hendrickson
Assistant to the President: Bob Harlan
Assistant to the President: Tom Miller
Executive Vice President, Football Operations: Tom Braatz
Public Relations Director: Lee Remmel
Assistant Director of Public Relations: Scott Berchtold
Ticket Director: Mark Wagner
Director of College Scouting: Dick Corrick
Pro Scout: Chuck Hutchison
Video Director: Al Treml
Trainer: Domenic Gentile
Equipment Manager: Bob Noel

Stadiums: (I) Lambeau Field (Capacity 57,091)
            (II) Milwaukee County Stadium (Capacity 56,051)
Playing Surfaces: Grass
Stadiums Addresses: (I) P.O. Box 10628,
  1265 Lombardi Avenue, Green Bay, Wisconsin 54307-0628
  (II) Highway 1-94, Milwaukee, Wisconsin 53214
Colours: Dark Green, Gold and White
Summer Training Camp: St. Norbert College, DePere,
  Wisconsin 54115

GREEN BAY PACKERS 1987 SCHEDULE

PRE-SEASON

Aug.	15	vs. Denver at Tempe, Ariz.	7:00
Aug.	22	vs. Washington at Madison, Wis.	1:00
Aug.	29	CINCINNATI	7:00
Sep.	5	vs. Cleveland at Milwaukee	7:00

REGULAR SEASON

Sep.	13	LOS ANGELES RAIDERS	3:00
Sep.	20	DENVER at Milwaukee	12:00
Sep.	27	at Tampa Bay	1:00
Oct.	4	at Minnesota	12:00
Oct.	11	DETROIT	12:00
Oct.	18	PHILADELPHIA	12:00
Oct.	25	at Detroit	1:00
Nov.	1	TAMPA BAY at Milwaukee	12:00
Nov.	8	CHICAGO	12:00
Nov.	15	at Seattle	1:00
Nov.	22	at Kansas City	12:00
Nov.	29	at Chicago	12:00
Dec.	6	SAN FRANCISCO	12:00
Dec.	13	MINNESOTA at Milwaukee	12:00
Dec.	19	at New York Giants	12:30
Dec.	27	at New Orleans	12:00

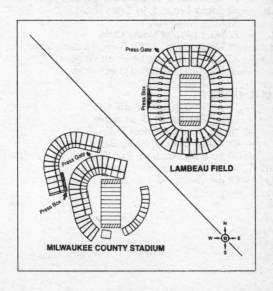

LAMBEAU FIELD

MILWAUKEE COUNTY STADIUM

GREEN BAY PACKERS
END OF SEASON DEPTH CHART

OFFENSE

WR	— 40 Eddie Lee Ivery, 87 Walter Stanley, 84 Nolan Franz
OLT	— 75 Ken Ruettgers, 77 Greg Feasel, 67 Karl Swanke
OLG	— 72 Tom Neville, 57 Rich Moran
C	— 67 Karl Swanke, 69 Bill Cherry
ORG	— 65 Ron Hallstrom, 72 Tom Neville, 57 Rich Moran
ORT	— 73 Alan Veingrad, 75 Ken Ruettgers
WR	— 87 Walter Stanley, 40 Eddie Lee Ivery, 82 Mike Moffitt
TE	— 81 Dan Ross, 86 Ed West, 89 Mark Lewis
QB	— 16 Randy Wright, 4 Chuck Fusina, 18 Joe Shield
H-B	— 31 Gerry Ellis, 36 Kenneth Davis, 42 Gary Ellerson, 40 Eddie Lee Ivery
F-B	— 30 Paul Ott Carruth, 31 Gerry Ellis

DEFENSE

DLE	— 76 Alphonso Carreker, 92 Ben Thomas
NT	— 79 Donnie Humphrey, 94 Charles Martin, 92 Ben Thomas
DRE	— 93 Robert Brown, 90 Ezra Johnson
LOLB	— 97 Tim Harris, 53 Bobby Leopold, 52 Mike Weddington
LILB	— 55 Randy Scott, 99 John Dorsey
RILB	— 91 Brian Noble, 99 John Dorsey, 56 Burnell Dent
ROLB	— 53 Bobby Leopold, 91 Brian Noble, 52 Mike Weddington
LCB	— 22 Mark Lee, 24 Mossy Cade
RCB	— 24 Mossy Cade, 20 Ed Berry, 32 John Simmons
SS	— 23 George Greene, 28 Elbert Watts
FS	— 29 Ken Stills, 49 David Greenwood

SPECIAL TEAMS

K	— 10 Al Del Greco, 31 Gerry Ellis
P	— 13 Bill Renner, 91 Brian Noble
H	— 18 Joe Shield, 4 Chuck Fusina
PR	— 87 Walter Stanley, 20 Ed Berry
KR	— 36 Kenneth Davis, 42 Gary Ellerson, 32 John Simmons
LSN(P)	— 69 Bill Cherry, 99 John Dorsey
LSN(F)	— 69 Bill Cherry, 99 John Dorsey

GREEN BAY PACKERS

INDIVIDUAL RUSHERS

	Att	Yards	Avg	Long	TD
Davis, Kenneth	114	519	4.6	50	0
Ellis, Gerry	84	345	4.1	24	2
Carruth, Paul Ott	81	308	3.8	42	2
Ellerson, Gary	90	287	3.2	18	3
Clark, Jessie	18	41	2.3	9	0
Wright, Randy	18	41	2.3	18	1
Ivery, Eddie Lee	4	25	6.3	15	0
Stanley, Walter	1	19	19.0	19	0
Epps, Phillip	4	18	4.5	20	0
Fusina, Chuck	7	11	1.6	6	0
Ferragamo, Vince	1	0	0.0	0	0
Renner, Bill	1	0	0.0	0	0
Swanke, Karl	1	0	0.0	0	0

INDIVIDUAL PASSING

	Att	Comp	Pct Comp	Yds	Avg Gain	TD	Pct TD	Long	Int	Pct Int	Rating Points
Wright, Randy	492	263	53.5	3247	6.60	17	3.5	62	23	4.7	66.2
Fusina, Chuck	32	19	59.4	178	5.56	0	0.0	42	1	3.1	61.7
Ferragamo, Vince	40	23	57.5	283	7.08	1	2.5	50	3	7.5	56.6
Lofton, James	1	0	0.0	0	0.00	0	0.0	0	0	0.0	39.6

INDIVIDUAL RECEIVERS

	No	Yards	Avg	Long	TD
Lofton, James	64	840	13.1	36	4
Epps, Phillip	49	612	12.5	t53	4
Stanley, Walter	35	723	20.7	62	2
Ivery, Eddie Lee	31	385	12.4	42	1
Ellis, Gerry	24	258	10.8	29	0
Carruth, Paul	24	134	5.6	19	2
Davis, Kenneth	21	142	6.8	18	1
Ross, Dan	17	143	8.4	16	1
West, Ed	15	199	13.3	t46	1
Ellerson, Gary	12	130	10.8	32	0
Clark, Jessie	6	41	6.8	12	0
Moffitt, Mike	4	87	21.8	34	0
Lewis, Mark	2	7	3.5	t4	2
Franz, Nolan	1	7	7.0	7	0

INDIVIDUAL INTERCEPTORS

	No	Yards	Avg	Long	TD
Lee, Mark	9	33	3.7	11	0
Cade, Mossy	4	26	6.5	18	0
Greene, George	2	0	0.0	0	0
Stills, Ken	1	58	58.0	t58	1
Leopold, Bobby	1	21	21.0	21	0
Watts, Elbert	1	6	6.0	6	0
Anderson, John	1	3	3.0	3	0
Flynn, Tom	1	0	0.0	0	0

INDIVIDUAL KICKOFF RETURNERS

	No	Yards	Avg	Long	TD
Stanley, Walter	28	559	20.0	55	0
Watts, Elbert	12	239	19.9	40	0
Davis, Kenneth	12	231	19.3	35	0
Stills, Ken	10	209	20.9	38	0
Ellerson, Gary	7	154	22.0	57	0
Carruth, Paul Ott	4	40	10.0	20	0
Epps, Phillip	1	21	21.0	21	0
Berry, Ed	1	16	16.0	16	0
Noble, Brian	1	1	1.0	1	0

INDIVIDUAL PUNTERS

	No	Yards	Long	Avg	Total Punts	TB	Blk	Opp Ret	Ret Yds	In 20	Net Avg
Bracken, Don	55	2203	63	40.1	57	5	2	33	235	6	32.8
Renner, Bill	15	622	50	41.5	18	1	3	11	52	2	30.6

INDIVIDUAL PUNT RETURNERS

	No	FC	Yards	Avg	Long	TD
Stanley, Walter	33	7	316	9.6	t83	1

INDIVIDUAL SCORERS

KICKERS	XP	XPA	FG	FGA	PTS
Del Greco, Al	29	29	17	27	80

NON-KICKERS	TD	TDR	TDP	TDM	PTS
Carruth, Paul	4	2	2	0	24
Epps, Phillip	4	0	4	0	24
Lofton, James	4	0	4	0	24
Ellerson, Gary	3	3	0	0	18
Stanley, Walter	3	0	2	1	18
Ellis, Gerry	2	2	0	0	12
Lewis, Mark	2	0	2	0	12
Davis, Kenneth	1	0	1	0	6
Ivery, Eddie Lee	1	0	1	0	6
Ross, Dan	1	0	1	0	6
Simmons, John	1	0	0	1	6
Stills, Ken	1	0	0	1	6
West, Ed	1	0	1	0	6
Wright, Randy	1	1	0	0	6

LOS ANGELES RAMS
NFC Western Division

Address: 2327 West Lincoln Ave., Anaheim, California 92801
Telephone: (714) 535-7267 or (213) 585-5400

CLUB OFFICIALS
President: Georgia Frontiere
Vice President, Finance: John Shaw
General Counsel: Jay Zygmunt
Administrator, Football Operations: Jack Faulkner
Director of Operations: Dick Beam
Director of Player Personnel: John Math
Director of Community Relations: Marshall Klein
Director of Administration: Barbara Robinson
Director of Promotions/Sales: Pete Donovan
Directors of Public Relations: John Oswald, Jerry Wilcox
Public Relations Assistant: Doug Ward
Trainers: George Menefee, Jim Anderson, Garrett Giemont
Equipment Manager: Don Hewitt
Assistant Equipment Manager: Todd Hewitt

Stadium: Anaheim Stadium (Capacity 69,007)
Playing Surface: Grass
Stadium Address: 1900 State College Blvd., Anaheim,
   California 92806
Colours: Royal Blue, Gold and White
Summer Training Camp: California State University, Fullerton,
   California 92634

LOS ANGELES RAMS 1987 SCHEDULE

PRE-SEASON

Aug.	9	vs. Denver at Wembley, London	6:00
Aug.	13	SEATTLE	7:30
Aug.	23	at San Diego	5:00
Aug.	29	DENVER	7:00
Sep.	5	WASHINGTON	6:00

REGULAR SEASON

Sep.	13	at Houston	12:00
Sep.	20	MINNESOTA	1:00
Sep.	27	CINCINNATI	1:00
Oct.	4	at New Orleans	12:00
Oct.	11	PITTSBURGH	1:00
Oct.	18	at Atlanta	1:00
Oct.	26	at Cleveland	9:00
Nov.	1	SAN FRANCISCO	1:00
Nov.	8	NEW ORLEANS	1:00
Nov.	15	at St. Louis	12:00
Nov.	23	at Washington	9:00
Nov.	29	TAMPA BAY	1:00
Dec.	6	at Detroit	1:00
Dec.	13	ATLANTA	1:00
Dec.	21	DALLAS	6:00
Dec.	27	at San Francisco	5:00

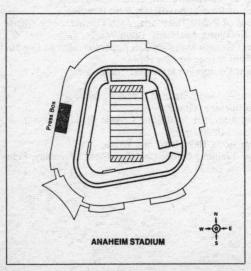

ANAHEIM STADIUM

LOS ANGELES RAMS
END OF SEASON DEPTH CHART

OFFENSE

WR	—	83 Kevin House, 89 Ron Brown
WR	—	80 Henry Ellard, 88 Michael Young
OLT	—	75 Irv Pankey, 67 Duval Love
OLG	—	66 Tom Newberry, 61 Tony Slaton
C	—	56 Doug Smith, 61 Tony Slaton
ORG	—	60 Dennis Harrah, 61 Tony Slaton
ORT	—	78 Jackie Slater, 67 Duval Love
TE	—	81 David Hill, 86 Damone Johnson, 45 Darren Long
QB	—	11 Jim Everett, 8 Steve Dils, 10 Steve Bartkowski
RB	—	30 Barry Redden, 32 Tim Tyrrell
RB	—	29 Eric Dickerson, 33 Charles White

DEFENSE

DLE	—	93 Doug Reed, 98 Shawn Miller
NT	—	98 Shawn Miller, 69 Greg Meisner, 99 Alvin Wright
DRE	—	71 Reggie Doss, 77 Gary Jeter
LOLB	—	58 Mel Owens, 91 Kevin Greene
RILB	—	59 Mark Jerue, 52 Cliff Thrift
LILB	—	55 Carl Ekern, 57 Jim Laughlin
ROLB	—	54 Mike Wilcher, 51 Norwood Vann
LCB	—	25 Jerry Gray, 20 Johnnie Johnson
RCB	—	47 LeRoy Irvin, 25 Jerry Gray, 49 Mickey Sutton
FS	—	22 Vince Newsome, 20 Johnnie Johnson
SS	—	21 Nolan Cromwell, 48 Tim Fox

SPECIAL TEAMS

K	—	1 Mike Lansford
P	—	3 Dale Hatcher
KR	—	49 Mickey Sutton, 33 Charles White, 89 Ron Brown
PR	—	80 Henry Ellard, 20 Johnnie Johnson, 49 Mickey Sutton
H	—	8 Steve Dils, 21 Nolan Cromwell
LSN	—	90 Mike McDonald, 57 Jim Laughlin

LOS ANGELES RAMS

INDIVIDUAL RUSHERS

	Att	Yards	Avg	Long	TD
Dickerson, Eric	404	1821	4.5	t42	11
Redden, Barry	110	467	4.2	t41	4
White, Charles	22	126	5.7	19	0
Everett, Jim	16	46	2.9	14	1
Brown, Ron	4	5	1.3	11	0
Dils, Steve	10	5	0.5	5	0
Bartkowski, Steve	6	3	0.5	7	0
Carpenter, Rob	2	3	1.5	3	0
Guman, Mike	2	2	1.0	3	0
Hunter, Tony	1	-6	-6.0	-6	0
Ellard, Henry	1	-15	-15.0	-15	0

INDIVIDUAL PASSING

	Att	Comp	Pct Comp	Yds	Avg Gain	TD	Pct TD	Long	Int	Pct Int	Rating Points
Everett, Jim	147	73	49.7	1018	6.93	8	5.4	t60	8	5.4	67.8
Dils, Steve	129	59	45.7	693	5.37	4	3.1	t65	4	3.1	60.0
Bartkowski, Steve	126	61	48.4	654	5.19	2	1.6	42	3	2.4	59.4
Dickerson, Eric	1	1	100.0	15	15.00	1	100.0	t15	0	0.0	158.3
House, Kevin	0	0	—	0	—	0	—	0	0	—	0.0

INDIVIDUAL RECEIVERS

	No	Yards	Avg	Long	TD
Ellard, Henry	34	447	13.1	t34	4
Redden, Barry	28	217	7.8	t24	1
Dickerson, Eric	26	205	7.9	28	0
Brown, Ron	25	396	15.8	t65	3
House, Kevin, T.B.-Rams	18	384	21.3	t60	2
Hunter, Tony	15	206	13.7	42	0
Young, Mike	15	181	12.1	21	3
Hill, David	14	202	14.4	33	1
Guman, Mike	9	68	7.6	13	0
Scott, Chuck	5	76	15.2	21	0
Long, Darren	5	47	9.4	13	0
Tyrrell, Tim	1	9	9.0	9	0
White, Charles	1	7	7.0	7	0

INDIVIDUAL INTERCEPTORS

	No	Yards	Avg	Long	TD
Gray, Jerry	8	101	12.6	28	0
Irvin, LeRoy	6	150	25.0	t50	1
Cromwell, Nolan	5	101	20.2	t80	1
Newsome, Vince	3	45	15.0	34	0
Sutton, Mickey	2	25	12.5	20	0
Jerue, Mark	2	23	11.5	t22	1
Johnson, Johnnie	1	13	13.0	13	0
Wilcher, Mike	1	0	0.0	0	0

INDIVIDUAL KICKOFF RETURNERS

	No	Yards	Avg	Long	TD
Brown, Ron	36	794	22.1	55	0
White, Charles	12	216	18.0	28	0
Sutton, Mickey	5	91	18.2	22	0
Guman, Mike	2	28	14.0	16	0
Carpenter, Rob	2	19	9.5	11	0
Ellard, Henry	1	18	18.0	18	0
Love, Duval	1	−6	−6.0	−6	0

INDIVIDUAL PUNTERS

	No	Yards	Long	Avg	Total Punts	TB	Blk	Opp Ret	Ret Yds	In 20	Net Avg
Hatcher, Dale	97	3740	57	38.6	98	5	1	47	416	26	32.9

INDIVIDUAL PUNT RETURNERS

	No	FC	Yards	Avg	Long	TD
Sutton, Mickey	28	5	234	8.4	32	0
Ellard, Henry	14	10	127	9.1	20	0
Johnson, Johnnie	0	7	0	—	0	0

INDIVIDUAL SCORERS

KICKERS	XP	XPA	FG	FGA	PTS
Lansford, Mike	34	35	17	24	85

NON-KICKERS	TD	TDR	TDP	TDM	PTS
Dickerson, Eric	11	11	0	0	66
Redden, Barry	5	4	1	0	30
Ellard, Henry	4	0	4	0	24
Brown, Ron	3	0	3	0	18
Irvin, LeRoy	3	0	0	3	18
Young, Mike	3	0	3	0	18
House, Kevin	2	0	2	0	12
Cromwell, Nolan	1	0	0	1	6
Duckworth, Bobby	1	0	1	0	6
Everett, Jim	1	1	0	0	6
Hill, David	1	0	1	0	6
Jerue, Mark	1	0	0	1	6
Newberry, Tom	1	0	0	1	6
Jeter, Gary	0	0	0	0	*2

MINNESOTA VIKINGS
NFC Central Division

Address: 9520 Viking Drive, Eden Prairie, Minnesota 55344
Telephone: (612) 828-6500

CLUB OFFICIALS
Chairman of the Board: John Skoglund
President: Max Winter
Senior Vice President: Jack Steele
Secretary/Treasurer: Sheldon Kaplan
Executive Vice President/General Manager: Mike Lynn
Assistant to the General Manager/Director of Operations:
  Jeff Diamond
Director of Administration: Harley Peterson
Ticket Manager: Harry Randolph
Director of Football Operations: Jerry Reichow
Director of Player Personnel: Frank Gilliam
Director of Pro Personnel: Bob Hollway
Head Scout: Ralph Kohl
Assistant Head Scout: Don Deisch
Regional Scout: John Carson
Director of Public Relations: Merrill Swanson
Director of Communications and Community Relations:
  Kernal Buhler
Public Relations Assistant: Katie Hogan
Public Relations Assistant: Daniel Endy
Trainer: Fred Zamberletti
Equipment Manager: Dennis Ryan

Stadium: Hubert H. Humphrey Metrodome (Capacity 63,000)
Playing Surface: AstroTurf
Stadium Address: 500 11th Avenue, So. Minneapolis,
  Minnesota 55415
Colours: Purple, Gold and White
Summer Training Camp: Mankato State University, Mankato,
  Minnesota 56001

MINNESOTA VIKINGS 1987 SCHEDULE

PRE-SEASON

Aug.	15	at New Orleans	7:00
Aug.	22	INDIANAPOLIS	7:00
Aug.	29	NEW ENGLAND	2:00
Sep.	3	at Denver	6:00

REGULAR SEASON

Sep.	13	DETROIT	12:00
Sep.	20	at Los Angeles Rams	1:00
Sep.	27	at Kansas City	12:00
Oct.	4	GREEN BAY	12:00
Oct.	11	at Chicago	12:00
Oct.	18	TAMPA BAY	12:00
Oct.	25	DENVER	12:00
Nov.	1	at Seattle	1:00
Nov.	8	LOS ANGELES RAIDERS	12:00
Nov.	15	at Tampa Bay	1:00
Nov.	22	ATLANTA	12:00
Nov.	26	at Dallas	3:00
Dec.	6	CHICAGO	7:00
Dec.	13	vs. Green Bay at Milwaukee	12:00
Dec.	20	at Detroit	1:00
Dec.	26	WASHINGTON	3:00

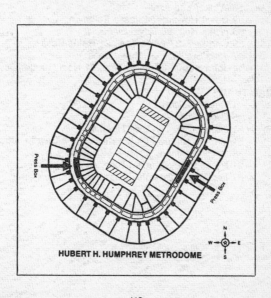

HUBERT H. HUMPHREY METRODOME

MINNESOTA VIKINGS
END OF SEASON DEPTH CHART

OFFENSE

WR	—	81 Anthony Carter, 84 Hassan Jones
OLT	—	65 Gary Zimmerman, 72 David Huffman
OLG	—	51 Jim Hough, 68 Curtis Rouse, 72 David Huffman
C	—	67 Dennis Swilley, 63 Kirk Lowdermilk
ORG	—	66 Terry Tausch, 63 Kirk Lowdermilk
ORT	—	76 Tim Irwin, 72 David Huffman
TE	—	83 Steve Jordan, 86 Mike Mularkey, 82 Carl Hilton
FL	—	87 Leo Lewis, 80 Jim Gustafson
QB	—	9 Tommy Kramer, 11 Wade Wilson
F-B	—	46 Alfred Anderson, 36 Allen Rice, 23 Ted Brown
RB	—	20 Darrin Nelson, 23 Ted Brown

DEFENSE

DLE	—	79 Doug Martin, 95 Gerald Robinson, 56 Chris Doleman
DLT	—	96 Tim Newton, 91 Joe Phillips
DRT	—	75 Keith Millard, 74 Mike Stensrud, 91 Joe Phillips
DRE	—	56 Chris Doleman, 95 Gerald Robinson, 77 Mark Mullaney
LLB	—	57 Chris Martin, 53 Jeff Schuh, 56 Chris Doleman
MLB	—	55 Scott Studwell, 54 Jesse Solomon, 58 Walker Lee Ashley
RLB	—	99 David Howard, 54 Jesse Solomon
LCB	—	30 Issiac Holt, 26 David Evans
RCB	—	39 Carl Lee, 37 Willie Teal, 21 Rufus Bess
SS	—	47 Joey Browner, 21 Rufus Bess
FS	—	44 John Harris, 37 Willie Teal, 41 Neal Guggemos

SPECIAL TEAMS

K	—	1 Chuck Nelson
P	—	8 Greg Coleman
LSN(P)	—	51 Jim Hough, 72 David Huffman
LSN(F)	—	51 Jim Hough, 63 Kirk Lowdermilk, 72 David Huffman
H	—	8 Greg Coleman, 86 Mike Mularkey
KR	—	21 Rufus Bess, 36 Allen Rice, 46 Alfred Anderson
PR	—	87 Leo Lewis, 21 Rufus Bess, 81 Anthony Carter

MINNESOTA VIKINGS

INDIVIDUAL RUSHERS

	Att	Yards	Avg	Long	TD
Nelson, Darrin	191	793	4.2	42	4
Anderson, Alfred	83	347	4.2	29	2
Brown, Ted	63	251	4.0	60	4
Rice, Allen	73	220	3.0	19	2
Kramer, Tommy	23	48	2.1	13	1
Coleman, Greg	2	46	23.0	30	0
Jones, Hassan	1	14	14.0	14	0
Carter, Anthony	1	12	12.0	12	0
Wilson, Wade	13	9	0.7	13	1
Lewis, Leo	3	−16	−5.3	−2	0

INDIVIDUAL PASSING

	Att	Comp	Pct Comp	Yds	Avg Gain	TD	Pct TD	Long	Int	Pct Int	Rating Points
Kramer, Tommy, Minn	372	208	55.9	3000	8.06	24	6.5	t76	10	2.7	92.6
Wilson, Wade	143	80	55.9	1165	8.15	7	4.9	39	3.5	84.4	
Anderson, Alfred	2	1	50.0	17	8.50	0	0.0	17	0	0.0	79.2
Bono, Steve	1	1	100.0	3	3.00	0	0.0	3	0	0.0	79.2
Rice, Allen	1	0	0.0	0	0.00	0	0.0	0	0	0.0	39.6

INDIVIDUAL RECEIVERS

	No	Yards	Avg	Long	TD
Jordan, Steve	58	859	14.8	t68	6
Nelson, Darrin	53	593	11.2	34	3
Carter, Anthony	38	686	18.1	t60	7
Lewis, Leo	32	600	18.8	t76	2
Rice, Allen	30	391	13.0	t32	3
Jones, Hassan	28	570	20.4	t55	4
Anderson, Alfred	17	179	10.5	t37	2
Brown, Ted	15	132	8.8	20	0
Mularkey, Mike	11	89	8.1	20	2
Gustafson, Jim	5	61	12.2	18	2
Rhymes, Buster	3	25	8.3	12	0

INDIVIDUAL INTERCEPTORS

	No	Yards	Avg	Long	TD
Holt, Issiac	8	54	6.8	27	0
Browner, Joey	4	62	15.5	t39	1
Harris, John	3	69	23.0	28	0
Lee, Carl	3	10	3.3	10	0
Solomon, Jesse	2	34	17.0	18	0
Doleman, Chris	1	59	59.0	t59	1

	No	Yards	Avg	Long	TD
Millard, Keith	1	17	17.0	17	0
Bess, Rufus	1	12	12.0	12	0
Studwell, Scott	1	2	2.0	2	0

INDIVIDUAL KICKOFF RETURNERS

	No	Yards	Avg	Long	TD
Bess, Rufus	31	705	22.7	43	0
Rhymes, Buster	9	213	23.7	34	0
Rice, Allen	5	88	17.6	23	0
Nelson, Darrin	3	105	35.0	40	0
Anderson, Alfred	3	38	12.7	17	0
Wilson, Wayne	2	33	16.5	26	0
Brown, Ted	2	18	9.0	17	0
Irwin, Tim	1	0	0.0	0	0

INDIVIDUAL PUNTERS

	No	Yards	Long	Avg	Total Punts	TB	Blk	Opp Ret	Ret Yds	In 20	Net Avg
Coleman, Greg	67	2774	69	41.4	67	4	0	39	353	15	34.9
Nelson, Chuck	3	72	31	24.0	3	0	0	0	0	0	24.0
Wilson, Wade	2	76	46	38.0	3	0	1	1	3	0	24.3

INDIVIDUAL PUNT RETURNERS

	No	FC	Yards	Avg	Long	TD
Bess, Rufus	23	10	162	7.0	15	0
Lewis, Leo	7	4	53	7.6	13	0
Rice, Allen	1	0	0	0.0	0	0
Carter, Anthony	0	1	0	—	0	0
Morrell, Kyle	0	2	0	—	0	0

INDIVIDUAL SCORERS
KICKERS

	XP	XPA	FG	FGA	PTS
Nelson, Chuck	44	47	22	28	110

NON-KICKERS

	TD	TDR	TDP	TDM	PTS
Carter, Anthony	7	0	7	0	42
Nelson, Darrin	7	4	3	0	42
Jordan, Steve	6	0	6	0	36
Rice, Allen	5	2	3	0	30
Anderson, Alfred	4	2	2	0	24
Brown, Ted	4	4	0	0	24
Jones, Hassan	4	0	4	0	24
Gustafson, Jim	2	0	2	0	12
Lewis, Leo	2	0	2	0	12
Mularkey, Mike	2	0	2	0	12
Browner, Joey	1	0	0	1	6
Doleman, Chris	1	0	0	1	6
Holt, Issiac	1	0	0	1	6
Kramer, Tommy	1	1	0	0	6
Wilson, Wade	1	1	0	0	6

NEW ORLEANS SAINTS
NFC Western Division

Address: 1500 Poydras Street, New Orleans, Louisiana 70112
Telephone: (504) 522-1500

CLUB OFFICIALS
Owner/General Partner: Tom Benson
President/General Manager: Jim Finks
Vice President/Administration: Jim Miller
Business Manager/Controller: Bruce Broussard
Director of Player Personnel: Bill Kuharich
Director of Public Relations/Marketing: Greg Suit
Director of Media Services: Rusty Kasmiersky
Director of Travel/Entertainment: Barra Birrcher
Assistant Director of Marketing: Bill Ferrante
Public Relations/Marketing Assistant: Sylvia Alfortish
Player Personnel Scouts: Bill Baker, Hamp Cook, Tom Marino, Carmen Piccone
Ticket Manager: Sandy King
Trainer: Dean Kleinschmidt
Equipment Manager: Dan Simmons

Stadium: Louisiana Superdome (Capacity 69,723)
Playing Surface: AstroTurf
Stadium Address: 1500 Poydras Street, New Orleans, Louisiana 70112
Colours: Old Gold, Black and White
Summer Training Camp: Southeastern Louisiana University, Hammond, Louisiana 70402

NEW ORLEANS SAINTS 1987 SCHEDULE

PRE-SEASON

Aug.	15	MINNESOTA	7:00
Aug.	22	HOUSTON	7:00
Aug.	29	PITTSBURGH	7:00
Sep.	4	at Cincinnati	7:35

REGULAR SEASON

Sep.	13	CLEVELAND	12:00
Sep.	20	at Philadelphia	1:00
Sep.	27	ATLANTA	12:00
Oct.	4	LOS ANGELES RAMS	12:00
Oct.	11	at St. Louis	12:00
Oct.	18	at Chicago	12:00
Oct.	25	SAN FRANCISCO	12:00
Nov.	1	at Atlanta	1:00
Nov.	8	at Los Angeles Rams	1:00
Nov.	15	at San Francisco	1:00
Nov.	22	NEW YORK GIANTS	3:00
Nov.	29	at Pittsburgh	1:00
Dec.	6	TAMPA BAY	3:00
Dec.	13	HOUSTON	12:00
Dec.	20	at Cincinnati	1:00
Dec.	27	GREEN BAY	12:00

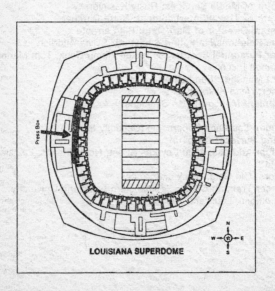

LOUISIANA SUPERDOME

NEW ORLEANS SAINTS
END OF SEASON DEPTH CHART

OFFENSE
WR   — 86 Mike Jones, 88 Eugene Goodlow
OLT   — 70 Bill Contz, 77 Daren Gilbert
OLG   — 63 Brad Edelman, 61 Joel Hilgenberg, 68 Pat Saindon
C   — 60 Steve Korte, 61 Joel Hilgenberg
ORG   — 66 Chuck Commiskey, 68 Pat Saindon
ORT   — 67 Stan Brock, 77 Daren Gilbert
TE   — 82 John Tice, 85 Hoby Brenner
WR   — 84 Eric Martin, 80 Herbert Harris, 83 Kelvin Edwards
QB   — 18 Dave Wilson, 3 Bobby Hebert
H-B   — 36 Rueben Mayes, 40 Dalton Hilliard, 37 Mel Gray
F-B   — 23 Buford Jordan, 30 Wayne Wilson

DEFENSE
DLE   — 75 Bruce Clark, 73 Frank Warren, 95 Joe Dumbauld
NT   — 94 Jim Wilks, 73 Frank Warren, 96 Sheldon Andrus
DRE   — 97 James Geathers, 95 Jon Dumbauld
LOLB   — 57 Rickey Jackson, 55 Joe Kohlbrand
LILB   — 51 Sam Mills, 53 Vaughan Johnson
RILB   — 54 Alvin Toles, 50 Jack Del Rio
ROLB   — 92 James Haynes, 56 Pat Swilling
LCB   — 44 Dave Waymer, 42 Dana McLemore
RCB   — 25 Johnnie Poe, 42 Dana McLemore
SS   — 27 Antonio Gibson, 24 Bobby Johnson
FS   — 49 Frank Wattelet, 39 Brett Maxie

SPECIAL TEAMS
P   — 10 Brian Hansen, 7 Morten Andersen
K   —   7 Morten Andersen
H   — 10 Brian Hansen, 49 Frank Wattelet
LSN(P) — 61 Joel Hilgenberg, 60 Steve Korte
LSN(F) — 61 Joel Hilgenberg, 60 Steve Korte
PR   — 42 Dana McLemore, 84 Eric Martin
KR   — 37 Mel Gray, 36 Ruben Mayes

NEW ORLEANS SAINTS

INDIVIDUAL RUSHERS

	Att	Yards	Avg	Long	TD
Mayes, Rueben	286	1353	4.7	50	8
Hilliard, Dalton	121	425	3.5	36	5
Jordan, Buford	68	207	3.0	10	1
Gray, Mel	6	29	4.8	11	0
Wilson, Dave	14	19	1.4	14	1
Wilson, Wayne, Minn.-N.O.	10	19	1.9	6	0
Del Rio, Jack	1	16	16.0	16	0
Hebert, Bobby	5	14	2.8	7	0
Edwards, Kelvin	1	6	6.0	6	0
Hansen, Brian	1	0	0.0	0	0

INDIVIDUAL PASSING

	Att	Comp	Pct Comp	Yds	Avg Gain	TD	Pct TD	Long	Int	Pct Int	Rating Points
Wilson, Dave	342	189	55.3	2353	6.88	10	2.9	t63	17	5.0	65.8
Hebert, Bobby	79	41	51.9	498	6.30	2	2.5	84	8	10.1	40.5
Hilliard, Dalton	3	1	33.3	29	9.67	1	33.3	t29	0	0.0	109.7
Wattelet, Frank	1	1	100.0	13	13.00	0	0.0	13	0	0.0	118.8

INDIVIDUAL RECEIVERS

	No	Yards	Avg	Long	TD
Jones, Mike	48	625	13.0	45	3
Martin, Eric	37	675	18.2	84	5
Tice, John	37	330	8.9	t29	3
Goodlow, Eugene	20	306	15.3	t29	2
Brenner, Hoby	18	286	15.9	34	0
Hilliard, Dalton	17	107	6.3	17	0
Mayes, Rueben	17	96	5.6	18	0
Harris, Herbert	11	148	13.5	27	0
Jordan, Buford	11	127	11.5	37	0
Edwards, Kelvin	10	132	13.2	24	0
Gray, Mel	2	45	22.5	38	0
Waymer, Dave	1	13	13.0	13	0
Williams, John	1	5	5.0	5	0
Hebert, Bobby	1	1	1.0	1	0
Wilson, Wayne	1	-3	-3.0	-3	0

INDIVIDUAL INTERCEPTORS

	No	Yards	Avg	Long	TD
Waymer, Dave	9	48	5.3	17	0
Poe, Johnnie	4	42	10.5	30	0
Wattelet, Frank	3	34	11.3	22	0
Gibson, Antonio	2	43	21.5	43	0
Maxie, Brett	2	15	7.5	15	0
Jakes, Van	2	6	3.0	4	0

	No	Yards	Avg	Long	TD
Haynes, James	1	17	17.0	17	0
Johnson, Vaughan	1	15	15.0	15	0
Gary, Russell	1	14	14.0	14	0
Jackson, Rickey	1	1	1.0	1	0

INDIVIDUAL KICKOFF RETURNERS

	No	Yards	Avg	Long	TD
Gray, Mel	31	866	27.9	t101	1
Mayes, Rueben	10	213	21.3	34	0
Harris, Herbert	7	122	17.4	22	0
Martin, Eric	3	64	21.3	27	0
McLemore, Dana	2	39	19.5	22	0
Tullis, Willie	2	28	14.0	19	0

INDIVIDUAL PUNTERS

	No	Yards	Long	Avg	Total Punts	TB	Blk	Opp Ret	Ret Yds	In 20	Net Avg
Hansen, Brian	81	3456	66	42.7	82	11	1	37	234	17	36.6

INDIVIDUAL PUNT RETURNERS

	No	FC	Yards	Avg	Long	TD
Martin, Eric	24	9	227	9.5	39	0
McLemore, Dana	10	3	67	6.7	23	0
Poe, Johnnie	8	3	71	8.9	17	0
Edwards, Kelvin	3	0	2	0.7	5	0
Tullis, Willie	2	0	10	5.0	7	0

INDIVIDUAL SCORERS

KICKERS	XP	XPA	FG	FGA	PTS
Andersen, Morten	30	30	26	30	108

NON-KICKERS	TD	TDR	TDP	TDM	PTS
Mayes, Rueben	8	8	0	0	48
Hilliard, Dalton	5	5	0	0	30
Martin, Eric	5	0	5	0	30
Jones, Mike	3	0	3	0	18
Tice, John	3	0	3	0	18
Goodlow, Eugene	2	0	2	0	12
Gray, Mel	1	0	0	1	6
Haynes, James	1	0	0	1	6
Jordan, Buford	1	1	0	0	6
Wilson, Dave	1	1	0	0	6

NEW YORK GIANTS
NFC Eastern Division

Address: Giants Stadium, East Rutherford, New Jersey 07073
Telephone: (201) 935-8111

CLUB OFFICIALS
President: Wellington T. Mara
Vice President-Treasurer: Timothy J. Mara
Vice President-Secretary: Raymond J. Walsh
Vice President-General Manager: George Young
Assistant General Manager: Harry Hulmes
Controller: John Pasquali
Director of Player Personnel: Tom Boisture
Director of Pro Personnel: Tim Rooney
Director of Media Services: Ed Croke
Director of Promotions: Tom Power
Director of Special Projects: Victor Del Guercio
Box Office Treasurer: Jim Gleason
Trainer Emeritus: John Dziegiel
Head Trainer: Ronnie Barnes
Assistant Trainers: John Johnson, Jim Madaleno
Equipment Manager: Ed Wagner, Jr.

Stadium: Giants Stadium (Capacity 76,891)
Playing Surface: AstroTurf
Stadium Address: East Rutherford, New Jersey 07073
Colours: Blue, Red and White
Summer Training Camp: Pace University, Pleasantville,
  N.Y. 10570

NEW YORK GIANTS 1987 SCHEDULE

PRE-SEASON

Aug.	16	at New England	1:30
Aug.	22	CLEVELAND	8:00
Aug.	29	NEW YORK JETS	9:00
Sep.	5	at Pittsburgh	9:00

REGULAR SEASON

Sep.	14	at Chicago	8:00
Sep.	20	DALLAS	4:00
Sep.	27	at Miami	1:00
Oct.	5	SAN FRANCISCO	9:00
Oct.	11	WASHINGTON	4:00
Oct.	18	at Buffalo	4:00
Oct.	25	ST. LOUIS	4:00
Nov.	2	at Dallas	8:00
Nov.	8	NEW ENGLAND	8:00
Nov.	15	at Philadelphia	4:00
Nov.	22	at New Orleans	3:00
Nov.	29	at Washington	4:00
Dec.	6	PHILADELPHIA	1:00
Dec.	13	at St. Louis	3:00
Dec.	19	GREEN BAY	12:30
Dec.	27	NEW YORK JETS	1:00

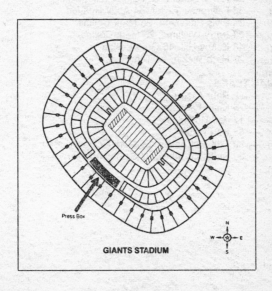

Press Box

GIANTS STADIUM

NEW YORK GIANTS
END OF SEASON DEPTH CHART

OFFENSE
WR	— 88 Bobby Johnson, 80 Phil McConkey, 86 Lionel Manuel
OLT	— 60 Brad Benson, 66 William Roberts
OLG	— 67 Bill Ard, 68 Damian Johnson
C	— 65 Bart Oates, 59 Brian Johnston
ORG	— 61 Chris Godfrey, 68 Damian Johnson
ORT	— 63 Karl Nelson, 66 William Roberts
TE	— 89 Mark Bavaro, 84 Zeke Mowatt
WR	— 81 Stacy Robinson, 87 Solomon Miller
QB	— 11 Phil Simms, 17 Jeff Rutledge
RB	— 20 Joe Morris, 22 Lee Rouson
RB	— 44 Maurice Carthon, 24 Ottis Anderson, 30 Tony Galbreath

DEFENSE
DLE	— 75 George Martin, 77 Eric Dorsey
NT	— 64 Jim Burt, 74 Erik Howard, 78 Jerome Sally
DRE	— 70 Leonard Marshall, 74 Erik Howard
LOLB	— 58 Carl Banks, 57 Byron Hunt
LILB	— 55 Gary Reasons, 51 Robbie Jones
RILB	— 53 Harry Carson, 52 Pepper Johnson
ROLB	— 56 Lawrence Taylor, 54 Andy Headen
LCB	— 34 Elvis Patterson, 25 Mark Collins
RCB	— 23 Perry Williams, 25 Mark Collins
SS	— 48 Kenny Hill, 46 Greg Lasker
FS	— 27 Herb Welch, 28 Tom Flynn

SPECIAL TEAMS
K	— 2 Raul Allegre
P	— 5 Sean Landeta
H	— 17 Jeff Rutledge
LSN	— 65 Bart Oates
PR	— 80 Phil McConkey, 25 Mark Collins
KR	— 80 Phil McConkey, 87 Solomon Miller

NEW YORK GIANTS

INDIVIDUAL RUSHERS

	Att	Yards	Avg	Long	TD
Morris, Joe	341	1516	4.4	54	14
Carthon, Maurice	72	260	3.6	12	0
Anderson, Ottis, St.L.-Giants	75	237	3.2	16	3
Rouson, Lee	54	179	3.3	t21	2
Simms, Phil	43	72	1.7	18	1
Galbreath, Tony	16	61	3.8	10	0
Johnson, Bobby	2	28	14.0	22	0
Manuel, Lionel	1	25	25.0	25	0
Rutledge, Jeff	3	19	6.3	18	0
Miller, Solomon	1	3	3.0	3	0
Hostetler, Jeff	1	1	1.0	1	0

INDIVIDUAL PASSING

	Att	Comp	Pct Comp	Yds	Avg Gain	TD	Pct TD	Long	Int	Pct Int	Rating Points
Simms, Phil	468	259	55.3	3487	7.45	21	4.5	49	22	4.7	74.6
Galbreath, Tony	1	0	0.0	0	0.00	0	0.0	0	0	0.0	39.6
Rutledge, Jeff	3	1	33.3	13	4.33	1	33.3	t13	0	0.0	87.5

INDIVIDUAL RECEIVERS

	No	Yards	Avg	Long	TD
Bavaro, Mark	66	1001	15.2	41	4
Galbreath, Tony	33	268	8.1	19	0
Johnson, Bobby	31	534	17.2	t44	5
Robinson, Stacy	29	494	17.0	49	2
Morris, Joe	21	233	11.1	23	1
Anderson, Ottis, St.L.-Giants	19	137	7.2	19	0
McConkey, Phil	16	279	17.4	46	1
Carthon, Maurice	16	67	4.2	10	0
Manuel, Lionel	11	181	16.5	35	3
Mowatt, Zeke	10	119	11.9	30	2
Miller, Solomon	9	144	16.0	t82	2
Rouson, Lee	8	121	15.1	t37	1
Carson, Harry	1	13	13.0	t13	1

INDIVIDUAL INTERCEPTORS

	No	Yards	Avg	Long	TD
Kinard, Terry	4	52	13.0	25	0
Williams, Perry	4	31	7.8	15	0
Hill, Kenny	3	25	8.3	23	0
Reasons, Gary	2	28	14.0	18	0
Patterson, Elvis	2	26	13.0	26	0
Welch, Herb	2	22	11.0	16	0
Martin, George	1	78	78.0	t78	1
Carson, Harry	1	20	20.0	20	0

	No	Yards	Avg	Long	TD
Johnson, Pepper	1	13	13.0	13	0
Headen, Andy	1	1	1.0	1	0
Collins, Mark	1	0	0.0	0	0
Lasker, Greg	1	0	0.0	0	0
Marshall, Leonard	1	0	0.0	0	0

INDIVIDUAL KICKOFF RETURNERS

	No	Yards	Avg	Long	TD
McConkey, Phil	24	471	19.6	27	0
Collins, Mark	11	204	18.5	26	0
Miller, Solomon	7	111	15.9	23	0
Hill, Kenny	5	61	12.2	30	0
Rouson, Lee	2	21	10.5	12	0
Lasker, Greg	1	0	0.0	0	0

INDIVIDUAL PUNTERS

	No	Yards	Long	Avg	Total Punts	TB	Blk	Opp Ret	Ret Yds	In 20	Net Avg
Landeta, Sean	79	3539	61	44.8	79	11	0	41	386	24	37.1

INDIVIDUAL PUNT RETURNERS

	No	FC	Yards	Avg	Long	TD
McConkey, Phil	32	12	253	7.9	22	0
Manuel, Lionel	3	6	22	7.3	12	0
Collins, Mark	3	1	11	3.7	6	0
Galbreath, Tony	3	1	1	0.3	1	0

INDIVIDUAL SCORERS

KICKERS

	XP	XPA	FG	FGA	PTS
Allegre, Raul	33	33	24	32	105
Cooper, Joe	4	4	2	4	10
Thomas, Bob	4	4	0	1	4

NON-KICKERS

	TD	TDR	TDP	TDM	PTS
Morris, Joe	15	14	1	0	90
Johnson, Bobby	5	0	5	0	30
Bavaro, Mark	4	0	4	0	24
Anderson, Ottis, St.L.-Giants	3	3	0	0	18
Manuel, Lionel	3	0	3	0	18
Rouson, Lee	3	2	1	0	18
Miller, Solomon	2	0	2	0	12
Mowatt, Zeke	2	0	2	0	12
Robinson, Stacy	2	0	2	0	12
Carson, Harry	1	0	1	0	6
Flynn, Tom	1	0	0	1	6
Martin, George	1	0	0	1	6
McConkey, Phil	1	0	1	0	6
Simms, Phil	1	1	0	0	6

PHILADELPHIA EAGLES
NFC Eastern Division

Address: Veterans Stadium, Broad Street and Pattison Avenue,
  Philadelphia, Pennsylvania 19148
Telephone: (215) 463-2500

CLUB OFFICIALS
Owner: Norman Braman
President-Chief Operating Officer: Harry Gamble
Vice President-Chief Financial Officer: Mimi Box
Vice President-Marketing and Development: Decker Uhlhorn
Assistants to the President: George Azar and Patrick Forte
Director of Player Personnel: Joe Woolley
Talent Scouts: Bill Baker, Lou Blumling
Director of Communications: Ed Wisneski
Assistant Director of Communications: Ron Howard
Associate Directors of Sales and Marketing: Jim Gallagher and
  Leslie Stephenson
Ticket Manager: Leo Carlin
Director of Penthouse Sales: Lou Scheinfeld
Trainer: Otho Davis
Assistant Trainer: David Price
Equipment Manager: Rusty Sweeney
Video Director: Mike Dougherty

Stadium: Veterans Stadium (Capacity 66,592)
Playing Surface: AstroTurf
Stadium Address: Broad Street and Pattison Avenue,
  Philadelphia, Pennsylvania 19148
Colours: Kelly Green, Silver and White
Summer Training Camp: West Chester University, West Chester,
  Pennsylvania 19382

PHILADELPHIA EAGLES 1987 SCHEDULE

PRE-SEASON

Aug.	15	at New York Jets	8:00
Aug.	23	at New England	7:00
Aug.	29	MIAMI	7:30
Sep.	3	DETROIT	7:30

REGULAR SEASON

Sep.	13	at Washington	1:00
Sep.	20	NEW ORLEANS	1:00
Sep.	27	at San Francisco	1:00
Oct.	4	CHICAGO	1:00
Oct.	11	at Dallas	12:00
Oct.	18	at Green Bay	12:00
Oct.	25	DALLAS	1:00
Nov.	1	at St. Louis	12:00
Nov.	8	WASHINGTON	1:00
Nov.	15	NEW YORK GIANTS	4:00
Nov.	22	ST. LOUIS	1:00
Nov.	29	at New England	1:00
Dec.	6	at New York Giants	1:00
Dec.	13	MIAMI	1:00
Dec.	20	at New York Jets	1:00
Dec.	27	BUFFALO	1:00

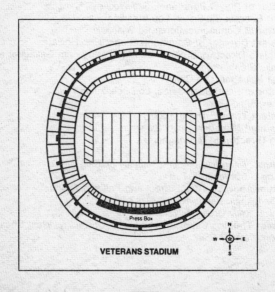

Press Box

VETERANS STADIUM

PHILADELPHIA EAGLES
END OF SEASON DEPTH CHART

OFFENSE

WR   — 82 Mike Quick, 85 Ron Johnson, 86 Gregg Garrity
OLT — 66 Ken Reeves, 77 Michael Black, 65 Bob Landsee
OLG — 65 Bob Landsee, 62 Nick Haden, 66 Ken Reeves
C   — 78 Matt Darwin, 65 Bob Landsee, 76 Adam Schreiber
ORG — 63 Ron Baker, 62 Nick Haden, 76 Adam Schreiber
ORT — 79 Joe Conwell, 77 Michael Black, 65 Bob Landsee
TE   — 88 John Spagnola, 89 Dave Little, 84 Byron Darby
WR   — 81 Kenny Jackson, 85 Ron Johnson, 86 Gregg Garrity
QB   — 12 Randall Cunningham, 6 Matt Cavanaugh,
         11 Kyle Mackey
RB   — 42 Keith Byars, 45 Charles Crawford,
         37 Junior Tautalatasi
F-B — 25 Anthony Toney, 26 Michael Haddix

DEFENSE

DLE — 92 Reggie White, 96 Clyde Simmons,
         93 Tom Strauthers
DLT — 71 Ken Clarke, 93 Tom Strauthers,
         97 Reggie Singletary
DRT — 97 Reggie Singletary, 93 Tom Strauthers,
         92 Reggie White
DRE — 98 Greg Brown, 96 Clyde Simmons, 69 Jeff Tupper
LLB — 50 Garry Cobb, 53 Dwayne Jiles, 95 Jody Schultz
MLB — 55 Mike Reichenbach, 50 Garry Cobb, 95 Jody Schultz
RLB — 59 Seth Joyner, 54 Alonzo Johnson, 95 Jody Schultz
LCB — 43 Roynell Young, 29 Elbert Foules
RCB — 29 Elbert Foules, 21 Evan Cooper
SS   — 20 Andre Waters, 22 Brenard Wilson,
         33 William Frizzell
FS   — 34 Terry Hoage, 22 Brenard Wilson, 33 William Frizzell

SPECIAL TEAMS

P   — 10 John Teltschik, 12 Randall Cunningham
K   — 8 Paul McFadden, 10 John Teltschik
H   — 10 John Teltschik, 6 Matt Cavanaugh,
            12 Randall Cunningham
KR   — 45 Charles Crawford, 37 Junior Tautalatasi,
            42 Keith Byars
PR   — 86 Gregg Garrity, 21 Evan Cooper
LSN(P) — 89 Dave Little, 76 Adam Schreiber
LSN(F) — 76 Adam Schreiber, 78 Matt Darwin

PHILADELPHIA EAGLES

INDIVIDUAL RUSHERS

	Att	Yards	Avg	Long	TD
Byars, Keith	177	577	3.3	32	1
Cunningham, Randall	66	540	8.2	20	5
Toney, Anthony	69	285	4.1	43	1
Haddix, Michael	79	276	3.5	18	0
Tautalatasi, Junior	51	163	3.2	50	0
Crawford, Charles	28	88	3.1	15	1
Jaworski, Ron	13	33	2.5	10	0
Cavanaugh, Matt	9	26	2.9	11	0
Waters, Mike	5	8	1.6	5	0
Jackson, Kenny	1	6	6.0	6	0
Teltschik, John	1	0	0.0	0	0

INDIVIDUAL PASSING

	Att	Comp	Pct Comp	Yds	Avg Gain	TD	Pct TD	Long	Int	Pct Int	Rating Points
Jaworski, Ron	245	128	52.2	1405	5.73	8	3.3	56	6	2.4	70.2
Cunningham, Randall	209	111	53.1	1391	6.66	9	3.8	t75	7	3.3	72.9
Cavanaugh, Matt	58	28	48.3	397	6.84	2	3.4	49	4	6.9	53.6
Byars, Keith	2	1	50.0	55	27.50	1	50.0	t55	0	0.0	135.4

INDIVIDUAL RECEIVERS

	No	Yards	Avg	Long	TD
Quick, Mike	60	939	15.7	t75	9
Tautalatasi, Junior Phil.	41	325	7.9	56	2
Spagnola, John, Phil	39	397	10.2	38	1
Jackson, Kenny	30	506	16.9	49	6
Haddix, Michael	26	150	5.8	29	0
Little, David, Phil	14	132	9.4	26	0
Toney, Anthony	13	177	13.6	47	0
Garrity, Gregg	12	227	18.9	34	0
Johnson, Ron	11	207	18.8	39	1
Byars, Keith	11	44	4.0	17	0
Duckworth, Bobby, Rams-Phil.	10	148	14.8	32	1
Smith, Phil.	6	94	15.7	36	0
Waters, Mike	2	27	13.5	19	0
Darby, Byron	2	16	8.0	13	0

INDIVIDUAL INTERCEPTORS

	No	Yards	Avg	Long	TD
Waters, Andre	6	39	6.5	21	0
Young, Roynell	6	9	1.5	9	0
Cooper, Evan	3	20	6.7	20	0
Johnson, Alonzo	3	6	2.0	9	0
Hoage, Terry	1	18	18.0	18	0
Foules, Elbert	1	14	14.0	14	0
Schulz, Jody	1	11	11.0	11	0
Joyner, Seth	1	4	4.0	4	0
Cobb, Garry	1	3	3.0	3	0

INDIVIDUAL KICKOFF RETURNERS

	No	Yards	Avg	Long	TD
Crawford, Charles	27	497	18.4	36	0
Tautalatasi, Junior	18	344	19.1	51	0
Byars, Keith	2	47	23.5	31	0
Cooper, Evan	2	42	21.0	24	0
Quick, Mike	2	6	3.0	6	0
Schulz, Jody	1	9	9.0	9	0
Simmons, Clyde	1	0	0.0	0	0

INDIVIDUAL PUNTERS

	No	Yards	Long	Avg	Total Punts	TB	Blk	Opp Ret	Ret Yds	In 20	Net Avg
Teltschik, John	108	4493	62	41.6	109	10	1	62	631	20	33.6
Cunningham, Randall	2	54	39	27.0	2	0	0	1	3	0	25.5

INDIVIDUAL PUNT RETURNERS

	No	FC	Yards	Avg	Long	TD
Garrity, Gregg	17	7	187	11.0	t76	1
Cooper, Evan	16	7	139	8.7	58	0
Waters, Mike	7	1	30	4.3	13	0
Smith, Phil	4	1	18	4.5	7	0

INDIVIDUAL SCORERS

KICKERS	XP	XPA	FG	FGA	PTS
McFadden, Paul	26	27	20	31	86

NON-KICKERS	TD	TDR	TDP	TDM	PTS
Quick, Mike	9	0	9	0	54
Jackson, Kenny	6	0	6	0	36
Cunningham, Randall	5	5	0	0	30
Tautalatasi, Junior	2	0	2	0	12
Byars, Keith	1	1	0	0	6
Crawford, Charles	1	1	0	0	6
Garrity, Gregg	1	0	0	1	6
Johnson, Ron	1	0	1	0	6
Spagnola, John	1	0	1	0	6
Toney, Anthony	1	1	0	0	6
Brown, Greg	0	0	0	0	*2

ST. LOUIS CARDINALS
NFC Eastern Division

Address: Busch Stadium, Box 888, St. Louis, Missouri 63188
Telephone: (314) 421-0777

CLUB OFFICIALS
Chairman/President: William V. Bidwill
Vice President/Administration: Curt Mosher
Secretary and General Counsel: Thomas J. Guilfoil
Treasurer: Charley Schlegel
Director of Pro Personnel: Larry Wilson
Director of Player Personnel: George Boone
Public Relations Director: Bob Rose
Media Coordinator: Greg Gladysiewski
Director of Community Relations: Adele Harris
Ticket Manager: Steve Walsh
Trainer: John Omohundro
Assistant Trainers: Jim Shearer, Jeff Herndon
Equipment Manager: Mark Ahlemeier

Stadium: Busch Stadium (Capacity 54,392)
Playing Surface: AstroTurf-8
Stadium Address: 200 Stadium Plaza, St. Louis, Missouri 63102
Colours: Cardinal Red, Black and White
Summer Training Camp: Eastern Illinois University, Charleston,
  Illinois 61920

ST. LOUIS CARDINALS 1987 SCHEDULE

PRE-SEASON

Aug.	15	at Cleveland	7:30
Aug.	22	SEATTLE	7:00
Aug.	31	at Chicago	7:00
Sep.	6	vs. Kansas City at Memphis, Tenn.	1:30

REGULAR SEASON

Sep.	13	DALLAS	12:00
Sep.	20	at San Diego	1:00
Sep.	27	INDIANAPOLIS	12:00
Oct.	4	at Washington	1:00
Oct.	11	NEW ORLEANS	12:00
Oct.	18	at San Francisco	1:00
Oct.	25	at New York Giants	4:00
Nov.	1	PHILADELPHIA	12:00
Nov.	8	TAMPA BAY	12:00
Nov.	15	LOS ANGELES RAMS	12:00
Nov.	22	at Philadelphia	1:00
Nov.	29	at Atlanta	1:00
Dec.	6	WASHINGTON	12:00
Dec.	13	NEW YORK GIANTS	3:00
Dec.	20	at Tampa Bay	4:00
Dec.	27	at Dallas	12:00

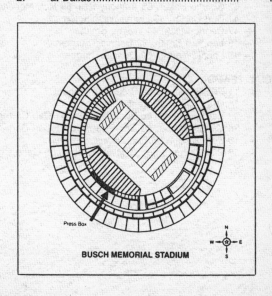

Press Box

BUSCH MEMORIAL STADIUM

ST. LOUIS CARDINALS
END OF SEASON DEPTH CHART

OFFENSE

WR	— 84 J.T. Smith, 87 Troy Johnson, 86 Eric Swanson
OLT	— 67 Luis Sharpe, 62 Ray Brown, 63 Tootie Robbins
OLG	— 62 Ray Brown, 70 Derek Kennard, 58 Gene Chilton
C	— 58 Gene Chilton, 64 Randy Clark, 51 Mike Ruether
ORG	— 61 Lance Smith, 70 Derek Kennard, 58 Gene Chilton
ORT	— 63 Tootie Robins, 61 Lance Smith, 62 Ray Brown
TE	— 80 Doug Marsh, 89 Cap Boso
WR	— 81 Roy Green, 82 Don Holmes, 86 Eric Swanson
QB	— 15 Neil Lomax, 18 Cliff Stoudt, 16 Kent Austin
H-B	— 30 Stump Mitchell, 36 Vai Sikahema, 39 Broderick Sargent
F-B	— 31 Earl Ferrell, 24 Ron Wolfley, 39 Broderick Sargent

DEFENSE

DLE	— 79 Bob Clasby, 76 Stafford Mays
NT	— 65 David Galloway, 73 Mark Duda, 78 Van Hughes
DRE	— 60 Al Baker, 76 Stafford Mays
OLB	— 53 Freddie Joe Nunn, 55 Anthony Bell
ILB	— 54 E.J. Junior, 59 Ron Monaco, 55 Anthony Bell
ILB	— 57 Niko Noga, 59 Ron Monaco, 56 Rick DiBernardo
OLB	— 52 Charlie Baker, 55 Anthony Bell, 59 Ron Monaco
LCB	— 41 Carl Carter, 48 Lionel Washington
RCB	— 47 Cedric Mack, 44 Wayne Smith
SS	— 45 Leonard Smith, 32 Dennis Thurman
FS	— 43 Lonnie Young, 32 Dennis Thurman

SPECIAL TEAMS

K	— 11 Eric Schubert, 39 Broderick Sargent
P	— 14 Greg Cater, 16 Kent Austin
KR	— 36 Vai Sikahema, 86 Eric Swanson, 41 Carl Carter
PR	— 36 Vai Sikahema, 86 Eric Swanson, 41 Carl Carter
H	— 16 Kent Austin, 86 Eric Swanson
LSN	— 56 Rick DiBernardo, 51 Mike Ruether, 58 Gene Chilton

ST. LOUIS CARDINALS

INDIVIDUAL RUSHERS

	Att	Yards	Avg	Long	TD
Mitchell, Stump	174	800	4.6	44	5
Ferrell, Earl	124	548	4.4	25	0
Lomax, Neil	35	148	4.2	18	1
Sikahema, Vai	16	62	3.9	23	0
Stoudt, Cliff	7	53	7.6	17	0
Wolfley, Ron	8	19	2.4	8	0
Marsh, Doug	1	5	5.0	5	0
Austin, Kent	1	0	0.0	0	0
Green, Roy	2	−4	−2.0	1	0

INDIVIDUAL PASSING

	Att	Comp	Pct Comp	Yds	Avg Gain	TD	Pct TD	Long	Int	Pct Int	Rating Points
Lomax, Neil	421	240	57.0	2583	6.14	13	3.1	t48	12	2.0	73.6
Stoudt, Cliff	91	52	57.1	542	5.96	3	3.3	t24	7	7.7	53.5
Arapostathis, Evan	1	0	0.0	0	0.00	0	0.0	0	0	0.0	39.6
Mitchell, Stump	3	1	33.3	15	5.00	1	33.3	t15	0	0.0	90.3

INDIVIDUAL RECEIVERS

	No	Yards	Avg	Long	TD
Smith, J.T.	80	1014	12.7	45	6
Ferrell, Earl	56	434	7.8	t30	3
Green, Roy	42	517	12.3	t48	6
Mitchell, Stump	41	276	6.7	24	0
Marsh, Doug	25	313	12.5	27	0
Johnson, Troy	14	203	14.5	39	0
Sikahema, Vai	10	99	9.9	27	1
Fox, Chas	5	59	11.8	t38	1
Tilley, Pat	3	51	17.0	18	0
Holman, Scott	3	41	13.7	18	0
Wolfley, Ron	2	32	16.0	28	0
Sargent, Broderick	1	8	8.0	8	0
Novacek, Jay	1	2	2.0	2	0

INDIVIDUAL INTERCEPTORS

	No	Yards	Avg	Long	TD
Mack, Cedric	4	42	10.5	24	0
Washington, Lionel	2	19	9.5	19	0
Carter, Carl	2	12	6.0	11	0
Smith, Wayne	1	35	35.0	35	0
Smith, Leonard	1	13	13.0	13	0

INDIVIDUAL KICKOFF RETURNERS

	No	Yards	Avg	Long	TD
Sikahema, Vai	37	847	22.9	44	0
Swanson, Eric	10	206	20.6	40	0
Mitchell, Stump	6	203	33.8	53	0
Fox, Chas	6	161	26.8	38	0
Johnson, Troy	3	46	15.3	25	0
Ferrell, Earl	3	41	13.7	27	0
Sargent, Broderick	2	27	13.5	14	0
Carter, Carl	2	21	10.5	14	0
Holmes, Don	1	2	2.0	2	0
Wolfley, Ron	0	-6	—	-6	0

INDIVIDUAL PUNTERS

	No	Yards	Long	Avg	Total Punts	TB	Blk	Opp Ret	Ret Yds	In 20	Net Avg
Cater, Greg	61	2271	52	37.2	62	4	1	24	130	16	33.2
Arapostathis, Evan	30	1140	50	38.0	30	0	0	20	166	5	32.5

INDIVIDUAL PUNT RETURNERS

	No	FC	Yards	Avg	Long	TD
Sikahema, Vai	43	16	522	12.1	t71	2
Smith, J.T.	1	0	6	6.0	6	0
Carter, Carl	1	0	0	0.0	0	0

INDIVIDUAL SCORERS

KICKERS	XP	XPA	FG	FGA	PTS
Lee, John	14	17	8	13	38
Schubert, Eric	9	9	3	11	18

NON-KICKERS	TD	TDR	TDP	TDM	PTS
Green, Roy	6	0	6	0	36
Smith, J.T.	6	0	6	0	36
Mitchell, Stump	5	5	0	0	30
Ferrell, Earl	3	0	3	0	18
Sikahema, Vai	3	0	1	2	18
Fox, Chas	1	0	1	0	6
Lomax, Neil	1	1	0	0	6

SAN FRANCISCO 49ERS
NFC Western Division

Address: 711 Nevada St., Redwood City, California 94061
Telephone: (415) 365-3420

CLUB OFFICIALS
Owner and Chairman of the Board: Edward J. DeBartolo, Jr.
President/Head Coach: Bill Walsh
Vice President/General Manager: John McVay
Business Manager: Keith Simon
Executive Administrative Assistant: Norb Hecker
Director of Pro Scouting: Alan Webb
Director of College Scouting: Tony Razzano
Director of Public Relations: Jerry Walker
Publications Coordinator: Rodney Knox
Coordinator of Football Operations: Neal Dahlen
Ticket Manager: Ken Dargel
Marketing/Promotions Coordinator: Laurie Welling
Trainer: Lindsy McLean
Equipment Manager: Bronco Hinek
Equipment Manager Emeritus: Chico Norton

Stadium: Candlestick Park (Capacity 61,891)
Playing Surface: Grass
Stadium Address: San Francisco, California 94124
Colours: Forty Niners Gold and Scarlet
Summer Training Camp: Sierra Community College, Rocklin,
  California 95677

SAN FRANCISCO 49ERS 1987 SCHEDULE

PRE-SEASON

Aug.	8	vs. Kansas City (Hall of Fame Game).....	12:00
Aug.	15	at Los Angeles Raiders.........................	7:00
Aug.	22	DALLAS..	6:00
Aug.	27	SAN DIEGO..	6:00
Sep.	4	at Seattle...	5:00

REGULAR SEASON

Sep.	13	at Pittsburgh.......................................	1:00
Sep.	20	at Cincinnati..	1:00
Sep.	27	PHILADELPHIA....................................	1:00
Oct.	5	at New York Giants..............................	9:00
Oct.	11	ATLANTA...	1:00
Oct.	18	ST. LOUIS...	1:00
Oct.	25	at New Orleans....................................	12:00
Nov.	1	at Los Angeles Rams	1:00
Nov.	8	HOUSTON	1:00
Nov.	15	NEW ORLEANS	1:00
Nov.	22	at Tampa Bay	1:00
Dec.	29	CLEVELAND	5:00
Dec.	6	at Green Bay	12:00
Dec.	14	CHICAGO	6:00
Dec.	20	at Atlanta...	1:00
Dec.	27	LOS ANGELES RAMS...........................	5:00

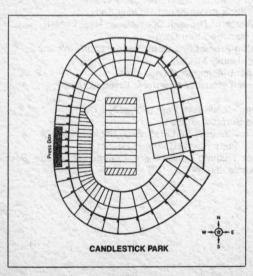

CANDLESTICK PARK

SAN FRANCISCO 49ERS
END OF SEASON DEPTH CHART

OFFENSE

WR	—	87 Dwight Clark, 84 Ken Margerum
OLT	—	77 "Bubba" Paris, 69 Bruce Collie, 74 Steve Wallace
OLG	—	68 John Ayers, 62 Guy McIntyre, 64 Michael Durrette
C	—	56 Fred Quillan, 51 Randy Cross
ORG	—	51 Randy Cross, 62 Guy McIntyre, 64 Michael Durrette
ORT	—	71 Keith Fahnhorst, 69 Bruce Collie, 74 Steve Wallace
WR	—	80 Jerry Rice, 3 Derrick Crawford
TE	—	81 Russ Francis, 86 John Frank
QB	—	16 Joe Montana, 9 Jeff Kemp, 15 Mike Moroski
RB	—	28 Joe Cribbs, 26 Wendell Tyler
RB	—	33 Roger Craig, 44 Tom Rathman, 30 Bill Ring

DEFENSE

DLE	—	72 Jeff Stover, 65 Doug Rogers
NT	—	95 Michael Carter, 78 Manu Tuiasosopo
DRE	—	76 Dwaine Board, 91 Larry Roberts
LOLB	—	53 Milt McColl, 94 Charles Haley
LILB	—	50 Riki Ellison, 99 Michael Walter
RILB	—	55 Jim Fahnhorst, 99 Michael Walter
ROLB	—	58 Keena Turner, 54 Ron Ferrari
LCB	—	22 Tim McKyer, 29 Don Griffin
RCB	—	29 Don Griffin, 20 Tory Nixon
SS	—	27 Carlton Williamson, 46 Tom Holmoe, 49 Jeff Fuller
FS	—	42 Ronnie Lott, 46 Tom Holmoe, 49 Jeff Fuller

SPECIAL TEAMS

P	—	4 Max Runager
K	—	14 Ray Wersching
H	—	15 Mike Moroski, 4 Max Runager, 9 Jeff Kemp
PR	—	29 Don Griffin, 22 Tim McKyer, 83 Derrick Crawford
KR	—	83 Derrick Crawford, 29 Don Griffin, 44 Tom Rathman
LSN(P)	—	51 Randy Cross, 56 Fred Quillan, 68 John Ayers
LSN(F)	—	51 Randy Cross, 56 Fred Quillan, 68 John Ayers

SAN FRANCISCO 49ERS

INDIVIDUAL RUSHERS

	Att	Yards	Avg	Long	TD
Craig, Roger	204	830	4.1	25	7
Cribbs, Joe	152	590	3.9	19	5
Rathman, Tom	33	138	4.2	t29	1
Tyler, Wendell	31	127	4.1	14	0
Harmon, Derrick	27	77	2.9	15	1
Rice, Jerry	10	72	7.2	18	1
Kemp, Jeff	15	49	3.3	12	0
Cherry, Tony	11	42	3.8	10	0
Montana, Joe	17	38	2.2	17	0
Moroski, Mike	6	22	3.7	12	1
Ring, Bill	3	4	1.3	4	0
Frank, John	1	-3	-3.0	-3	0

INDIVIDUAL PASSING

	Att	Comp	Pct Comp	Yds	Avg Gain	TD	Pct TD	Long	Int	Pct Int	Rating Points
Montana, Joe	307	191	62.2	2236	7.28	8	2.6	48	9	2.9	80.7
Kemp, Jeff	200	119	59.5	1554	7.77	11	5.5	t66	8	4.0	85.7
Moroski, Mike	73	42	57.5	493	6.75	2	2.7	42	3	4.1	70.2
Rice, Jerry	2	1	50.0	16	8.00	0	0.0	16	0	0.0	77.1

INDIVIDUAL RECEIVERS

	No	Yards	Avg	Long	TD
Rice, Jerry	86	1570	18.3	t66	15
Craig, Roger	81	624	7.7	48	0
Clark, Dwight	61	794	13.0	t45	2
Francis, Russ	41	505	12.3	52	1
Cribbs, Joe	35	346	9.9	33	0
Rathman, Tom	13	121	9.3	14	0
Wilson, Mike	9	104	11.6	18	1
Frank, John	9	61	6.8	17	2
Harmon, Derrick	8	78	9.8	15	0
Crawford, Derrick	5	70	14.0	42	0
Margerum, Ken	2	12	6.0	6	0
Monroe, Carl	2	6	3.0	5	0
Ring, Bill	1	8	8.0	8	0

INDIVIDUAL INTERCEPTORS

	No	Yards	Avg	Long	TD
Lott, Ronnie	10	134	13.4	t57	1
McKyer, Tim	6	33	5.5	t21	1
Fahnhorst, Jim	4	52	13.0	46	0
Fuller, Jeff	4	44	11.0	26	0
Holmoe, Tom	3	149	49.7	t78	2
Williamson, Carlton	3	3	1.0	2	0
Griffin, Don	3	0	0.0	0	0
Nixon, Tory	2	106	53.0	t88	1
Tuiasosopo, Manu	1	22	22.0	22	0
Cousineau, Tom	1	18	18.0	18	0
Turner, Keena	1	9	9.0	9	0
Haley, Charles	1	8	8.0	8	0

INDIVIDUAL KICKOFF RETURNERS

	No	Yards	Avg	Long	TD
Crawford, Derrick	15	280	18.7	34	0
Monroe, Carl	8	139	17.4	25	0
Griffin, Don	5	97	19.4	28	0
Harmon, Derrick	4	82	20.5	28	0
Rathman, Tom	3	66	22.0	22	0
Cherry, Tony	2	29	14.5	17	0
Frank, John	2	24	12.0	16	0
McKyer, Tim	1	15	15.0	15	0
Ring, Bill	1	15	15.0	15	0
Wilson, Mike	1	10	10.0	10	0

INDIVIDUAL PUNTERS

	No	Yards	Long	Avg	Total Punts	TB	Blk	Opp Ret	Ret Yds	In 20	Net Avg
Runager, Max	83	3450	62	41.6	85	8	2	49	373	23	34.3

INDIVIDUAL PUNT RETURNERS

	No	FC	Yards	Avg	Long	TD
Griffin, Don	38	18	377	9.9	t76	1
Crawford, Derrick	4	0	15	3.8	9	0
McKyer, Tim	1	1	5	5.0	5	0

INDIVIDUAL SCORERS

KICKERS

	XP	XPA	FG	FGA	PTS
Wersching, Ray	41	42	25	35	116

NON-KICKERS

	TD	TDR	TDP	TDM	PTS
Rice, Jerry	16	1	15	0	96
Craig, Roger	7	7	0	0	42
Cribbs, Joe	5	5	0	0	30
Clark, Dwight	2	0	2	0	12
Frank, John	2	0	2	0	12
Holmoe, Tom	2	0	0	2	12
Francis, Russ	1	0	1	0	6
Griffin, Don	1	0	0	1	6
Harmon, Derrick	1	1	0	0	6
Lott, Ronnie	1	0	0	1	6
McKyer, Tim	1	0	0	1	6
Moroski, Mike	1	1	0	0	6
Nixon, Tory	1	0	0	1	6
Rathman, Tom	1	1	0	0	6
Wilson, Mike	1	0	1	0	6

TAMPA BAY BUCCANEERS
NFC Central Division

Address: One Buccaneer Place, Tampa, Florida 33607
Telephone: (813) 870-2700

CLUB OFFICIALS
Owner/President: Hugh F. Culverhouse
Vice President: Joy Culverhouse
Vice President-Head Coach: Ray Perkins
Vice President-Community Relations: Gay Culverhouse
Secretary-Treasurer: Ward Holland
Director of Administration: Jim McVay
Assistant to the President: Phil Krueger
Director of Player Personnel: Jerry Angelo
Director of Pro Personnel: Erik Widmark
Director of Ticket Operations: Terry Wooten
Director of Public Relations: Rick Odioso
Director of Marketing and Advertising: Fred Doremus
Assistant Director-Community Relations: Jill Massicotte
Assistant Director-Media Relations: John Gerdes
College Personnel: Gary Horton, Leland Kendall, Dean Rossi
Controller: Ed Easom
Trainer: Chris Smith
Assistant Trainer: Joe Joe Petrone
Equipment Manager: Frank Pupello
Assistant Equipment Manager: Carl Melchior
Video Director: Marvin Scott

Stadium: Tampa Stadium (Capacity 74,315)
Playing Surface: Grass
Stadium Address: North Dale Mabry, Tampa, Florida 33607
Colours: Florida Orange, White and Red
Summer Training Camp: University of Tampa,
  401 West Kennedy Boulevard, Tampa, Florida 33606

TAMPA BAY BUCCANEERS 1987 SCHEDULE

PRE-SEASON

Aug.	15	CINCINNATI	7:00
Aug.	22	NEW YORK JETS	7:00
Aug.	29	WASHINGTON	7:00
Sep.	5	at Indianapolis	7:30

REGULAR SEASON

Sep.	13	ATLANTA	1:00
Sep.	20	at Chicago	12:00
Sep.	27	GREEN BAY	1:00
Oct.	4	at Detroit	1:00
Oct.	11	SAN DIEGO	1:00
Oct.	18	at Minnesota	12:00
Oct.	25	CHICAGO	1:00
Nov.	1	Green Bay at Milwaukee	12:00
Nov.	8	at St. Louis	12:00
Nov.	15	MINNESOTA	1:00
Nov.	22	SAN FRANCISCO	1:00
Nov.	29	at Los Angeles Rams	1:00
Dec.	6	at New Orleans	3:00
Dec.	13	DETROIT	4:00
Dec.	20	ST. LOUIS	4:00
Dec.	27	at Indianapolis	1:00

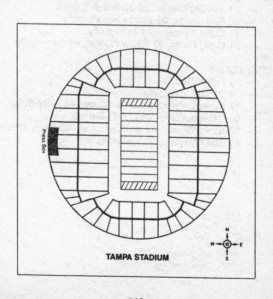

Press Box

N
W — E
S

TAMPA STADIUM

TAMPA BAY BUCCANEERS
END OF SEASON DEPTH CHART

OFFENSE

WR	—	89 Vince Heflin, 81 Phil Freeman, 83 Willie Gillespie
OLT	—	72 Rob Taylor, 77 J.D. Maarleveld, 64 Greg Robinson
OLG	—	66 George Yarno, 68 Rick Mallory, 72 Rob Taylor
C	—	60 Randy Grimes, 66 George Yarno
ORG	—	62 Sean Farrell, 68 Rick Mallory
ORT	—	73 Ron Heller, 77 J.D. Maarleveld, 64 Greg Robinson
TE	—	86 Calvin Magee, 85 K.D. Dunn
WR	—	87 Gerald Carter, 80 David Williams
QB	—	8 Steve Young, 17 Steve DeBerg
F-B	—	20 Ron Springs, 35 Pat Franklin, 38 Dennis Bligen
RB	—	32 James, Wilder, 25 Bobby Howard, 20 Ron Springs, 28 Greg Allen

DEFENSE

DLE	—	71 Bob Nelson, 78 John Cannon, 75 Kevin Kellin
NT	—	76 David Logan, 71 Bob Nelson
DRE	—	90 Ron Holmes, 71 Bob Nelson
LOLB	—	56 Jackie Walker, 57 Keith Browner
LILB	—	58 Jeff Davis, 54 Ervin Randle
RILB	—	52 Scott Brantley, 54 Ervin Randle
ROLB	—	51 Chris Washington, 59 Kevin Murphy
LCB	—	21 Vito McKeever, 23 Jeremiah Castille
RCB	—	22 Rod Jones, 35 Bobby Futrell
SS	—	41 Craig Swoope, 44 Ivory Sully
FS	—	31 Craig Curry, 37 Kevin Walker, 44 Ivory Sully

SPECIAL TEAMS

P	—	5 Frank Garcia
K	—	1 Donald Igwebuike
H	—	17 Steve DeBerg, 8 Steve Young, 44 Ivory Sully
LSN	—	66 George Yarno, 86 Calvin Magee
PR	—	37 Kevin Walker, 36 Bobby Futrell, 83 Willie Gillespie
KR	—	81 Phil Freeman, 37 Kevin Walker

TAMPA BAY BUCCANEERS

INDIVIDUAL RUSHERS

	Att	Yards	Avg	Long	TD
Wilder, James	190	704	3.7	t45	2
Young, Steve	74	425	5.7	31	5
Wonsley, Nathan	73	339	4.6	t59	3
Springs, Ron	74	285	3.9	40	0
Howard, Bobby	30	110	3.7	16	1
Franklin, Pat	7	7	1.0	4	0
House, Kevin	2	5	2.5	4	0
Allen Greg	1	3	3.0	3	0
DeBerg, Steve	2	1	0.5	t1	1
Carter, Gerald	1	−5	−5.0	−5	0
Garcia, Frank	1	-11	-11.0	−11	0

INDIVIDUAL PASSING

	Att	Comp	Pct Comp	Yds	Avg Gain	TD	Pct TD	Long	Int	Pct Int	Rating Points
Young, Steve	363	195	53.7	2282	6.29	8	2.2	46	13	3.6	65.5
DeBerg, Steve	96	50	52.1	610	6.35	5	5.2	45	12	12.5	49.7

INDIVIDUAL RECEIVERS

	No	Yards	Avg	Long	TD
Magee, Calvin	45	564	12.5	45	5
Wilder, James	43	326	7.6	25	1
Carter, Gerald	42	640	15.2	46	2
Springs, Ron	24	187	7.8	46	0
Freeman, Phil	14	229	16.4	t33	2
Bell, Jerry	10	120	12.0	25	0
Wonsley, Nathan	8	57	7.1	11	0
Franklin, Pat	7	29	4.1	9	1
Williams, David	6	91	15.2	25	0
Howard, Bobby	5	60	12.0	29	0
Dunn, K.D.	3	83	27.7	38	0
Harris, Leonard	3	52	17.3	23	0
Heflin, Vince	3	42	14.0	15	0
Gillespie, Willie	1	18	18.0	18	0
Mallory, Rick	1	9	9.0	9	0
Heller, Ron	1	1	1.0	t1	1

INDIVIDUAL INTERCEPTORS

	No	Yards	Avg	Long	TD
McKeever, Vito	3	12	4.0	10	0
Brantley, Scot	2	65	32.5	57	0
Curry, Craig	2	0	0.0	0	0
Swoope, Craig	1	23	23.0	23	0

	No	Yards	Avg	Long	TD
Browner, Keith	1	16	16.0	16	0
Washington, Chris	1	12	12.0	12	0
Davis, Jeff	1	0	0.0	0	0
Easmon, Ricky	1	0	0.0	0	0
Jones, Rod	1	0	0.0	0	0

INDIVIDUAL KICKOFF RETURNERS

	No	Yards	Avg	Long	TD
Freeman, Phil	31	582	18.8	33	0
Wonsley, Nathan	10	208	20.8	29	0
Walker, Kevin	8	146	18.3	26	0
Futrell, Bobby	5	115	23.0	30	0
Howard, Bobby	4	71	17.8	24	0
Harris, Leonard	4	63	15.8	23	0
Franklin, Pat	3	23	7.7	18	0
Williams, David	2	29	14.5	15	0
Magee, Calvin	2	21	10.5	11	0
Allen, Greg	1	21	21.0	21	0
Heflin, Vince	1	15	15.0	15	0
Curry, Craig	1	6	6.0	6	0
Boatner, Mack	1	2	2.0	2	0
Dunn, K.D.	1	0	0.0	0	0
Randle, Ervin	1	0	0.0	0	0

INDIVIDUAL PUNTERS

	No	Yards	Long	Avg	Total Punts	TB	Blk	Opp Ret	Ret Yds	In 20	Net Avg
Garcia, Frank	77	3089	60	40.1	77	8	0	38	410	19	32.7
Springs, Ron	1	43	43	43.0	1	0	0	1	4	0	39.0

INDIVIDUAL PUNT RETURNERS

	No	FC	Yards	Avg	Long	TD
Futrell, Bobby	14	5	67	4.8	12	0
Walker, Kevin	9	0	27	3.0	10	0
Harris, Leonard	3	0	16	5.3	8	0

INDIVIDUAL SCORERS

KICKERS	XP	XPA	FG	FGA	PTS
Igwebuike, Donald	26	27	17	24	77

NON-KICKERS	TD	TDR	TDP	TDM	PTS
Magee, Calvin	5	0	5	0	30
Young, Steve	5	5	0	0	30
Wilder, James	3	2	1	0	18
Wonsley, Nathan	3	3	0	0	18
Carter, Gerald	2	0	2	0	12
Franklin, Pat	2	0	1	1	12
Freeman, Phil	2	0	2	0	12
DeBerg, Steve	1	1	0	0	6
Heflin, Vince	1	0	0	1	6
Heller, Ron	1	0	1	0	6
Howard, Bobby	1	1	0	0	6

WASHINGTON REDSKINS
NFC Eastern Division

Address: Redskin Park, PO Box 17247, Dulles International
Airport, Washington, D.C. 20041
Telephone: (703) 471-9100

CLUB OFFICIALS
Chairman of the Board and Chief Operating Executive:
Jack Kent Cooke
Executive Vice President: John Kent Cooke
Secretary: Robert N. Eisman
Controller: Doug Porter
Board of Directors: Jack Kent Cooke, John Kent Cooke,
James Lacher, William A. Shea, Esq.,
The Honorable John W. Warner
General Manager: Bobby Beathard
Assistant General Managers: Bobby Mitchell, Charles Casserly
Director of Player Personnel: Dick Daniels
Director of Pro Scouting: Kirk Mee
Talent Scouts: Billy Devaney, George Saimes, Jerry Fauls
Director of Media Relations: John C. Konoza
Director of Publications: Ronn Levine
Director of Marketing: Paul Denfeld
Director of Photography: Nate Fine
Ticket Manager: Sue Barton
Head Trainer: Lamar 'Bubba' Tyer
Assistant Trainers: Joe Kuczo, Keoki Kamau
Equipment Manager: Jay Brunetti

Stadium: Robert F. Kennedy Stadium (Capacity 55,750)
Playing Surface: Grass (PAT)
Stadium Address: East Capitol Street, Washington DC 20003
Colours: Burgundy and Gold
Summer Training Camp: Dickinson College, Carlisle,
Pennsylvania 17013

WASHINGTON REDSKINS 1987 SCHEDULE

PRE-SEASON

Aug.	14	PITTSBURGH	8:00
Aug.	22	vs. Green Bay at Madison, Wis.	1:00
Aug.	29	at Tampa Bay	7:00
Sep.	5	at Los Angeles Rams	6:00

REGULAR SEASON

Sep.	13	PHILADELPHIA	1:00
Sep.	20	at Atlanta	1:00
Sep.	27	NEW ENGLAND	1:00
Oct.	4	ST. LOUIS	1:00
Oct.	11	at New York Giants	4:00
Oct.	19	at Dallas	8:00
Oct.	25	NEW YORK JETS	1:00
Nov.	1	at Buffalo	1:00
Nov.	8	at Philadelphia	1:00
Nov.	15	DETROIT	1:00
Nov.	23	LOS ANGELES RAMS	9:00
Nov.	29	NEW YORK GIANTS	4:00
Dec.	6	at St. Louis	12:00
Dec.	13	DALLAS	1:00
Dec.	20	at Miami	8:00
Dec.	26	at Minnesota	3:00

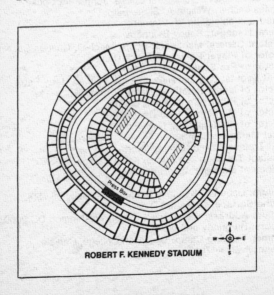

ROBERT F. KENNEDY STADIUM

WASHINGTON REDSKINS
END OF SEASON DEPTH CHART

OFFENSE

WR	— 81 Art Monk, 46 Ricky Sanders, 80 Eric Yarber
TE	— 85 Don Warren, 87 Terry Orr
OLT	— 66 Joe Jacoby, 60 Dan McQuaid, 68 Russ Grimm
OLG	— 68 Russ Grimm, 63 Raleigh McKenzie, 76 Ron Tilton
C	— 53 Jeff Bostic , 63 Raleigh McKenzie, 68 Russ Grimm
ORG	— 69 R C Thielemann, 63 Raleigh McKenzie, 76 Ron Tilton
ORT	— 73 Mark May, 60 Dan McQuaid, 66 Joe Jacoby
TE	— 86 Clint Didier, 87 Terry Orr
WR	— 84 Gary Clark, 46 Ricky Sanders, 80 Eric Yarber
QB	— 10 Jay Schroeder, 17 Doug Williams
RB	— 38 George Rogers, 24 Kelvin Bryant, 38 Keith Griffin, 29 Reggie Branch

DEFENSE

DLE	— 71 Charles Mann, 74 Markus Koch, 64 Steve Hamilton
DLT	— 65 Dave Butz, 77 Darryl Grant, 64 Steve Hamilton
DRT	— 77 Darryl Grant, 78 Dean Hamel, 64 Steve Hamilton
DRE	— 72 Dexter Manley, 74 Markus Koch, 64 Steve Hamilton
LLB	— 51 Monte Coleman, 56 Calvin Daniels
MLB	— 52 Neal Olkewicz, 58 Shawn Burks
RLB	— 57 Rich Milot, 51 Monte Coleman
LCB	— 28 Darrell Green, 45 Barry Wilburn, 32 Vernon Dean
RCB	— 32 Vernon Dean, 41 Tim Morrison, 45 Barry Wilburn
SS	— 40 Alvin Walton, 48 Ken Coffey, 23 Todd Bowles
FS	— 22 Curtis Jordan, 23 Todd Bowles

SPECIAL TEAMS

P	— 12 Steve Cox, 10 Jay Schroeder, 57 Rich Milot
K	— 4 Jess Atkinson, 12 Steve Cox
LSN(P)	— 53 Jeff Bostic, 77 Darryl Grant
LSN(F)	— 53 Jeff Bostic, 77 Darryl Grant
PR	— 80 Eric Yarber, 28 Darrell Green, 46 Ricky Sanders
KR	— 30 Dwight Garner, 80 Eric Yarber, 35 Keith Griffin
H	— 10 Jay Schroeder, 17 Doug Williams

WASHINGTON REDSKINS

INDIVIDUAL RUSHERS

	Att	Yards	Avg	Long	TD
Rogers, George	303	1203	4.0	42	18
Bryant, Kelvin	69	258	3.7	t22	4
Griffin, Keith	62	197	3.2	12	0
Schroeder, Jay	36	47	1.3	20	1
Monk, Art	4	27	6.8	21	0

INDIVIDUAL PASSING

	Att	Comp	Pct Comp	Yds	Avg Gain	TD	Pct TD	Long	Int	Pct Int	Rating Points
Schroeder, Jay	541	276	51.0	4109	7.60	22	4.1	t71	22	4.1	72.9
Williams, Doug	1	0	0.0	0	0.00	0	0.0	0	0	0.0	39.6

INDIVIDUAL RECEIVERS

	No	Yards	Avg	Long	TD
Clark, Gary	74	1265	17.1	55	7
Monk, Art	73	1068	14.6	69	4
Bryant, Kelvin	43	449	10.4	40	3
Didier, Clint	34	691	20.3	t71	4
Warren, Don	20	164	8.2	20	1
Sanders, Ricky	14	286	20.4	71	2
Griffin, Keith	11	110	10.0	28	0
Orr, Terry	3	45	15.0	t22	1
Rogers, George	3	24	8.0	13	0
Holloway, Derek	1	7	7.0	7	0

INDIVIDUAL INTERCEPTORS

	No	Yards	Avg	Long	TD
Green, Darrell	5	9	1.8	7	0
Jordan, Curtis	3	46	15.3	20	0
Milot, Rich	2	33	16.5	31	0
Wilburn, Barry	2	14	7.0	14	0
Bowles, Todd	2	0	0.0	0	0
Coffey, Ken	2	0	0.0	0	0
Olkewicz, Neal	1	15	15.0	15	0
Dean, Vernon	1	5	5.0	5	0
Daniels, Calvin	1	4	4.0	4	0

INDIVIDUAL KICKOFF RETURNERS

	No	Yards	Avg	Long	TD
Jenkins, Ken	27	554	20.5	37	0
Verdin, Clarence	12	240	20.0	29	0
Griffin, Keith	8	156	19.5	35	0
Garner, Dwight	7	142	20.3	26	0
Holloway, Derek	3	44	14.7	18	0
Orr, Terry	2	31	15.5	16	0
Krakoski, Joe	1	8	8.0	8	0

INDIVIDUAL PUNTERS

	No	Yards	Long	Avg	Total Punts	TB	Blk	Opp Ret	Ret Yds	In 20	Net Avg
Cox, Steve	75	3271	58	43.6	75	16	0	36	220	21	36.4

INDIVIDUAL PUNT RETURNERS

	No	FC	Yards	Avg	Long	TD
Jenkins, Ken	28	11	270	9.6	39	0
Green, Darrell	12	2	120	10.0	23	0
Yarber, Eric	9	4	143	15.9	44	0
Clark, Gary	1	3	14	14.0	14	0
Milot, Rich	1	0	3	3.0	3	0

INDIVIDUAL SCORERS

KICKERS

	XP	XPA	FG	FGA	PTS
Zendejas, Max	23	28	9	14	50
Cox, Steve	0	0	3	5	9
Atkinson, Jess	3	3	0	0	3

NON-KICKERS

	TD	TDR	TDP	TDM	PTS
Rogers, George	18	18	0	0	108
Bryant, Kelvin	7	4	3	0	42
Clark, Gary	7	0	7	0	42
Didier, Clint	4	0	4	0	24
Monk, Art	4	0	4	0	24
Sanders, Ricky	2	0	2	0	12
Manley, Dexter	1	0	0	1	6
Orr, Terry	1	0	1	0	6
Schroeder, Jay	1	1	0	0	6
Warren, Don	1	0	1	0	6

ACTIVE COACHES' CAREER RECORDS

Coach	Team(s)	Yrs	W	L	T	Pct.	W	L	T	Pct.	W	L	T	Pct.
			Regular Season				Postseason				Career			
Joe Gibbs	WASH.	6	63	26	0	.708	8	3	0	.727	71	29	0	.710
Don Shula	Balt., MIA.	24	247	94	6	.720	16	13	0	.552	263	107	6	.707
Mike Ditka	CHI.	5	50	23	0	.685	4	2	0	.667	54	25	0	.684
Tom Flores	RAIDERS	8	78	43	0	.645	8	3	0	.727	86	46	0	.652
Raymond Berry	N. ENG.	3	26	14	0	.650	3	2	0	.600	29	16	0	.644
Tom Landry	DALL.	27	240	141	6	.628	20	16	0	.556	260	157	6	.622
Chuck Knox	Rams, Buff., SEA.	14	130	76	1	.630	7	9	0	.438	137	85	1	.617
Dan Reeves	DEN.	6	56	33	0	.629	2	3	0	.400	58	36	0	.617
John Robinson	RAMS	4	40	24	0	.625	2	4	0	.333	42	28	0	.600
Al Saunders	S.D.	1	3	5	0	.600	0	0	0	.000	3	5	0	.600
Chuck Noll	PITT.	18	155	107	1	.591	15	7	0	.682	170	114	1	.598
Bill Walsh	S.F.	8	69	51	1	.574	7	3	0	.700	76	54	1	.584
M. Schottenheimer	CLE.	3	24	16	0	.600	1	2	0	.333	25	18	0	.581
Bill Parcells	N.Y.G.	4	36	27	1	.570	5	2	0	.714	41	29	1	.577
Ron Meyer	N.Eng., IND.	4	21	15	0	.583	0	1	0	.000	21	16	0	.568
Jerry Burns	MINN.	1	9	7	0	.563	0	0	0	.000	9	7	0	.563
Joe Walton	N.Y.J.	4	35	29	0	.547	1	2	0	.333	36	31	0	.537
Sam Wyche	CIN.	3	25	23	0	.521	0	0	0	.000	25	23	0	.521
Forrest Gregg	Cle., Cin., G.B.	10	70	76	0	.479	2	2	0	.500	72	78	0	.480
Jim Mora	N.O.	1	7	9	0	.438	0	0	0	.000	7	9	0	.438
Marv Levy	Kan.C., BUFF.	6	33	47	0	.413	0	0	0	.000	33	47	0	.413
Ray Perkins	N.Y.Gi., T.B.	4	23	34	0	.404	1	1	0	.500	24	35	0	.407
Darryl Rogers	DET.	2	12	20	0	.375	0	0	0	.000	12	20	0	.375
Buddy Ryan	PHIL.	1	5	10	1	.344	0	0	0	.000	5	10	1	.344
Marion Campbell	Atl., Phil., ATL.	6	23	48	1	.326	0	0	0	.000	23	48	1	.326
Gene Stallings	ST. L.	1	4	11	1	.281	0	0	0	.000	4	11	1	.281
Jerry Glanville	HOU.	2	5	13	0	.278	0	0	0	.000	5	13	0	.278
Frank Gansz	K.C.	0	0	0	0	.000	0	0	0	.000	0	0	0	.000

COACHES WITH 100 CAREER VICTORIES

Coach	Team(s)	Yrs	W	L	T	Pct.	W	L	T	Pct.	W	L	T	Pct.
			Regular Season				Postseason				Career			
George Halas	CHI.	40	319	148	31	.672	6	3	0	.667	325	151	31	.672
Don Shula	Balt., MIA.	24	247	94	6	.720	16	13	0	.552	263	107	6	.707
Tom Landry	DALL.	27	240	141	6	.628	20	16	0	.556	260	157	6	.622
Earl Lambeau	G.B., Chi. Card., WASH.	33	226	132	22	.623	3	2	0	.600	229	134	22	.623
Paul Brown	Cle., CIN.	21	166	100	6	.621	4	8	0	.333	170	108	6	.609
Chuck Noll	PITT.	18	155	107	1	.591	15	7	0	.682	170	114	1	.598
Bud Grant	MINN.	18	158	96	5	.620	10	12	0	.455	168	108	5	.607
Steve Owen	N.Y.G.	23	151	100	17	.605	2	8	0	.682	164	104	1	.612
Chuck Knox	Rams, Bills, SEA.	14	130	76	1	.630	7	9	0	.438	137	85	1	.617
Hank Stram	Chiefs, N.O.	17	131	97	10	.571	5	3	0	.625	136	100	10	.573
Weeb Ewbank	Colts, N.Y.J.	20	130	129	7	.502	4	1	0	.800	134	130	7	.507
Sid Gillman	Rams, S.D., HOU.	18	122	99	7	.550	1	5	0	.167	123	104	7	.541
George Allen	Rams, WASH.	12	116	47	5	.705	2	7	0	.222	118	54	5	.681
Don Coryell	St.L., S.D.	14	111	83	1	.572	3	6	0	.333	114	89	1	.561
John Madden	Oakland	10	103	32	7	.750	9	7	0	.563	112	39	7	.731
Ray Parker	Chi.Card.Det., PITT	15	104	75	9	.577	3	1	0	.750	107	76	9	.581
Vince Lombardi	G.B., WASH.	10	96	34	6	.728	9	1	0	.900	105	35	6	.740

Current team in capitals

AMERICAN FOOTBALL CONFERENCE

INDIVIDUAL PLAYER
STATISTICS

AFC — INDIVIDUAL RUSHERS

	Att	Yards	Avg	Long	TD
Warner, Curt, Sea.	319	1481	4.6	t60	13
Brooks, James, Cin.	205	1087	5.3	t56	5
Jackson, Earnest, Pitt.	216	910	4.2	31	5
Abercrombie, Walter, Pitt.	214	877	4.1	t38	6
McNeil, Freeman, Jets.	214	856	4.0	40	5
Hampton, Lorenzo, Mia.	186	830	4.5	t54	9
Winder, Sammy, Den.	240	789	3.3	31	9
Allen, Marcus, Raiders	208	759	3.6	t28	5
Mack, Kevin, Clev.	174	665	3.8	20	10
Rozier, Mike, Hou.	199	662	3.3	t19	4
Riddick, Robb, Buff.	150	632	4.2	t4t	4
McMillan, Randy, Ind.	189	609	3.2	28	3
Hector, Johnny, Jets	164	605	3.7	41	8
Williams, John L., Sea.	129	538	4.2	36	0
McCallum, Napoleon, Raiders	142	536	3.8	18	1
Dickey, Curtis, Clev.	135	523	3.9	47	6
Kinnebrew, Larry, Cin.	131	519	4.0	39	8
Pruitt, Mike, K.C.	139	448	3.2	16	2
Anderson, Gary, S.D.	127	442	3.5	17	1
James, Craig, N.E.	154	427	2.8	16	4
Collins, Tony, N.E.	156	412	2.6	17	3
Wilson, Stanley, Cin.	68	379	5.6	t58	8
Bell, Greg, Buff.	90	377	4.2	42	4
Adams, Curtis, S.D.	118	366	3.1	22	4
Willhite, Gerald, Den.	85	365	4.3	42	5
Bentley, Albert, Ind.	73	351	4.8	t70	3
Spencer, Tim, S.D.	99	350	3.5	23	6
Davenport, Ron, Mia.	75	314	4.2	35	0
Green, Boyce, K.C.	90	314	3.5	27	3
Heard, Herman, K.C.	71	295	4.2	40	2
Byner, Earnest, Clev.	94	277	2.9	37	2
Elway, John, Den.	52	257	4.9	24	1
Moriarty, Larry, Hou.-K.C.	90	252	2.8	11	1
Hawkins, Frank, Raiders	58	245	4.2	15	0
Smith, Jeff, K.C.	54	238	4.4	t32	3
Gill, Owen, Ind.	53	228	4.3	18	1
Johnson, Bill, Cin.	39	226	5.8	34	0
Pinkett, Allen, Hou.	77	225	2.9	14	2
James, Lionel, S.D.	51	224	4.4	24	0
Wallace, Ray, Hou.	52	218	4.2	19	3
Wonsley, George, Ind.	60	214	3.6	46	1
Nathan, Tony, Mia.	27	203	7.5	20	0
Kelly, Jim, Buff.	41	199	4.9	20	0
McGee, Buford, S.D.	63	187	3.0	20	7
Harmon, Ronnie, Buff.	54	172	3.2	38	0

	Att	Yards	Avg	Long	TD
Tatupu, Mosi, N.E.	71	172	2.4	13	1
Eason, Tony, N.E.	35	170	4.9	26	0
Erenberg, Rich, Pitt.	42	170	4.0	17	1
Bennett, Woody, Mia.	36	162	4.5	16	0
Moon, Warren, Hou.	42	157	3.7	19	2
Byrum, Carl, Buff.	38	156	4.1	18	0
Morris, Randall, Sea.	19	149	7.8	t49	1
Givins, Earnest, Hou.	9	148	16.4	t43	1
Esiason, Boomer, Cin.	44	146	3.3	23	1
Sewell, Steve, Den.	23	123	5.3	15	1
Krieg, Dave, Sea.	35	122	3.5	19	1
Paige, Tony, Jets	47	109	2.3	9	2
Malone, Mark, Pitt.	31	107	3.5	45	5
Fontenot, Herman, Clev.	25	105	4.2	16	1
Moore, Ricky, Buff.	33	104	3.2	14	1
Lang, Gene, Den.	29	94	3.2	14	1
Hayes, Jeff, Cin.	3	92	30.7	t61	1
Pollard, Frank, Pitt.	24	86	3.6	12	0
Banks, Chuck, Hou.	29	80	2.8	9	0
Fryar, Irving, N.E.	4	80	20.0	31	0
Bligen, Dennis, Jets	20	65	3.3	10	1
Blackledge, Todd, K.C.	23	60	2.6	14	0
Weathers, Robert, N.E.	21	58	2.8	t16	1
Woolfolk, Butch, Hou.	23	57	2.5	15	0
Jennings, Stanford, Cin.	16	54	3.4	10	1
Strachan, Steve, Raiders	18	53	2.9	10	0
Hilger, Rusty, Raiders	6	48	8.0	16	0
Plunkett, Jim, Raiders	12	47	3.9	11	0
O'Brien, Ken, Jets	17	46	2.7	11	0
Wilson, Marc, Raiders	14	45	3.2	13	0
Everett, Major, Clev.	12	43	3.6	8	0
Dupard, Reggie, N.E.	15	39	2.6	11	0
Clayton, Mark, Mia.	2	33	16.5	22	0
Brown, Eddie, Cin.	8	32	4.0	17	0
Hughes, David, Pitt.	14	32	2.3	8	0
Mueller, Vance, Raiders	13	30	2.3	8	0
Ryan, Pat, Jets	8	28	3.5	18	0
Barber, Marion, Jets	11	27	2.5	8	0
Williams, Dokie, Raiders	3	27	9.0	19	0
Grogan, Steve, N.E.	9	23	2.6	10	1
Kubiak, Gary, Den.	6	22	3.7	10	0
Trudeau, Jack, Ind.	13	21	1.6	8	1
Hogeboom, Gary, Ind.	10	20	2.0	6	1
Kiel, Blair, Ind.	3	20	6.7	9	0
Reeder, Dan, Pitt.	6	20	3.3	6	0
Kosar, Bernie, Clev.	24	19	0.8	17	0
Carter, Joe, Mia.	4	18	4.5	9	0

	Att	Yards	Avg	Long	TD
Wilkins, Gary, Buff.	3	18	6.0	11	0
Bell, Ken, Den.	9	17	1.9	12	0
Holt, Harry, Clev.	1	16	16.0	t16	1
Johnson, Vance, Den.	5	15	3.0	6	0
Bouza, Matt, Ind.	1	12	12.0	12	0
Luck, Oliver, Hou.	2	12	6.0	8	0
McNeil, Gerald, Clev.	1	12	12.0	12	0
Sanders, Chuck, Pitt.	4	12	3.0	13	0
Capers, Wayne, Ind.	1	11	11.0	11	0
Lane, Eric, Sea.	6	11	1.8	4	0
Brister, Bubby, Pitt.	6	10	1.7	9	1
King, Bruce, Buff.	4	10	2.5	7	0
McGee, Tim, Cin.	4	10	2.5	8	0
Gilbert, Gale, Sea.	3	8	2.7	12	0
Ellis, Craig, Mia.	3	6	2.0	2	0
Herrmann, Mark, S.D.	2	6	3.0	6	0
Jackson, Mark, Den.	2	6	3.0	5	0
Brooks, Bill, Ind.	4	5	1.3	12	0
Faaola, Nuu, Jets	3	5	1.7	2	0
Flick, Tom, S.D.	6	5	0.8	7	1
Hawthorne, Greg, N.E.	1	5	5.0	5	0
Gaynor, Doug, Cin.	1	4	4.0	4	0
Edwards, Stan, Hou.	1	3	3.0	3	0
Boddie, Tony, Den.	1	2	2.0	2	0
Franklin, Byron, Sea.	1	2	2.0	2	0
Seitz, Warren, Pitt.	3	2	0.7	2	0
Townsell, JoJo, Jets	1	2	2.0	2	0
Oliver, Hubert, Hou.	1	1	1.0	1	0
Slaughter, Webster, Clev.	1	1	1.0	1	0
Guy, Ray, Raiders	1	0	0.0	0	0
Horan, Mike, Den.	1	0	0.0	0	0
Jennings, Dave, Jets	1	0	0.0	0	0
Kenney, Bill, K.C.	18	0	0.0	9	0
Kidd, John, Buff.	1	0	0.0	0	0
Pagel, Mike, Clev.	2	0	0.0	0	0
Reich, Frank, Buff.	1	0	0.0	0	0
Starring, Stephen, N.E.	1	0	0.0	0	0
Strock, Don, Mia.	1	0	0.0	0	0
Mathison, Bruce, S.D.	1	−1	−1.0	−1	0
Mobley, Orson, Den.	1	−1	−1.0	−1	0
Paige, Stephone, K.C.	2	−2	−1.0	12	0
Fouts, Dan, S.D.	4	−3	−0.8	0	0
Lipps, Louis, Pitt.	4	−3	−0.8	8	0
Marino, Dan, Mia.	12	−3	−0.3	13	0
Toon, Al, Jets	2	−3	−1.5	2	0
Broughton, Walter, Buff.	1	−6	−6.0	−6	0
Ramsey, Tom, N.E.	1	−6	−6.0	−6	0

	Att	Yards	Avg	Long	TD
Jones, Cedric, N.E.	1	−7	−7.0	−7	0
Reed, Andre, Buff.	3	−8	−2.7	4	0
Roby, Reggie, Mia.	2	−8	−4.0	0	0
Duper, Mark, Mia.	1	−10	−10.0	−10	0
Edmonds, Bobby Joe, Sea.	1	−11	−11.0	−11	0
Langhorne, Reggie, Clev.	1	−11	−11.0	−11	0
Norman, Chris, Den.	1	−11	−11.0	−11	0
Sohn, Kurt, Jets	2	−11	−5.5	−3	0
Collinsworth, Cris, Cin.	2	−16	−8.0	−6	0

t = touchdown
Leader based on most yards gained

AFC — TEAM RUSHING

	Att	Yards	Avg	Long	TD
Cincinnati	521	2533	4.9	t61	24
Seattle	513	2300	4.5	t60	15
Pittsburgh	564	2223	3.9	45	18
Raiders	475	1790	3.8	t28	6
Jets	490	1729	3.5	41	16
Houston	490	1700	3.5	t43	13
Denver	455	1678	3.7	42	17
Buffalo	419	1654	3.9	42	9
Cleveland	470	1650	3.5	47	20
'San Diego	471	1576	3.3	24	19
Miami	349	1545	4.4	t54	9
Indianapolis	407	1491	3.7	t70	10
Kansas City	432	1468	3.4	40	10
New England	469	1373	2.9	31	10
Conference Total	6525	24710	—	t70	196
Conference Average	466.1	1765.0	3.8	—	14.0

AFC — INDIVIDUAL PASSING

QUALIFIERS

	Att	Comp	Pct Comp	Yds	Avg Gain	TD	Pct TD	Long	Int	Pct Int	Rating Points
Marino, Dan, Mia.	623	378	60.7	4746	7.62	44	7.1	t85	23	3.7	92.5
Krieg, Dave, Sea.	375	225	60.0	2921	7.79	21	5.6	t72	11	2.9	91.0
Eason, Tony, N.E.	448	276	61.6	3328	7.43	19	4.2	49	10	2.2	89.2
Esiason, Boomer, Cin.	469	273	58.2	3959	8.44	24	5.1	57	17	3.6	87.7
O'Brien, Ken, Jets	482	300	62.2	3690	7.66	25	5.2	t83	20	4.1	85.8
Kosar, Bernie, Clev.	531	310	58.4	3854	7.26	17	3.2	t72	10	1.9	83.8
Kelly, Jim Buff.	480	285	59.4	3593	7.49	22	4.6	t84	17	3.5	83.3
Plunkett, Jim, Raiders	252	133	52.8	1986	7.88	14	5.6	t81	9	3.6	82.5
Elway, John, Den.	504	280	55.6	3485	6.91	19	3.8	53	13	2.6	79.0
Fouts, Dan, S.D.	430	252	58.6	3031	7.05	16	3.7	t65	22	5.1	71.4
Kenney, Bill, K.C.	308	161	52.3	1922	6.24	13	4.2	53	11	3.6	70.8
Wilson, Marc, Raiders	240	129	53.8	1721	7.17	12	5.0	t57	15	6.3	67.4
Malone, Mark, Pitt	425	216	50.8	2444	5.75	15	3.5	48	18	4.2	62.5
Moon, Warren, Hou.	488	256	52.5	3489	7.15	13	2.7	t81	26	5.3	62.3
Trudeau, Jack, Ind.	417	204	48.9	2225	5.34	8	1.9	t84	18	4.3	53.5

NON-QUALIFIERS

	Att	Comp	Pct Comp	Yds	Avg Gain	TD	Pct TD	Long	Int	Pct Int	Rating Points
Strock, Don, Mia.	20	14	70.0	152	7.60	2	10.0	21	0	0.0	125.4
Grogan, Steve, N.E.	102	62	60.8	976	9.57	9	8.8	t69	2	2.0	113.8
Kiel, Blair, Ind.	25	11	44.0	236	9.44	2	8.0	50	0	0.0	104.8
Ryan, Pat, Jets	55	34	61.8	342	6.22	2	3.6	36	1	1.8	84.1
Hogeboom, Gary, Ind.	144	85	59.0	1154	8.01	6	4.2	60	6	4.2	81.2
Gilbert, Gale, Sea.	76	42	55.3	485	6.38	3	3.9	t38	3	3.9	71.4
Hilger, Rusty, Raiders	38	19	50.0	266	7.00	1	2.6	54	1	2.6	70.7
Blackledge, Todd, K.C.	211	96	45.5	1200	5.69	10	4.7	t70	6	2.8	67.6
Herrmann, Mark, S.D.	97	51	52.6	627	6.46	2	2.1	28	3	3.1	66.8
Kubiak, Gary, Den.	38	23	60.5	249	6.55	1	2.6	26	3	7.9	55.7
Anderson, Ken, Cin.	23	11	47.8	171	7.43	1	4.3	43	2	8.7	51.2
Luck, Oliver, Hou.	60	31	51.7	341	5.68	1	1.7	27	5	8.3	39.7
Brister, Bubby, Pitt.	60	21	35.0	291	4.85	0	0.0	58	2	3.3	37.6
Flick, Tom, S.D.	73	33	45.2	361	4.95	2	2.7	26	8	11.0	29.9
Reich, Frank, Buff.	19	9	47.4	104	5.47	0	0.0	37	2	10.5	24.8
(Less than 10 attempts)											
Anderson, Gary, S.D.	1	1	100.0	4	4.00	1	100.0	t4	0	0.0	122.9
Bentley, Albert, Ind.	0	0	—	0	—	0	—	0	0	—	0.0
Brennan, Brian, Clev.	1	1	100.0	35	35.00	0	0.0	35	0	0.0	118.8
Brooks, James, Cin.	1	0	0.0	0	0.00	0	0.0	0	0	0.0	39.6
Fontenot, Herman, Clev.	1	1	100.0	46	46.00	1	100.0	t46	0	0.0	158.3
Gaynor, Doug, Cin.	3	3	100.0	30	10.00	0	0.0	16	0	0.0	108.3
Givins, Earnest, Hou.	2	0	0.0	0	0.00	0	0.0	0	0	0.0	39.6
Gossett, Jeff, Clev.	2	1	50.0	30	15.00	0	0.0	30	1	50.0	56.3
Green, Boyce, K.C.	1	0	0.0	0	0.00	0	0.0	0	1	100.0	0.0
Holohan, Pete, S.D.	2	1	50.0	21	10.50	0	0.0	21	0	0.0	87.5
James, Craig, N.E.	4	1	25.0	10	2.50	1	25.0	t10	1	25.0	39.6
Jensen, Jim, Mia.	2	0	0.0	0	0.00	0	0.0	0	0	0.0	39.6
Johnson, Vance, Den.	1	0	0.0	0	0.00	0	0.0	0	0	0.0	39.6
Kreider, Steve, Cin.	1	0	0.0	0	0.00	0	0.0	0	1	100.0	0.0
Largent, Steve, Sea.	1	1	100.0	18	18.00	0	0.0	18	0	0.0	118.8
Marshall, Henry, K.C.	1	0	0.0	0	0.00	0	0.0	0	0	0.0	39.6

	Att	Comp	Pct Comp	Yds	Avg Gain	TD	Pct TD	Long	Int	Pct Int	Rating Points
McGee, Buford, S.D.	1	1	100.0	1	1.00	0	0.0	1	0	0.0	79.2
Morris, Randall, Sea.	1	0	0.0	0	0.00	0	0.0	0	0	0.0	39.6
Newsome, Harry, Pitt.	2	1	50.0	12	6.00	1	50.0	t12	0	0.0	108.3
Norman, Chris, Den.	1	1	100.0	43	43.00	1	100.0	t43	0	0.0	158.3
Pagel, Mike, Clev.	3	2	66.7	53	17.67	0	0.0	45	0	0.0	109.7
Ramsey, Tom, N.E.	3	1	33.3	7	2.33	0	0.0	7	0	0.0	42.4
Rozier, Mike, Hou.	1	1	100.0	13	13.00	0	0.0	13	0	0.0	118.8
Sewell, Steve, Den.	1	1	100.0	23	23.00	1	100.0	t23	0	0.0	158.3
Willhite, Gerald, Den.	41	1	25.0	11	2.75	0	0.0	11	0	0.0	39.6

t = touchdown
Leader based on rating points, minimum 224 attempts

AFC — TEAM PASSING

	Att	Comp	Pct Comp	Gross Yards	Tkd	Yds Lost	Net Yards	Avg Yds Att	Avg Yds Comp	TD	Pct TD	Long	Int	Pct Int
Miami	645	392	60.8	4898	17	119	4779	7.59	12.49	46	7.1	t85	23	3.6
Cincinnati	497	287	57.7	4160	28	203	3957	8.37	14.49	25	5.0	57	20	4.0
New England	557	340	61.0	4321	47	367	3954	7.76	12.71	29	5.2	t69	13	2.3
San Diego	604	339	56.1	4045	32	265	3780	6.70	11.93	21	3.5	t65	33	5.5
Cleveland	538	315	58.6	4018	39	274	3744	7.47	12.76	18	3.3	t72	11	2.0
Jets	537	334	62.2	4032	45	386	3646	7.51	12.07	27	5.0	t83	21	3.9
Denver	549	306	55.7	3811	38	273	3538	6.94	12.45	22	4.0	53	16	2.9
Raiders	530	281	53.0	3973	64	464	3509	7.50	14.14	27	5.1	t81	25	4.7
Houston	551	288	52.3	3843	48	394	3449	6.97	13.34	14	2.5	t81	31	5.6
Buffalo	499	294	58.9	3697	45	334	3363	7.41	12.57	22	4.4	t84	19	3.8
Indianapolis	586	300	51.2	3615	53	406	3209	6.17	12.05	16	2.7	t84	24	4.1
Seattle	453	268	59.2	3424	39	315	3109	7.56	12.78	24	5.3	t72	14	3.1
Kansas City	521	257	49.3	3122	50	372	2750	5.99	12.15	23	4.4	t70	18	3.5
Pittsburgh	491	238	48.5	2747	20	159	2588	5.59	11.54	16	3.3	58	20	4.1
Conf. Total	7558	4239	—	53706	565	4331	49375	—	—	330	—	t85	288	—
Conf. Average	539.9	302.8	56.1	3836.1	40.4	309.4	3526.8	7.11	12.67	23.6	4.4	—	20.6	3.8

AFC — INDIVIDUAL RECEIVERS

	No	Yards	Avg	Long	TD
Christensen, Todd, Raiders	95	1153	12.1	35	8
Toon, Al, Jets	85	1176	13.8	t62	8
Morgan, Stanley, N.E.	84	1491	17.8	t44	10
Anderson, Gary, S.D.	80	871	10.9	t65	8
Collins, Tony, N.E.	77	684	8.9	49	5
Bouza, Matt, Ind.	71	830	11.7	33	5
Largent, Steve, Sea.	70	1070	15.3	t38	9
Shuler, Mickey, Jets	69	675	9.8	t36	4
Duper, Mark, Mia.	67	1313	19.6	t85	11
Brooks, Bill, Ind.	65	1131	17.4	t84	8
Hill, Drew, Hou.	65	1112	17.1	t81	5
Winslow, Kellen, S.D.	64	728	11.4	t28	5
Willhite, Gerald, Den.	64	529	8.3	31	4
Collinsworth, Cris, Cin.	62	1024	16.5	t46	10
Givins, Earnest, Hou.	61	1062	17.4	60	3
Hampton, Lorenzo, Mia.	61	446	7.3	19	3
Clayton, Mark, Mia.	60	1150	19.2	t68	10
Brown, Eddie, Cin.	58	964	16.6	57	4
Chandler, Wes, S.D.	56	874	15.6	40	4
Brennan, Brian, Clev.	55	838	15.2	t57	6
Brooks, James, Cin.	54	686	12.7	54	4
Hardy, Bruce, Mia.	54	430	8.0	t18	5
Reed, Andre, Buff.	53	739	13.9	t55	7
Paige, Stephone, K.C.	52	829	15.9	51	11
Walker, Wesley, Jets	49	1016	20.7	t83	12
Metzelaars, Pete, Buff.	49	485	9.9	t44	3
Riddick, Robb, Buff.	49	468	9.6	t31	1
McNeil, Freeman, Jets	49	410	8.4	26	1
Nathan, Tony, Mia.	48	457	9.5	t23	2
Fontenot, Herman, Clev.	47	559	11.9	t72	1
Abercrombie, Walter, Pitt.	47	395	8.4	27	2
Marshall, Henry, K.C.	46	652	14.2	31	1
Allen, Marcus, Raiders	46	453	9.8	36	2
Watson, Steve, Den.	45	699	15.5	46	3
Williams, Dokie, Raiders	43	843	19.6	53	8
Fryar, Irving, N.E.	43	737	17.1	t69	6
Warner, Curt, Sea.	41	342	8.3	26	0
Slaughter, Webster, Clev.	40	577	14.4	t47	4
Holman, Rodney, Cin.	40	570	14.3	t34	2
Langhorne, Reggie, Clev.	39	678	17.4	66	1
Newsome, Ozzie, Clev.	39	417	10.7	31	3
Jackson, Mark, Den.	38	738	19.4	53	1
Lipps, Louis, Pitt.	38	590	15.5	48	3
Moore, Nat, Mia.	38	431	11.3	t38	7
Baty, Greg, N.E.	37	331	8.9	22	2

	No	Yards	Avg	Long	TD
Byner, Earnest, Clev.	37	328	8.9	40	2
Pinkett, Allen, Hou.	35	248	7.1	20	1
Burkett, Chris, Buff.	34	778	22.9	t84	4
Stallworth, John, Pitt.	34	466	13.7	t40	1
Joiner, Charlie, S.D.	34	440	12.9	33	2
McMillan, Randy, Ind.	34	289	8.5	45	0
Franklin, Byron, Sea.	33	547	16.6	49	2
Hector, Johnny, Jets	33	302	9.2	23	0
Smith, Jeff, K.C.	33	230	7.0	18	3
Williams, John L., Sea.	33	219	6.6	23	0
Johnson, Vance, Den.	31	363	11.7	t34	2
Johnson, Trumaine, S.D.	30	399	13.3	30	1
Holohan, Pete, S.D.	29	356	12.3	34	1
Woolfolk, Butch, Hou.	28	314	11.2	30	2
Mack, Kevin, Clev.	28	292	10.4	44	0
Erenberg, Rich, Pitt.	27	217	8.0	19	3
Winder, Sammy, Den.	26	171	6.6	t20	5
Beach, Pat, Ind.	25	265	10.6	26	1
Bentley, Albert, Ind.	25	230	9.2	38	0
Hawkins, Frank, Raiders	25	166	6.6	16	0
Hawthorne, Greg, N.E.	24	192	8.0	17	0
Rozier, Mike, Hou.	24	180	7.5	23	0
Hester, Jessie, Raiders	23	632	27.5	t81	6
Sewell, Steve, Den.	23	294	12.8	40	1
Moore, Ricky, Buff.	23	184	8.0	27	0
James, Lionel, S.D.	23	173	7.5	18	0
Mobley, Orson, Den.	22	332	15.1	32	1
Skansi, Paul, Sea.	22	271	12.3	30	0
Boyer, Mark, Ind.	22	237	10.8	38	1
Williams, Jamie, Hou.	22	227	10.3	33	1
Harmon, Ronnie, Buff.	22	185	8.4	27	1
Carson, Carlos, K.C.	21	497	23.7	t70	4
Sweeney, Calvin, Pitt.	21	337	16.0	58	1
Sampson, Clinton, Den.	21	259	12.3	43	0
Gothard, Preston, Pitt.	21	246	11.7	34	1
Davenport, Ron, Mia.	20	177	8.9	27	1
Arnold, Walt, K.C.	20	169	8.5	27	1
Butler, Raymond, Sea.	19	351	18.5	t67	4
Johnson, Dan, Mia.	19	170	8.9	20	4
Green, Boyce, K.C.	19	137	7.2	17	0
Barksdale, Rod, Raiders	18	434	24.1	t57	2
Turner, Daryl, Sea.	18	334	18.6	t72	7
Drewrey, Willie, Hou.	18	299	16.6	31	0
James, Craig, N.E.	18	129	7.2	17	0
Paige, Tony, Jets	18	121	6.7	18	0
Thompson, Weegie, Pitt.	17	191	11.2	20	5
Wallace, Ray, Hou.	17	177	10.4	t35	2

	No	Yards	Avg	Long	TD
Jackson, Earnest, Pitt.	17	169	9.9	28	0
Heard, Herman, K.C.	17	83	4.9	13	0
Starring, Stephen, N.E.	16	295	18.4	47	2
McGee, Tim, Cin.	16	276	17.3	51	1
Wonsley, George, Ind.	16	175	10.9	60	0
Gill, Owen, Ind.	16	137	8.6	15	0
Butler, Jerry, Buff.	15	302	20.1	53	2
Pruitt, James, Mia.	15	235	15.7	27	2
Kay, Clarence, Den.	15	195	13.0	34	1
Klever, Rocky, Jets	15	150	10.0	21	0
Tice, Mike, Sea.	15	150	10.0	25	0
Tatupu, Mosi, N.E.	15	145	9.7	25	0
Jones, Cedric, N.E.	14	222	15.9	28	1
Kinnebrew, Larry, Cin.	13	136	10.5	31	1
Hudson, Gordon, Sea.	13	131	10.1	30	1
Lang, Gene, Den.	13	105	8.1	26	2
Byrum, Carl, Buff.	13	104	8.0	17	1
Johnson, Bill, Cin.	13	103	7.9	17	0
McCallum, Napoleon, Raiders	13	103	7.9	22	0
Bell, Greg, Buff.	12	142	11.8	t40	2
Coffman, Paul, K.C.	12	75	6.3	10	2
Kattus, Eric, Cin.	11	99	9.0	28	1
McGee, Buford, S.D.	10	105	10.5	18	0
Hughes, David, Pitt.	10	98	9.8	22	0
Dickey, Curtis, Clev.	10	78	7.8	12	0
Harry, Emile, K.C.	9	211	23.4	53	1
Capers, Wayne, Ind.	9	118	13.1	27	0
Weathers, Clarence, Clev.	9	100	11.1	16	0
Moriarty, Larry, Hou.-K.C.	9	67	7.4	19	0
Sohn, Kurt, Jets	8	129	16.1	t24	2
Wilkins, Gary, Buff.	8	74	9.3	26	0
Hayes, Jonathan, K.C.	8	69	8.6	16	0
Pruitt, Mike, K.C.	8	56	7.0	13	0
Scott, Willie, N.E.	8	41	5.1	t8	3
Banks, Chuck, Hou.	7	71	10.1	17	0
LaFleur, Greg, Ind.	7	56	8.0	11	0
Jennings, Stanford, Cin.	6	86	14.3	34	0
Moffett, Tim, Raiders	6	77	12.8	17	0
Teal, Jimmy, Buff.	6	60	10.0	20	1
Mueller, Vance, Raiders	6	54	9.0	20	0
Spencer, Tim, S.D.	6	48	8.0	15	0
Kreider, Steve, Cin.	5	96	19.2	23	0
Jensen, Jim, Mia.	5	50	10.0	t20	1
Barber, Marion, Jets	5	36	7.2	16	0
Smith, Tim, Hou.	4	72	18.0	25	0
Akiu, Mike, Hou.	4	67	16.8	27	0
Hancock, Anthony, K.C.	4	63	15.8	25	0

	No	Yards	Avg	Long	TD
Holt, Harry, Clev.	4	61	15.3	34	1
Rolle, Butch, Buff.	4	56	14.0	20	0
Harbour, James, Ind.	4	46	11.5	28	0
Wilson, Stanley, Cin.	4	45	11.3	34	0
Bennett, Woody, Mia.	4	33	8.3	13	0
Adams, Curtis, S.D.	4	26	6.5	10	0
Broughton, Walter, Buff.	3	71	23.7	57	0
Martin, Mike, Cin.	3	68	22.7	51	0
Greer, Terry, Clev.	3	51	17.0	22	0
Richardson, Eric, Buff.	3	49	16.3	32	0
Hackett, Joey, Den.	3	48	16.0	19	0
Sherwin, Tim, Ind.	3	26	8.7	15	1
Lane, Eric, Sea.	3	6	2.0	4	0
Junkin, Trey, Raiders	2	38	19.0	19	0
Williams, Derwin, N.E.	2	35	17.5	26	0
Murray, Walter, Ind.	2	34	17.0	24	0
Tucker, Travis, Clev.	2	29	14.5	16	0
Sanders, Chuck, Pitt.	2	19	9.5	10	0
Pollard, Frank, Pitt.	2	15	7.5	10	0
Sievers, Eric, S.D.	2	14	7.0	9	0
Pattison, Mark, Raiders	2	12	6.0	6	0
Bell, Ken, Den.	2	10	5.0	7	0
Parker, Andy, Raiders	2	8	4.0	6	1
Munoz, Anthony, Cin.	2	7	3.5	t5	2
Bligen, Dennis, Jets	2	6	3.0	4	0
Reeder, Dan, Pitt.	2	4	2.0	3	0
Wilson, Steve, Den.	1	43	43.0	t43	1
Martin, Robbie, Ind.	1	41	41.0	41	0
Elway, John, Den.	1	23	23.0	t23	1
Weathers, Robert, N.E.	1	14	14.0	14	0
Townsell, JoJo, Jets	1	11	11.0	11	0
Ware, Timmie, S.D.	1	11	11.0	11	0
McNeil, Gerald, Clev.	1	9	9.0	9	0
Carter, Joe, Mia.	1	6	6.0	6	0
Holloway, Brian, N.E.	1	5	5.0	5	0
Bailey, Edwin, Sea.	1	3	3.0	3	0
Studdard, Dave, Den.	1	2	2.0	t2	1
Kosar, Bernie, Clev.	1	1	1.0	1	0
Kenney, Bill, K.C.	1	0	0.0	0	0
Oliver, Hubert, Hou.	1	-2	-2.0	-2	0

t = touchdown
Leader based on most passes caught

AFC — TOP 25 RECEIVERS BY YARDS

	Yards	No	Avg	Long	TD
Morgan, Stanley, N.E.	1491	84	17.8	t44	10
Duper, Mark, Mia.	1313	67	19.6	t85	11
Toon, Al, Jets	1176	85	13.8	t62	8
Christensen, Todd, Raiders	1153	95	12.1	35	8
Clayton, Mark, Mia.	1150	60	19.2	t68	10
Brooks, Bill, Ind	1131	65	17.4	t84	8
Hill, Drew, Hou.	1112	65	17.1	t81	5
Largent, Steve, Sea.	1070	70	15.3	t38	9
Givins, Earnest, Hou.	1062	61	17.4	60	3
Collinsworth, Cris, Cin.	1024	62	16.5	t46	10
Walker, Wesley, Jets	1016	49	20.7	t83	12
Brown, Eddie, Cin.	964	58	16.6	57	4
Chandler, Wes, S.D.	874	56	15.6	40	4
Anderson, Gary, S.D.	871	80	10.9	t65	8
Williams, Dokie, Raiders	843	43	19.6	53	8
Brennan, Brian, Clev.	838	55	15.2	t57	6
Bouza, Matt, Ind.	830	71	11.7	33	5
Paige, Stephone, K.C.	829	52	15.9	51	11
Burkett, Chris, Buff.	778	34	22.9	t84	4
Reed, Andre, Buff.	739	53	13.9	t55	7
Jackson, Mark, Den.	738	38	19.4	53	1
Fryar, Irving, N.E.	737	43	17.1	t69	6
Winslow, Kellen, S.D.	728	64	11.4	t28	5
Watson, Steve, Den.	699	45	15.5	46	3
Brooks, James, Cin.	686	54	12.7	54	4

AFC — INDIVIDUAL INTERCEPTORS

	No	Yards	Avg	Long	TD
Cherry, Deron, K.C.	9	150	16.7	49	0
Lippett, Ronnie, N.E.	8	76	9.5	43	0
McElroy, Vann, Raiders	7	105	15.0	28	0
Breeden, Louis, Cin.	7	72	10.3	t36	1
Harden, Mike, Den.	6	179	29.8	52	2
Holmes, Jerry, Jets	6	29	4.8	28	0
Burruss, Lloyd, K.C.	5	193	38.6	t72	3
Brown, Dave, Sea.	5	58	11.6	24	1
Byrd, Gill, S.D.	5	45	9.0	18	0
Lyles, Lester, Jets	5	36	7.2	22	0
Lynn, Johnny, Jets	5	36	7.2	26	0
Dixon, Hanford, Clev.	5	35	7.0	19	0
Dale, Jeffery, S.D.	4	153	38.3	50	0
Ross, Kevin, K.C.	4	66	16.5	35	0
Robinson, Jerry, Raiders	4	42	10.5	t32	1
Coleman, Leonard, Ind.	4	36	9.0	31	0
Justin, Kerry, Sea.	4	29	7.3	18	0
Romes, Charles, Buff.	4	23	5.8	23	0
Fulcher, David, Cin.	4	20	5.0	15	0
Lewis, Albert, K.C.	4	18	4.5	13	0
Seale, Sam, Raiders	4	2	0.5	2	0
Sanchez, Lupe, Pitt.	3	71	23.7	t67	1
Hill, Greg, K.C.	3	64	21.3	t26	1
Wright, Louis, Den.	3	56	18.7	56	0
Williams, Eric, Pitt.	3	44	14.7	25	0
Robinson, Eugene, Sea.	3	39	13.0	25	0
Moyer, Paul, Sea.	3	38	12.7	20	0
Wright, Felix, Clev.	3	33	11.0	33	0
Cocroft, Sherman, K.C.	3	32	10.7	13	0
Shell, Donnie, Pitt.	3	29	9.7	17	0
Woods, Rick, Pitt.	3	26	8.7	23	0
Lyday, Allen, Hou.	3	24	8.0	24	0
Lilly, Tony, Den.	3	22	7.3	15	0
Allen, Patrick, Hou.	3	20	6.7	18	0
Minnifield, Frank, Clev.	3	20	6.7	20	0
Clayton, Harvey, Pitt.	3	18	6.0	14	0
Daniel, Eugene, Ind.	3	11	3.7	5	0
Hinkle, Bryan, Pitt.	3	7	2.3	6	0
Clayborn, Ray, N.E.	3	4	1.3	4	0
Rose, Don, Mia.	2	63	31.5	36	0
Marion, Fred, N.E.	2	56	28.0	t37	1
Burroughs, Derrick, Buff.	2	49	24.5	41	0
McNeal, Don, Mia.	2	46	23.0	29	0
McGrew, Larry, N.E.	2	44	22.0	27	0
Rockins, Chris, Clev.	2	41	20.5	24	0
Foley, Steve, Den.	2	39	19.5	24	0

	No	Yards	Avg	Long	TD
James, Roland, N.E.	2	39	19.5	21	0
Brown, Steve, Hou.	2	34	17.0	38	0
Easley, Ken, Sea.	2	34	17.0	24	0
Glenn, Vencie, S.D.	2	31	15.5	31	0
Haynes, Mike, Raiders	2	28	14.0	22	0
Toran, Stacey, Raiders	2	28	14.0	19	0
O'Neal, Leslie, S.D.	2	22	11.0	17	1
Nelson, Steve, N.E.	2	21	10.5	17	0
Eason, Bo, Hou.	2	16	8.0	11	0
Hicks, Dwight, Ind.	2	16	8.0	16	0
Merriweather, Mike, Pitt.	2	14	7.0	11	0
Ellis, Ray, Clev.	2	12	6.0	7	0
Matthews, Clay, Clev.	2	12	6.0	8	0
Bickett, Duane, Ind.	2	10	5.0	10	0
Blackwood, Glenn, Mia.	2	10	5.0	7	0
Scholtz, Bruce, Sea.	2	10	5.0	10	0
Clifton, Kyle, Jets.	2	8	4.0	7	0
Barker, Leo, Cin.	2	7	3.5	7	0
Barnes, Jeff, Raiders	2	7	3.5	7	0
Hayes, Lester, Raiders	2	7	3.5	7	0
Johnson, Richard, Hou.	2	6	3.0	6	0
Judson, William, Mia.	2	0	0.0	0	0
Lyles, Robert, Hou.	2	0	0.0	0	0
Taylor, Terry, Sea.	2	0	0.0	0	0
Holt, John, Ind.	1	80	80.0	80	0
Rembert, Johnny, N.E.	1	37	37.0	37	0
Adams, Stefon, Raiders	1	32	32.0	32	0
Harper, Mark, Clev.	1	31	31.0	31	0
Hamilton, Harry, Jets	1	29	29.0	29	0
Crable, Bob, Jets.	1	26	26.0	26	0
Spani, Gary, K.C.	1	24	24.0	24	0
Brown, Donald, S.D.	1	23	23.0	23	0
Hunley, Ricky, Den.	1	22	22.0	22	0
Radecic, Scott, K.C.	1	20	20.0	20	0
Bussey, Barney, Cin.	1	19	19.0	19	0
Zander, Carl, Cin.	1	18	18.0	18	0
Martin, Rod, Raiders	1	15	15.0	15	0
Bellinger, Rodney, Buff.	1	14	14.0	14	0
Blackwood, Lyle, Mia.	1	14	14.0	14	0
Offerdahl, John, Mia.	1	14	14.0	14	0
McKenzie, Reggie, Raiders	1	9	9.0	9	0
Gaines, Greg, Sea.	1	8	8.0	8	0
Hand, Jon, Ind.	1	8	8.0	8	0
Kelly, Joe, Cin.	1	6	6.0	6	0
Dennison, Rick, Den.	1	5	5.0	5	0
Armstrong, Harvey, Ind.	1	4	4.0	4	0
Horton, Ray, Cin.	1	4	4.0	4	0
Brown, Bud, Mia.	1	3	3.0	3	0

	No	Yards	Avg	Long	TD
McSwain, Rod, N.E.	1	3	3.0	3	0
Smerlas, Fred, Buff.	1	3	3.0	3	0
Charles, Mike, Mia.	1	2	2.0	2	0
Cooks, Johnie, Ind.	1	1	1.0	1	0
Bayless, Martin, Buff.	1	0	0.0	0	0
Bostic, Keith, Hou.	1	0	0.0	0	0
Daniel, Kenny, Ind.	1	0	0.0	0	0
Donaldson, Jeff, Hou.	1	0	0.0	0	0
Freeman, Steve, Buff.	1	0	0.0	0	0
Hackett, Dino, K.C.	1	0	0.0	0	0
Kozlowski, Mike, Mia.	1	0	0.0	0	0
Smith, Dennis, Den.	1	0	0.0	0	0
Taylor, Ken, S.D.	1	0	0.0	0	0
Wilson, Steve, Den.	1	−5	−5.0	−5	0
Tippett, Andre, N.E.	0	32	—	32	0
Swain, John, Pitt.	0	9	—	9	0

t = touchdown
Leader based on most interceptions

AFC — TEAM INTERCEPTIONS

	Att	Yards	Avg	Long	TD
Kansas City	31	567	18.3	t72	4
Raiders	26	275	10.6	t32	1
Seattle	22	215	9.8	25	1
New England	21	312	14.9	69	1
Pittsburgh	20	218	10.9	t67	1
Jets	20	164	8.2	29	0
Denver	18	318	17.7	56	2
Cleveland	18	184	10.2	33	0
Cincinnati	17	146	8.6	t36	1
Indianapolis	16	166	10.4	80	0
Houston	16	100	6.3	38	0
San Diego	15	274	18.3	50	1
Miami	13	152	11.7	36	0
Buffalo	10	89	8.9	41	0
Conference Total	263	3181	—	80	12
Conference Average	18.8	227.2	12.1	—	0.9

AFC — INDIVIDUAL PUNTERS

	No	Yards	Long	Avg	Total Punts	TB	Blk	Opp Ret	Ret Yds	In 20	Net Avg
Stark, Rohn, Ind..........	76	3432	63	45.2	76	5	0	48	502	22	37.2
Roby, Reggie, Mia.	56	2476	73	44.2	56	9	0	23	200	13	37.4
Camarillo, Rich, N.E. ...	89	3746	64	42.1	92	7	3	60	565	16	33.1
Mojsiejenko, Ralf, S.D..	72	3026	62	42.0	74	11	2	42	368	15	32.9
Gossett, Jeff, Clev.	83	3423	61	41.2	83	10	0	44	268	21	35.6
Johnson, Lee, Hou.......	88	3623	66	41.2	88	9	0	40	303	26	35.7
Colbert, Lewis, K.C.	99	4033	56	40.7	99	6	0	52	572	23	33.7
Kidd, John, Buff..........	75	3031	57	40.4	75	9	0	32	260	14	34.5
Guy, Ray, Raiders........	90	3620	64	40.2	90	11	0	42	357	20	33.8
Newsome, Harry, Pitt...	86	3447	64	40.1	89	11	3	34	364	18	32.2
Jennings, Dave, Jets....	85	3353	55	39.4	85	6	0	36	165	27	36.1
Gamache, Vince, Sea..	79	3048	55	38.6	79	7	0	38	298	10	33.0
Hayes, Jeff, Cin.	56	1965	52	35.1	58	3	2	19	182	11	29.7
(Non-Qualifiers)											
Weil, Jack, Den...........	34	1344	55	39.5	34	3	0	20	169	5	32.8
Norman, Chris, Den. ...	30	1168	57	38.9	31	4	1	9	94	2	32.1
Horan, Mike, Den........	21	864	50	41.1	21	2	0	11	99	8	34.5
Chandler, Wes, S.D.	5	167	38	33.4	5	0	0	1	2	0	33.0
Kiel, Blair, Ind.	5	190	43	38.0	5	0	0	4	31	0	31.8
Esiason, Boomer, Cin. .	1	31	31	31.0	1	0	0	0	0	1	31.0
Zendejas, Tony, Hou....	1	36	36	36.0	1	0	0	0	0	1	36.0

Leader based on gross average, minimum 40 punts

AFC — TEAM PUNTING

	Total Punts	Yards	Long	Avg	TB	Blk	Opp Ret	Ret Yds	In 20	Net Avg
Indianapolis	81	3622	63	44.7	5	0	52	533	22	36.9
Miami........................	56	2476	73	44.2	9	0	23	200	13	37.4
Cleveland..................	83	3423	61	41.2	10	0	44	268	21	35.6
Houston	89	3659	66	41.1	9	0	40	303	27	35.7
Kansas City..............	99	4033	56	40.7	6	0	52	572	23	33.7
New England	92	3746	64	40.7	7	3	60	565	16	33.1
San Diego.................	79	3193	62	40.4	11	2	43	370	15	32.9
Buffalo	75	3031	57	40.4	9	0	32	260	14	34.5
Raiders	90	3620	64	40.2	11	0	42	357	20	33.8
Jets..........................	85	3353	55	39.4	6	0	36	165	27	36.1
Denver	86	3376	57	39.3	9	1	40	362	15	33.0
Pittsburgh	89	3447	64	38.7	11	3	34	364	18	32.2
Seattle	79	3048	55	38.6	7	0	38	298	10	33.0
Cincinnati..................	59	1996	52	33.8	3	2	19	182	12	29.7
Conference Total	1142	46023	73	—	113	11	555	4799	253	—
Conference Average .	81.6	3287.4	—	40.3	8.1	0.8	39.6	342.8	18.1	34.1

AFC — INDIVIDUAL PUNT RETURNERS

	No	FC	Yards	Avg	Long	TD
Edmonds, Bobby Joe, Sea.........	34	14	419	12.3	t75	1
Willhite, Gerald, Den.................	42	8	468	11.1	t70	1
Fryar, Irving, N.E.	35	10	366	10.5	t59	1
Anderson, Gary, S.D................	25	10	227	9.1	30	0
Walker, Fulton, Raiders	49	15	440	9.0	t70	1
Woods, Rick, Pitt.	33	12	294	8.9	41	0
McNeil, Gerald, Clev.................	40	10	348	8.7	t84	1
Smith, Jeff, K.C.	29	11	245	8.4	48	0
Sohn, Kurt, Jets......................	35	8	289	8.3	27	0
Drewrey, Willie, Hou.	34	13	262	7.7	25	0
Ellis, Craig, Mia.	24	1	149	6.2	17	0
(Non-Qualifiers)						
Pitts, Ron, Buff.	18	11	194	10.8	t49	1
Brooks, Bill, Ind.	18	7	141	7.8	18	0
Martin, Robbie, Ind.	17	5	109	6.4	25	0
Martin, Mike, Cin.	13	6	96	7.4	14	0
Broughton, Walter, Buff.	12	2	53	4.4	13	0
Pruitt, James, Mia....................	11	1	150	13.6	t71	1
Horton, Ray, Cin......................	11	3	111	10.1	25	0
James, Lionel, S.D.	9	6	94	10.4	21	0
Givins, Earnest, Hou................	8	0	80	10.0	17	0
McCallum, Napoleon, Raiders....	7	1	44	6.3	13	0
Harry, Emile, K.C.....................	6	7	20	3.3	7	0
Starring, Stephen, N.E..............	6	0	18	3.0	12	0
Skansi, Paul, Sea.	5	0	38	7.6	14	0
Townsell, JoJo, Jets	4	1	52	13.0	28	0
Johnson, Vance, Den................	3	0	36	12.0	19	0
McGee, Tim, Cin.	3	4	21	7.0	9	0
Lipps, Louis, Pitt......................	3	1	16	5.3	10	0
Chandler, Wes, S.D.	3	0	13	4.3	10	0
Jackson, Mark, Den.	2	0	7	3.5	6	0
Simmons, John, Cin.	2	4	7	3.5	6	0
Harden, Mike, Den....................	1	0	41	41.0	t41	1
Marion, Fred, N.E.	1	1	12	12.0	12	0
Slaughter, Webster, Clev.	1	0	2	2.0	2	0
Blackwood, Glenn, Mia.	1	0	0	0.0	0	0
Blackwood, Lyle, Mia................	1	0	0	0.0	0	0
Clayton, Mark, Mia...................	1	0	0	0.0	0	0
Hill, Rod, Buff.	1	0	0	0.0	0	0
Richardson, Eric, Buff...............	1	0	0	0.0	0	0
Thompson, Reyna, Mia.	1	0	0	0.0	0	0
Pinkett, Allen, Hou...................	1	2	-1	-1.0	-1	0
Moore, Nat, Mia........................	1	6	-2	-2.0	0	0
Jackson, Victor, Ind.	0	1	0	—	0	0

	No	FC	Yards	Avg	Long	TD
James, Roland, N.E.	0	1	0	—	0	0
Kozlowski, Mike, Mia.	0	3	0	—	0	0

t = touchdown
Leader based on average return, minimum 20 returns

AFC — TEAM PUNT RETURNS

	Att	FC	Yards	Avg	Long	TD
Seattle	39	14	457	11.7	t75	1
Denver	48	8	552	11.5	t70	2
New England	42	12	396	9.4	t59	1
San Diego	37	16	334	9.0	30	0
Jets	39	9	341	8.7	28	0
Raiders	56	16	484	8.6	t70	1
Pittsburgh	36	13	310	8.6	41	0
Cleveland	41	10	350	8.5	t84	1
Cincinnati	29	17	235	8.1	25	0
Houston	43	15	341	7.9	25	0
Buffalo	32	13	247	7.7	t49	1
Kansas City	35	18	265	7.6	48	0
Miami	40	11	297	7.4	t71	1
Indianapolis	35	13	250	7.1	25	0
Conference Total	552	185	4859	—	t84	8
Conference Average	39.4	13.2	347.1	8.8	—	0.6

AFC — INDIVIDUAL KICKOFF RETURNERS

	No	Yards	Avg	Long	TD
Sanchez, Lupe, Pitt.	25	591	23.6	64	0
McGee, Tim, Cin.	43	1007	23.4	94	0
Humphery, Bobby, Jets	28	655	23.4	t96	1
Bell, Ken, Den.	23	531	23.1	42	0
Lang, Gene, Den.	21	480	22.9	42	0
Edmonds, Bobby Joe, Sea.	34	764	22.5	46	0
Starring, Stephen, N.E.	36	802	22.3	52	0
Ellis, Craig, Mia.	25	541	21.6	41	0
Bentley, Albert, Ind.	32	687	21.5	37	0
Adams, Stefon, Raiders	27	573	21.2	51	0
McNeil, Gerald, Clev.	47	997	21.2	t100	1
Morris, Randall, Sea.	23	465	20.2	38	0
Anderson, Gary, S.D.	24	482	20.1	35	0
Drewrey, Willie, Hou.	25	500	20.0	32	0
Pinkett, Allen, Hou.	26	519	20.0	48	0
Smith, Jeff, K.C.	29	557	19.2	29	0
Martin, Robbie, Ind.	21	385	18.3	27	0
Walker, Fulton, Raiders	23	368	16.0	27	0
(Non-Qualifiers)					
Harmon, Ronnie, Buff.	18	321	17.8	32	0
James, Lionel, S.D.	18	315	17.5	31	0
Davenport, Ron, Mia.	16	285	17.8	37	0
Townsell, JoJo, Jets	13	322	24.8	t93	1
Jennings, Stanford, Cin.	12	257	21.4	41	0
Tasker, Steve, Hou.-Buff.	12	213	17.8	24	0
Broughton, Walter, Buff.	11	243	22.1	39	0
Green, Boyce, K.C.	10	254	25.4	t97	1
Fryar, Irving, N.E.	10	192	19.2	33	0
Hampton, Lorenzo, Mia.	9	182	20.2	25	0
Carter, Joe, Mia.	9	133	14.8	22	0
Riddick, Robb, Buff.	8	200	25.0	49	0
McCallum, Napoleon, Raiders	8	183	22.9	59	0
Sanders, Chuck, Pitt.	8	148	18.5	29	0
Brooks, Bill, Ind.	8	143	17.9	24	0
Sohn, Kurt, Jets	7	124	17.7	36	0
Fontenot, Herman, Clev.	7	99	14.1	19	0
Harper, Michael, Jets	7	71	10.1	19	0
Richardson, Eric, Buff.	6	123	20.5	28	0
Harry, Emile, K.C.	6	115	19.2	26	0
Daniel, Kenny, Ind.	5	109	21.8	30	0
Adams, Curtis, S.D.	5	100	20.0	25	0
Carson, Carlos, K.C.	5	88	17.6	29	0
Spencer, Tim, S.D.	5	81	16.2	21	0
Wyatt, Kevin, S.D.	5	74	14.8	23	0
Gill, Owen, Ind.	5	73	14.6	28	0

	No	Yards	Avg	Long	TD
Martin, Mike, Cin.	4	83	20.8	21	0
Moriarty, Larry, K.C.	4	80	20.0	23	0
Jones, Cedric, N.E.	4	63	15.8	20	0
Langhorne, Reggie, Clev.	4	57	14.3	20	0
Reeder, Dan, Pitt.	4	52	13.0	17	0
Dupard, Reggie, N.E.	3	50	16.7	21	0
Johnson, Trumaine, S.D.	3	48	16.0	21	0
Millen, Matt, Raiders	3	40	13.3	19	0
Hardy, Bruce, Mia.	3	39	13.0	16	0
Scholtz, Bruce, Sea.	3	39	13.0	16	0
Willhite, Gerald, Den.	3	35	11.7	23	0
Nicolas, Scott, Clev.	3	28	9.3	13	0
Rembert, Johnny, N.E.	3	27	9.0	14	0
Rudolph, Ben, Jets	3	17	5.7	10	0
Mueller, Vance, Raiders	2	73	36.5	46	0
Woolfolk, Butch, Hou.	2	38	19.0	21	0
Bellinger, Rodney, Buff.	2	32	16.0	16	0
Wonsley, George, Ind.	2	31	15.5	20	0
Seitz, Warren, Pitt.	2	25	12.5	14	0
Simpkins, Ron, Cin.	2	24	12.0	15	0
Johnson, Vance, Den.	2	21	10.5	21	0
Riley, Avon, Hou.	2	17	8.5	10	0
Hughes, David, Pitt.	2	16	8.0	16	0
Hawthorne, Greg, N.E.	2	13	6.5	13	0
Hunley, Ricky, Den.	2	11	5.5	6	0
Winslow, Kellen, S.D.	2	11	5.5	8	0
Baldwin, Tom, Jets	2	3	1.5	4	0
Shuler, Mickey, Jets	2	-3	-1.5	0	0
Puzzuoli, Dave, Clev.	1	32	32.0	32	0
Merriweather, Mike, Pitt.	1	27	27.0	27	0
Cocroft, Sherman, K.C.	1	23	23.0	23	0
Skansi, Paul, Sea.	1	21	21.0	21	0
Holman, Rodney, Cin.	1	18	18.0	18	0
Tice, Mike, Sea.	1	17	17.0	17	0
Woods, Rick, Pitt.	1	17	17.0	17	0
Jackson, Mark, Den.	1	16	16.0	16	0
Hawkins, Frank, Raiders	1	15	15.0	15	0
McGee, Buford, S.D.	1	15	15.0	15	0
Williams, Oliver, Ind.	1	15	15.0	15	0
Edwards, Randy, Sea.	1	13	13.0	13	0
Chandler, Wes, S.D.	1	11	11.0	11	0
Pitts, Ron, Buff.	1	7	7.0	7	0
Lee, Larry, Mia.	1	5	5.0	5	0
Lane, Eric, Sea.	1	3	3.0	3	0
Rostosky, Pete, Pitt.	1	3	3.0	3	0
Johnson, Dan, Mia.	1	0	0.0	0	0
Lynn, Johnny, Jets	1	0	0.0	0	0

	No	Yards	Avg	Long	TD
Madsen, Lynn, Hou.	1	0	0.0	0	0
Pearson, Aaron, K.C.	1	0	0.0	0	0
Plummer, Gary, S.D.	1	0	0.0	0	0
Ryan, Jim, Den.	1	0	0.0	0	0
Simmons, John, Cin.	1	0	0.0	0	0
Sweeney, Calvin, Pitt.	1	0	0.0	0	0
Toth, Tom, Mia.	1	0	0.0	0	0

t = touchdown
Leader based on average return, minimum 20 returns

AFC — TEAM KICKOFF RETURNS

	No	Yards	Avg	Long	TD
Cincinnati	63	1389	22.0	94	0
Seattle	64	1322	20.7	46	0
Denver	53	1094	20.6	42	0
Kansas City	56	1117	19.9	t97	1
New England	58	1147	19.8	52	0
Pittsburgh	66	1304	19.8	64	0
Cleveland	62	1213	19.6	t100	1
Raiders	64	1252	19.6	59	0
Buffalo	55	1074	19.5	49	0
Indianapolis	74	1443	19.5	37	0
Houston	59	1139	19.3	48	0
Jets	63	1189	18.9	t96	2
Miami	65	1185	18.2	41	0
San Diego	65	1137	17.5	35	0
Conference Total	867	17005	—	t100	4
Conference Average	61.9	1214.6	19.6	—	0.3

AFC — INDIVIDUAL SCORERS

KICKERS	XP	XPA	FG	FGA	PTS
Franklin, Tony, N.E.	44	45	32	41	140
Johnson, Norm, Sea.	42	42	22	35	108
Karlis, Rich, Den.	44	45	20	28	104
Breech, Jim, Cin.	50	51	17	32	101
Lowery, Nick, K.C.	43	43	19	26	100
Bahr, Chris, Raiders	36	36	21	28	99
Anderson, Gary, Pitt.	32	32	21	32	95
Reveiz, Fuad, Mia.	52	55	14	22	94
Zendejas, Tony, Hou.	28	29	22	27	94
Leahy, Pat, Jets	44	44	16	19	92
Bahr, Matt, Clev.	30	30	20	26	90
Benirschke, Rolf, S.D.	39	41	16	25	87
Norwood, Scott, Buff.	32	34	17	27	83
Biasucci, Dean, Ind.	26	27	13	25	65
Moseley, Mark, Wash.-Clev.	25	28	12	19	61

NON-KICKERS	TD	TDR	TDP	TDM	PTS
Winder, Sammy, Den.	14	9	5	0	84
Warner, Curt, Sea.	13	13	0	0	78
Hampton, Lorenzo, Mia.	12	9	3	0	72
Walker, Wesley, Jets	12	0	12	0	72
Duper, Mark, Mia.	11	0	11	0	66
Paige, Stephone, K.C.	11	0	11	0	66
Clayton, Mark, Mia.	10	0	10	0	60
Collinsworth, Cris, Cin.	10	0	10	0	60
Mack, Kevin, Clev.	10	10	0	0	60
Morgan, Stanley, N.E.	10	0	10	0	60
Anderson, Gary, S.D.	9	1	8	0	54
Brooks, James, Cin.	9	5	4	0	54
Kinnebrew, Larry, Cin.	9	8	1	0	54
Largent, Steve, Sea.	9	0	9	0	54
Willhite, Gerald, Den.	9	5	3	1	54
Abercrombie, Walter, Pitt.	8	6	2	0	48
Brooks, Bill, Ind.	8	0	8	0	48
Christensen, Todd, Raiders	8	0	8	0	48
Collins, Tony, N.E.	8	3	5	0	48
Hector, Johnny, Jets	8	8	0	0	48
Toon, Al, Jets	8	0	8	0	48
Williams, Dokie, Raiders	8	0	8	0	48
Wilson, Stanley, Cin.	8	8	0	0	48
Allen, Marcus, Raiders	7	5	2	0	42
Brennan, Brian, Clev.	7	0	6	1	42
Fryar, Irving, N.E.	7	0	6	1	42
McGee, Buford, S.D.	7	7	0	0	42
Moore, Nat, Mia.	7	0	7	0	42

	TD	TDR	TDP	TDM	PTS
Reed, Andre, Buff.	7	0	7	0	42
Turner, Daryl, Sea.	7	0	7	0	42
Bell, Greg, Buff.	6	4	2	0	36
Dickey, Curtis, Clev.	6	6	0	0	36
Hester, Jessie, Raiders	6	0	6	0	36
McNeil, Freeman, Jets	6	5	1	0	36
Smith, Jeff, K.C.	6	3	3	0	36
Spencer, Tim, S.D.	6	6	0	0	36
Bouza, Matt, Ind.	5	0	5	0	30
Hardy, Bruce, Mia.	5	0	5	0	30
Hill, Drew, Hou.	5	0	5	0	30
Jackson, Earnest, Pitt.	5	5	0	0	30
Malone, Mark, Pitt.	5	5	0	0	30
Riddick, Robb, Buff.	5	4	1	0	30
Slaughter, Webster, Clev.	5	0	4	1	30
Thompson, Weegie, Pitt.	5	0	5	0	30
Wallace, Ray, Hou.	5	3	2	0	30
Winslow, Kellen, S.D.	5	0	5	0	30
Adams, Curtis, S.D.	4	4	0	0	24
Brown, Eddie, Cin.	4	0	4	0	24
Burkett, Chris, Buff.	4	0	4	0	24
Burruss, Lloyd, K.C.	4	0	0	4	24
Butler, Raymond, Sea.	4	0	4	0	24
Byner, Earnest, Clev.	4	2	2	0	24
Carson, Carlos, K.C.	4	0	4	0	24
Chandler, Wes, S.D.	4	0	4	0	24
Erenberg, Rich, Pitt.	4	1	3	0	24
Givins, Earnest, Hou.	4	1	3	0	24
Green, Boyce, K.C.	4	3	0	1	24
James, Craig, N.E.	4	4	0	0	24
Johnson, Dan, Mia.	4	0	4	0	24
Metzelaars, Pete, Buff.	4	0	3	1	24
Rozier, Mike, Hou.	4	4	0	0	24
Shuler, Mickey, Jets	4	0	4	0	24
Bentley, Albert, Ind.	3	3	0	0	18
Harden, Mike, Den.	3	0	0	3	18
Lang, Gene, Den.	3	1	2	0	18
Lipps, Louis, Pitt.	3	0	3	0	18
McMillan, Randy, Ind.	3	3	0	0	18
Newsome, Ozzie, Clev.	3	0	3	0	18
Pinkett, Allen, Hou.	3	2	1	0	18
Pruitt, James, Mia.	3	0	2	1	18
Scott, Willie, N.E.	3	0	3	0	18
Watson, Steve, Den.	3	0	3	0	18
Arnold, Walt, K.C.	2	0	1	1	12
Barksdale, Rod, Raiders	2	0	2	0	12
Baty, Greg, N.E.	2	0	2	0	12

	TD	TDR	TDP	TDM	PTS
Butler, Jerry, Buff.	2	0	2	0	12
Cherry, Deron, K.C.	2	0	0	2	12
Coffman, Paul, K.C.	2	0	2	0	12
Elway, John, Den.	2	1	1	0	12
Fontenot, Herman, Clev.	2	1	1	0	12
Franklin, Byron, Sea.	2	0	2	0	12
Heard, Herman, K.C.	2	2	0	0	12
Holman, Rodney, Cin.	2	0	2	0	12
Holt, Harry, Clev.	2	1	1	0	12
Johnson, Vance, Den.	2	0	2	0	12
Joiner, Charlie, S.D.	2	0	2	0	12
Lane, Eric, Sea.	2	0	1	1	12
McNeil, Gerald, Clev.	2	0	0	2	12
Moon, Warren, Hou.	2	2	0	0	12
Munoz, Anthony, Cin.	2	0	2	0	12
Nathan, Tony, Mia.	2	0	2	0	12
Paige, Tony, Jets	2	2	0	0	12
Pruitt, Mike, K.C.	2	2	0	0	12
Robinson, Jerry, Raiders	2	0	0	2	12
Sewell, Steve, Den.	2	1	1	0	12
Sohn, Kurt, Jets	2	0	2	0	12
Starring, Stephen, N.E.	2	0	2	0	12
Tatupu, Mosi, N.E.	2	1	0	1	12
Woolfolk, Butch, Hou.	2	0	2	0	12
Humphery, Bobby, Jets	1	0	0	1	*8
Beach, Pat, Ind.	1	0	1	0	6
Bellinger, Rodney, Buff.	1	0	0	1	6
Bligen, Dennis, Jets	1	1	0	0	6
Boyer, Mark, Ind.	1	0	1	0	6
Breeden, Louis, Cin.	1	0	0	1	6
Brister, Bubby, Pitt.	1	1	0	0	6
Brown, Dave, Sea.	1	0	0	1	6
Byrum, Carl, Buff.	1	0	1	0	6
Daniel, Eugene, Ind.	1	0	0	1	6
Davenport, Ron, Mia.	1	0	1	0	6
Donaldson, Jeff, Hou.	1	0	0	1	6
Edmonds, Bobby Joe, Sea.	1	0	0	1	6
Edwards, Eddie, Cin.	1	0	0	1	6
Esiason, Boomer, Cin.	1	1	0	0	6
Flick, Tom, S.D.	1	1	0	0	6
Gill, Owen, Ind.	1	1	0	0	6
Gothard, Preston, Pitt.	1	0	1	0	6
Grogan, Steve, N.E.	1	1	0	0	6
Gross, Al, Clev.	1	0	0	1	6
Harmon, Ronnie, Buff.	1	0	1	0	6
Harry, Emile, K.C.	1	0	1	0	6
Hayes, Jeff, Cin.	1	1	0	0	6

	TD	TDR	TDP	TDM	PTS
Hayes, Lester, Raiders............	1	0	0	1	6
Hill, Greg, K.C.	1	0	0	1	6
Hogeboom, Gary, Ind.............	1	1	0	0	6
Holohan, Pete, S.D.	1	0	1	0	6
Hudson, Gordon, Sea.	1	0	1	0	6
Jackson, Mark, Den.	1	0	1	0	6
Jennings, Stanford, Cin.	1	1	0	0	6
Jensen, Jim, Mia.	1	0	1	0	6
Johnson, Trumaine, S.D.	1	0	1	0	6
Jones, Cedric, N.E.................	1	0	1	0	6
Kattus, Eric, Cin....................	1	0	1	0	6
Kay, Clarence, Den................	1	0	1	0	6
Krieg, Dave, Sea.	1	1	0	0	6
Langhorne, Reggie, Clev.	1	0	1	0	6
Lyles, Robert, Hou.	1	0	0	1	6
Marion, Fred, N.E.	1	0	0	1	6
Marshall, Henry, K.C..............	1	0	1	0	6
McCallum, Napoleon, Raiders.	1	1	0	0	6
McGee, Tim, Cin....................	1	0	1	0	6
McSwain, Rod, N.E.	1	0	0	1	6
Minnifield, Frank, Clev.	1	0	0	1	6
Mobley, Orson, Den.	1	0	1	0	6
Moore, Ricky, Buff.	1	1	0	0	6
Moriarty, Larry, Hou................	1	1	0	0	6
Morris, Randall, Sea.	1	1	0	0	6
Moyer, Paul, Sea.	1	0	0	1	6
Munchak, Mike, Hou...............	1	0	0	1	6
O'Neal, Leslie, S.D.	1	0	0	1	6
Parker, Andy, Raiders.............	1	0	1	0	6
Pitts, Ron, Buff.	1	0	0	1	6
Rembert, Johnny, N.E.	1	0	0	1	6
Ross, Kevin, K.C....................	1	0	0	1	6
Sanchez, Lupe, Pitt.	1	0	0	1	6
Sherwin, Tim, Ind.	1	0	1	0	6
Stallworth, John, Pitt..............	1	0	1	0	6
Studdard, Dave, Den.	1	0	1	0	6
Sweeney, Calvin, Pitt.	1	0	1	0	6
Teal, Jimmy, Buff...................	1	0	1	0	6
Townsell, JoJo, Jets	1	0	0	1	6
Townsend, Andre, Den.	1	0	0	1	6
Trudeau, Jack, Ind.................	1	1	0	0	6
Walker, Fulton, Raiders	1	0	0	1	6
Weathers, Robert, N.E............	1	1	0	0	6
Williams, Brent, N.E...............	1	0	0	1	6
Williams, Jamie, Hou..............	1	0	1	0	6
Wilson, Steve, Den.	1	0	1	0	6
Wonsley, George, Ind.	1	1	0	0	6

	TD	TDR	TDP	TDM	PTS
Woodard, Ken, Den.	1	0	0	1	6
Wright, Felix, Clev.	1	0	0	1	6
Edwards, David, Pitt.	0	0	0	0	*2
Jones, Rulon, Den.	0	0	0	0	*2
Leiding, Jeff, Ind.	0	0	0	0	*2
Townsend, Greg, Raiders	0	0	0	0	*2
White, Leon, Cin.	0	0	0	0	*2

* Safety (also Team Safeties: Den., N.E., S.D.)

AFC — TEAM SCORING

	TD	TDR	TDP	TDM	XP	XPA	FG	FGA	SAF	PTS
Miami	56	9	46	1	52	55	14	22	0	430
New England	45	10	29	6	44	45	32	41	1	412
Cincinnati	51	24	25	2	50	51	17	32	1	409
Cleveland	45	20	18	7	43	44	26	33	0	391
Denver..........	45	17	22	6	44	45	20	28	2	378
Seattle..........	43	15	24	4	42	43	22	35	0	366
Jets	45	16	27	2	44	44	16	19	1	364
Kansas City ..	43	10	23	10	43	43	19	26	0	358
San Diego	41	19	21	1	39	41	16	25	1	335
Raiders.........	37	6	27	4	36	36	21	28	1	323
Pittsburgh.....	35	18	16	1	32	34	21	32	1	307
Buffalo..........	34	9	22	3	32	34	17	27	0	287
Houston........	30	13	14	3	28	30	22	27.	0	274
Indianapolis..	27	10	16	1	26	27	13	25	1	229
Conf. Total.......	577	196	330	51	555	572	276	400	9	4863
Conf. Average .	41.2	14.0	23.6	3.6	39.6	40.9	19.7	28.6	0.6	347.4

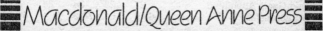

AFC — Team-by-Team Summary

AFC Offense	Buff.	Cin.	Clev.	Den.	Hou.
Rushes	419	521	470	455	490
Net Yds. Gained	1654	2533	1650	1678	1700
Avg. Gain	3.9	4.9	3.5	3.7	3.5
Avg. Yds. per Game	103.4	158.3	103.1	104.9	106.3
Passes Attempted	499	497	538	549	551
Completed	294	287	315	306	288
% Completed	58.9	57.7	58.6	55.7	52.3
Total Yds. Gained	3697	4160	4018	3811	3843
Times Sacked	45	28	39	38	48
Yds. Lost	334	203	274	273	394
Net Yds. Gained	3363	3957	3744	3538	3449
Avg. Yds. per Game	210.2	247.3	234.0	221.1	215.6
Net Yds. per Pass Play	6.18	7.54	6.49	6.03	5.76
Yds. Gained per Comp.	12.57	14.49	12.76	12.45	13.34
Combined Net Yds. Gained	5017	6490	5394	5216	5149
% Total Yds. Rushing	33.0	39.0	30.6	32.2	33.0
% Total Yds. Passing	67.0	61.0	69.4	67.8	67.0
Avg. Yds. per Game	313.6	405.6	337.1	326.0	321.8
Had Intercepted	19	20	11	16	31
Yds. Opp. Returned	284	189	135	363	325
Ret. by Opp. for TD	0	0	1	2	1
Punts	75	59	83	86	89
Yds. Punted	3031	1996	3423	3376	3659
Avg. Yds. per Punt	40.4	33.8	41.2	39.3	41.1
Punt Returns	32	29	41	48	43
Yds. Returned	247	235	350	552	341
Avg. Yds. per Return	7.7	8.1	8.5	11.5	7.9
Returned for TD	1	0	1	2	0
Kickoff Returns	55	63	62	53	59
Yds. Returned	1074	1389	1213	1094	1139
Avg. Yds. per Return	19.5	22.0	19.6	20.6	19.3
Returned for TD	0	0	1	0	0
Total Points Scored	287	409	391	378	274
Total TDs	34	51	45	45	30
TDs Rushing	9	24	20	17	13
TDs Passing	22	25	18	22	14
TDs on Ret. and Rec.	3	2	7	6	3
Extra Points	32	50	43	44	28
Safeties	0	1	0	2	0
Field Goals Made	17	17	26	20	22
Field Goals Attempted	27	32	33	28	27
% Successful	63.0	53.1	78.8	71.4	81.5

Ind.	K.C.	Raid.	Mia.	N.E.	N.Y.J.	Pitt.	S.D.	Sea
407	432	475	349	469	490	564	471	513
1491	1468	1790	1545	1373	1729	2223	1576	2300
3.7	3.4	3.8	4.4	2.9	3.5	3.9	3.3	4.5
93.2	91.8	111.9	96.6	85.8	108.1	138.9	98.5	143.8
586	521	530	645	557	537	491	604	453
300	257	281	392	340	334	238	339	268
51.2	49.3	53.0	60.8	61.0	62.2	48.5	56.1	59.2
3615	3122	3973	4898	4321	4032	2747	4045	3424
53	50	64	17	47	45	20	32	39
406	372	464	119	367	386	159	265	315
3209	2750	3509	4779	3954	3646	2588	3780	3109
200.6	171.9	219.3	298.7	247.1	227.9	161.8	236.3	194.3
5.02	4.82	5.91	7.22	6.55	6.26	5.06	5.94	6.32
12.05	12.15	14.14	12.49	12.71	12.07	11.54	11.93	12.78
4700	4218	5299	6324	5327	5375	4811	5356	5409
31.7	34.8	33.8	24.4	25.8	32.2	46.2	29.4	42.5
68.3	65.2	66.2	75.6	74.2	67.8	53.8	70.6	57.5
293.8	263.6	331.2	395.3	332.9	335.9	300.7	334.8	338.1
24	18	25	23	13	21	20	33	14
310	181	282	221	151	230	244	421	216
2	1	1	1	0	1	2	2	1
81	99	90	56	92	85	89	79	79
3622	4033	3620	2476	3746	3353	3447	3193	3048
44.7	40.7	40.2	44.2	40.7	39.4	38.7	40.4	38.6
35	35	56	40	42	39	36	37	39
250	265	484	297	396	341	310	334	457
7.1	7.6	8.6	7.4	9.4	8.7	8.6	9.0	11.7
0	0	1	1	1	0	0	0	1
74	56	64	65	58	63	66	65	64
1443	1117	1252	1185	1147	1189	1304	1137	1322
19.5	19.9	19.6	18.2	19.8	18.9	19.8	17.5	20.7
0	1	0	0	0	2	0	0	0
229	358	323	430	412	364	307	335	366
27	43	37	56	45	45	35	41	43
10	10	6	9	10	16	18	19	15
16	23	27	46	29	27	16	21	24
1	10	4	1	6	2	1	1	4
26	43	36	52	44	44	32	39	42
1	0	1	0	1	1	1	1	0
13	19	21	14	32	16	21	16	22
25	26	28	22	41	19	32	25	35
52.0	73.1	75.0	63.6	78.0	84.2	65.6	64.0	62.9

AFC Defense	Buff.	Cin.	Clev.	Den.	Hou.
Rushes	465	514	494	432	532
Net Yds. Gained	1721	2122	1981	1651	2035
Avg. Gain	3.7	4.1	4.0	3.8	3.8
Avg. Yds. per Game	107.6	132.6	123.8	103.2	127.2
Passes Attempted	570	495	518	545	490
Completed	343	278	291	301	228
% Completed	60.2	56.2	56.2	55.2	46.5
Total Yds. Gained	4069	3520	3546	3755	3200
Times Sacked	36	42	35	49	32
Yds. Lost	267	368	258	459	201
Net Yds. Gained	3802	3152	3288	3296	2999
Avg. Yds. per Game	237.6	197.0	205.5	206.0	187.4
Net Yds. per Pass Play	6.27	5.87	5.95	5.55	5.75
Yds. Gained per Comp.	11.86	12.66	12.19	12.48	14.04
Combined Net Yds. Gained	5523	5274	5269	4947	5034
% Total Yds. Rushing	31.2	40.2	37.6	33.4	40.4
% Total Yds. Passing	68.8	59.8	62.4	66.6	59.6
Avg. Yds. per Game	345.2	329.6	329.3	309.2	314.6
Intercepted by	10	17	18	18	16
Yds. Returned by	89	146	184	318	100
Returned for TD	0	1	0	2	0
Punts	83	77	80	86	94
Yds. Punted	3162	3068	3033	3689	3713
Avg. Yds. per Punt	38.1	39.8	37.9	42.9	39.5
Punt Returns	32	19	44	40	40
Yds. Returned	260	182	268	362	303
Avg. Yds. per Return	8.1	9.6	6.1	9.1	7.6
Returned for TD	0	0	0	0	0
Kickoff Returns	56	80	78	65	32
Yds. Returned	1157	1611	1476	1299	695
Avg. Yds. per Return	20.7	20.1	18.9	20.0	21.7
Returned for TD	0	1	1	0	0
Total Points Scored	348	394	310	327	329
Total TDs	40	47	36	36	39
TDs Rushing	18	23	12	13	13
TDs Passing	21	17	21	21	25
TDs on Ret. and Rec.	1	7	3	2	1
Extra Points	38	44	34	35	38
Safeties	2	1	0	2	0
Field Goals Made	22	22	20	24	19
Field Goals Attempted	33	30	29	32	29
% Successful	66.7	73.3	69.0	75.0	65.5

Ind.	K.C.	Raid.	Mia.	N.E.	N.Y.J.	Pitt.	S.D.	Sea
517	485	439	540	510	450	471	475	471
1962	1739	1728	2493	2203	1661	1872	1678	1759
3.8	3.6	3.9	4.6	4.3	3.7	4.0	3.5	3.7
122.6	108.7	108.0	155.8	137.7	103.8	117.0	104.9	109.9
510	569	501	485	473	603	536	509	535
306	303	271	290	255	348	311	288	301
60.0	53.3	54.1	59.8	53.9	57.7	58.0	56.6	56.3
3933	3555	3539	3825	3324	4567	3669	4128	3888
24	44	63	33	48	28	43	62	47
194	360	463	268	346	178	289	440	306
3739	3195	3076	3557	2978	4389	3380	3688	3582
233.7	199.7	192.3	222.3	186.1	274.3	211.3	230.5	223.9
7.00	5.21	5.45	6.87	5.72	6.96	5.84	6.46	6.15
12.85	11.73	13.06	13.19	13.04	13.12	11.80	14.33	12.92
5701	4934	4804	6050	5181	6050	5252	5366	5341
34.4	35.2	36.0	41.2	42.5	27.5	35.6	31.3	32.9
65.6	64.8	64.0	58.8	57.5	72.5	64.4	68.7	67.1
356.3	308.4	300.3	378.1	323.8	378.1	328.3	335.4	333.8
16	31	26	13	21	20	20	15	22
166	567	275	152	312	164	218	274	216
0	4	1	0	1	0	1	1	1
67	83	97	64	90	75	82	81	81
2725	3067	4087	2648	3585	2977	3194	3304	3270
40.7	37.0	42.1	41.4	39.8	39.7	39.0	40.8	40.4
52	52	42	23	60	36	34	43	38
533	572	357	200	565	165	364	370	298
10.3	11.0	8.5	8.7	9.4	4.6	10.7	8.6	7.8
1	1	1	0	0	0	0	1	0
43	71	63	53	81	62	56	60	59
827	1278	1064	997	1480	1307	1362	1088	1002
19.2	18.0	16.9	18.8	18.3	21.1	24.3	18.1	17.0
0	0	0	0	0	0	3	0	0
400	326	346	405	307	386	336	396	293
47	38	43	47	35	48	39	47	34
14	13	19	23	19	12	10	14	12
28	21	21	22	15	35	22	27	20
5	4	3	2	1	1	7	6	2
46	36	40	45	34	48	36	45	32
0	1	0	0	0	1	0	0	0
24	20	16	26	21	16	22	23	19
35	31	21	31	28	27	39	31	28
68.6	64.5	76.2	83.9	75.0	59.3	56.4	74.2	67.9

NATIONAL FOOTBALL CONFERENCE

INDIVIDUAL PLAYER
STATISTICS

NFC — INDIVIDUAL RUSHERS

	Att	Yards	Avg	Long	TD
Dickerson, Eric, Rams	404	1821	4.5	t42	11
Morris, Joe, Giants	341	1516	4.4	54	14
Mayes, Rueben, N.O.	286	1353	4.7	50	8
Payton, Walter, Chi.	321	1333	4.2	41	8
Riggs, Gerald, Atl.	343	1327	3.9	31	9
Rogers, George, Wash.	303	1203	4.0	42	18
Jones, James, Det.	252	903	3.6	39	8
Craig, Roger, S.F.	204	830	4.1	25	7
Mitchell, Stump, St.L.	174	800	4.6	44	5
Nelson, Darrin, Minn.	191	793	4.2	42	4
Dorsett, Tony, Dall.	184	748	4.1	33	5
Walker, Herschel, Dall.	151	737	4.9	t84	12
Wilder, James, T.B.	190	704	3.7	t45	2
James, Garry, Det.	159	688	4.3	t60	3
Cribbs, Joe, S.F.	152	590	3.9	19	5
Byars, Keith, Phil.	177	577	3.3	32	1
Ferrell, Earl, St.L.	124	548	4.4	25	0
Cunningham, Randall, Phil.	66	540	8.2	20	5
Davis, Kenneth, G.B.	114	519	4.6	50	0
Redden, Barry, Rams	110	467	4.2	t41	4
Hilliard, Dalton, N.O.	121	425	3.5	36	5
Young, Steve, T.B.	74	425	5.7	31	5
Anderson, Alfred, Minn.	83	347	4.2	29	2
Ellis, Gerry, G.B.	84	345	4.1	24	2
Wonsley, Nathan, T.B.	73	339	4.6	t59	3
Carruth, Paul Ott, G.B.	81	308	3.8	42	2
Archer, David, Atl.	52	298	5.7	22	0
Ellerson, Gary, G.B.	90	287	3.2	18	3
Springs, Ron, T.B.	74	285	3.9	40	0
Toney, Anthony, Phil.	69	285	4.1	43	1
Austin, Cliff, Atl.	62	280	4.5	22	1
Haddix, Michael, Phil.	79	276	3.5	18	0
Suhey, Matt, Chi.	84	270	3.2	17	2
Carthon, Maurice, Giants	72	260	3.6	12	0
Bryant, Kelvin, Wash.	69	258	3.7	t22	4
Pelluer, Steve, Dall.	41	255	6.2	21	1
Brown, Ted, Minn.	63	251	4.0	60	4
Anderson, Ottis, St.L.-Giants	75	237	3.2	16	3
Sanders, Thomas, Chi.	27	224	8.3	t75	5
Thomas, Calvin, Chi.	56	224	4.0	23	0
Rice, Allen, Minn.	73	220	3.0	19	2
Stamps, Sylvester, Atl.	30	220	7.3	48	0
Andrews, William, Atl.	52	214	4.1	13	1
Jordan, Buford, N.O.	68	207	3.0	10	1
Griffin, Keith, Wash.	62	197	3.2	12	0

	Att	Yards	Avg	Long	TD
Rouson, Lee, Giants	54	179	3.3	t21	2
Tautalatasi, Junior, Phil.	51	163	3.2	50	0
McMahon, Jim, Chi.	22	152	6.9	23	1
Lomax, Neil, St.L.	35	148	4.2	18	1
Anderson, Neal, Chi.	35	146	4.2	23	0
Rathman, Tom, S.F.	33	138	4.2	t29	1
Tyler, Wendell, S.F.	31	127	4.1	14	0
White, Charles, Rams	22	126	5.7	19	0
Tomczak, Mike, Chi.	23	117	5.1	16	3
Howard, Bobby, T.B.	30	110	3.7	16	1
Newsome, Tim, Dall.	34	110	3.2	13	2
Gentry, Dennis, Chi.	11	103	9.4	29	1
Crawford, Charles, Phil.	28	88	3.1	15	1
Gault, Willie, Chi.	8	79	9.9	33	0
Harmon, Derrick, S.F.	27	77	2.9	15	1
Moore, Alvin, Det.	19	73	3.8	18	0
Rice, Jerry, S.F.	10	72	7.2	18	1
Simms, Phil, Giants	43	72	1.7	18	1
Dixon, Floyd, Atl.	11	67	6.1	23	0
Sikahema, Vai, St.L.	16	62	3.9	23	0
Galbreath, Tony, Giants	16	61	3.8	10	0
Collier, Reggie, Dall.	6	53	8.8	21	0
Stoudt, Cliff, St.L.	7	53	7.6	17	0
Kemp, Jeff, S.F.	15	49	3.3	12	0
Kramer, Tommy, Minn.	23	48	2.1	13	1
Schroeder, Jay, Wash.	36	47	1.3	20	1
Coleman, Greg, Minn.	2	46	23.0	30	0
Everett, Jim, Rams	16	46	2.9	14	1
Hipple, Eric, Det.	16	46	2.9	13	0
Cherry, Tony, S.F.	11	42	3.8	10	0
Clark, Jessie, G.B.	18	41	2.3	9	0
Wright, Randy, G.B.	18	41	2.3	18	1
Montana, Joe, S.F.	17	38	2.2	17	0
Flutie, Doug, Chi.	9	36	4.0	19	1
Jaworski, Ron, Phil.	13	33	2.5	10	0
Fuller, Steve, Chi.	8	30	3.8	10	0
Gray, Mel, N.O.	6	29	4.8	11	0
Johnson, Bobby, Giants	2	28	14.0	22	0
Monk, Art, Wash.	4	27	6.8	21	0
Cavanaugh, Matt, Phil.	9	26	2.9	11	0
Ferguson, Joe, Det.	5	25	5.0	14	0
Ivery, Eddie Lee, G.B.	4	25	6.3	15	0
Johnson, Billy, Atl.	6	25	4.2	10	0
Manuel, Lionel, Giants	1	25	25.0	25	0
Hunter, Herman, Det.	3	22	7.3	18	0
Moroski, Mike, S.F.	6	22	3.7	12	1
Williams, Scott, Det.	13	22	1.7	5	2

	Att	Yards	Avg	Long	TD
Whisenhunt, Ken, Atl.	1	20	20.0	20	0
Clack, Darryl, Dall.	4	19	4.8	8	0
Rutledge, Jeff, Giants	3	19	6.3	18	0
Stanley, Walter, G.B.	1	19	19.0	19	0
Wilson, Dave, N.O.	14	19	1.4	14	1
Wilson, Wayne, Minn.-N.O.	10	19	1.9	6	0
Wolfley, Ron, St.L.	8	19	2.4	8	0
Epps, Phillip, G.B.	4	18	4.5	20	0
Williams, Keith, Atl.	3	18	6.0	8	0
Del Rio, Jack, N.O.	1	16	16.0	16	0
White, Danny, Dall.	8	16	2.0	10	1
Hebert, Bobby, N.O.	5	14	2.8	7	0
Jones, Hassan, Minn.	1	14	14.0	14	0
Carter, Anthony, Minn.	1	12	12.0	12	0
Matthews, Aubrey, Atl.	1	12	12.0	12	0
Schonert, Turk, Atl.	11	12	1.1	7	1
Fusina, Chuck, G.B.	7	11	1.6	6	0
Sherrard, Mike, Dall.	2	11	5.5	8	0
Cosbie, Doug, Dall.	1	9	9.0	9	0
Wilson, Wade, Minn.	13	9	0.7	13	1
Clark, Bret, Atl.	2	8	4.0	6	0
Waters, Mike, Phil.	5	8	1.6	5	0
Campbell, Scott, Atl.	1	7	7.0	7	0
Franklin, Pat, T.B.	7	7	1.0	4	0
Jones, Joey, Atl.	1	7	7.0	7	0
Bailey, Stacey, Atl.	1	6	6.0	6	0
Edwards, Kelvin, N.O.	1	6	6.0	6	0
Jackson, Kenny, Phil.	1	6	6.0	6	0
Lavette, Robert, Dall.	10	6	0.6	5	0
Brown, Ron, Rams	4	5	1.3	11	0
Dils, Steve, Rams	10	5	0.5	5	0
Fowler, Todd, Dall.	6	5	0.8	2	0
House, Kevin, T.B.	2	5	2.5	4	0
Marsh, Doug, St.L.	1	5	5.0	5	0
Ring, Bill, S.F.	3	4	1.3	4	0
Allen Greg, T.B.	1	3	3.0	3	0
Baker, Tony, Atl.	1	3	3.0	3	0
Bartkowski, Steve, Rams	6	3	0.5	7	0
Carpenter, Rob, Rams	2	3	1.5	3	0
Miller, Solomon, Giants	1	3	3.0	3	0
Guman, Mike, Rams	2	2	1.0	3	0
DeBerg, Steve, T.B.	2	1	0.5	t1	1
Hostetler, Jeff, Giants	1	1	1.0	1	0
Austin, Kent, St.L.	1	0	0.0	0	0
Ferragamo, Vince, G.B.	1	0	0.0	0	0
Hansen, Brian, N.O.	1	0	0.0	0	0
Long, Chuck, Det.	2	0	0.0	0	0

	Att	Yards	Avg	Long	TD
Renner, Bill, G.B.	1	0	0.0	0	0
Swanke, Karl, G.B.	1	0	0.0	0	0
Teltschik, John, Phil.	1	0	0.0	0	0
Perry, William, Chi.	1	−1	−1.0	−1	0
Frank, John, S.F.	1	−3	−3.0	−3	0
Green, Roy, St.L.	2	−4	−2.0	1	0
Carter, Gerald, T.B.	1	−5	−5.0	−5	0
Hunter, Tony, Rams	1	−6	−6.0	−6	0
Black, Mike, Det.	1	−8	−8.0	−8	0
Garcia, Frank, T.B.	1	−11	−11.0	−11	0
Buford, Maury, Chi.	1	−13	−13.0	−13	0
Ellard, Henry, Rams	1	−15	−15.0	−15	0
Lewis, Leo, Minn.	3	−16	−5.3	−2	0

t = touchdown
Leader based on most yards gained

NFC — TEAM RUSHING

	Att	Yards	Avg	Long	TD
Chicago	606	2700	4.5	t75	21
Atlanta	578	2524	4.4	48	12
Rams	578	2457	4.3	t42	16
Giants	558	2245	4.0	54	18
New Orleans	505	2074	4.1	50	15
Philadelphia	499	2002	4.0	50	8
San Francisco	510	1986	3.9	t29	16
Dallas	447	1969	4.4	t84	21
Tampa Bay	455	1863	4.1	t59	12
St. Louis	419	1787	4.3	44	8
Detroit	470	1771	3.8	t60	13
Minnesota	461	1738	3.8	60	14
Washington	474	1732	3.7	42	23
Green Bay	424	1614	3.8	50	8
Conference Total	6984	28462	—	t84	205
Conference Average	498.9	2033.0	4.1	—	14.6

NFC — INDIVIDUAL PASSING

QUALIFIERS

	Att	Comp	Pct Comp	Yds	Avg Gain	TD	Pct TD	Long	Int	Pct Int	Rating Points
Kramer, Tommy, Minn	372	208	55.9	3000	8.06	24	6.5	t76	10	2.7	92.6
Montana, Joe, S.F.	307	191	62.2	2236	7.28	8	2.6	48	9	2.9	80.7
Hipple, Eric, Det.	305	192	63.0	1919	6.29	9	3.0	46	11	3.6	75.6
Simms, Phil, Giants	468	259	55.3	3487	7.45	21	4.5	49	22	4.7	74.6
Lomax, Neil, St.L.	421	240	57.0	2583	6.14	13	3.1	t48	12	2.9	73.6
Schroeder, Jay, Wash.	541	276	51.0	4109	7.60	22	4.1	t71	22	4.1	72.9
Archer, David, Atl.	294	150	51.0	2007	6.83	10	3.4	65	9	3.1	71.6
Jaworski, Ron, Phil.	245	128	52.2	1405	5.73	8	3.3	56	6	2.4	70.2
Pelluer, Steve, Dall.	378	215	56.9	2727	7.21	8	2.1	t84	17	4.5	67.9
Wright, Randy, G.B.	492	263	53.5	3247	6.60	17	3.5	62	23	4.7	66.2
Wilson, Dave, N.O.	342	189	55.3	2353	6.88	10	2.9	t63	17	5.0	65.8
Young, Steve, T.B.	363	195	53.7	2282	6.29	8	2.2	46	13	3.6	65.5

NON-QUALIFIERS

	Att	Comp	Pct Comp	Yds	Avg Gain	TD	Pct TD	Long	Int	Pct Int	Rating Points
White, Danny, Dall.	153	95	62.1	1157	7.56	12	7.8	63	5	3.3	97.9
Kemp, Jeff, S.F.	200	119	59.5	1554	7.77	11	5.5	t66	8	4.0	85.7
Wilson, Wade, Minn.	143	80	55.9	1165	8.15	7	4.9	39	5	3.5	84.4
Flutie, Doug, Chi.	46	23	50.0	361	7.85	3	6.5	t58	2	4.3	80.1
Cunningham, Randall, Phil.	209	111	53.1	1391	6.66	8	3.8	t75	7	3.3	72.9
Moroski, Mike, S.F.	73	42	57.5	493	6.75	2	2.7	52	3	4.1	70.2
Schonert, Turk, Atl.	154	95	61.7	1032	6.70	4	2.6	41	8	5.2	68.4
Everett, Jim, Rams	147	73	49.7	1018	6.93	8	5.4	t60	8	5.4	67.8
Long, Chuck, Det.	40	21	52.5	247	6.18	2	5.0	t34	2	5.0	67.4
Ferguson, Joe, Det.	155	73	47.1	941	6.07	7	4.5	73	7	4.5	62.9
Fusina, Chuck, G.B.	32	19	59.4	178	5.56	0	0.0	42	1	3.1	61.7
McMahon, Jim, Chi.	150	77	51.3	995	6.63	5	3.3	t58	8	5.3	61.4
Fuller, Steve, Chi.	64	34	53.1	451	7.05	2	3.1	t50	4	6.3	60.1
Dils, Steve, Rams	129	59	45.7	693	5.37	4	3.1	t65	4	3.1	60.0
Bartkowski, Steve, Rams	126	61	48.4	654	5.19	2	1.6	42	3	2.4	59.4
Ferragamo, Vince, G.B.	40	23	57.5	283	7.08	1	2.5	50	3	7.5	56.6
Collier, Reggie, Dall.	15	8	53.3	96	6.40	1	6.7	27	2	13.3	55.8
Cavanaugh, Matt, Phil.	58	28	48.3	397	6.84	2	3.4	49	4	6.9	53.6
Stoudt, Cliff, St.L.	91	52	57.1	542	5.96	3	3.3	t24	7	7.7	53.5
Tomczak, Mike, Chi.	151	74	49.0	1105	7.32	2	1.3	85	10	6.6	50.2
DeBerg, Steve, T.B.	96	50	52.1	610	6.35	5	5.2	45	12	12.5	49.7
Hebert, Bobby, N.O.	79	41	51.9	498	6.30	2	2.5	84	8	10.1	40.5
(Less than 10 attempts)											
Anderson, Alfred, Minn.	2	1	50.0	17	8.50	0	0.0	17	0	0.0	79.2
Arapostathis, Evan, St.L.	1	0	0.0	0	0.00	0	0.0	0	0	0.0	39.6
Bono, Steve, Minn.	1	1	100.0	3	3.00	0	0.0	3	0	0.0	79.2
Byars, Keith, Phil.	2	1	50.0	55	27.50	1	50.0	t55	0	0.0	135.4
Campbell, Scott, Pitt.-Atl.	7	1	14.3	7	1.00	0	0.0	7	0	0.0	39.6
Dickerson, Eric, Rams	1	1	100.0	15	15.00	1	100.0	t15	0	0.0	158.3
Galbreath, Tony, Giants	1	0	0.0	0	0.00	0	0.0	0	0	0.0	39.6
Hilliard, Dalton, N.O.	3	1	33.3	29	9.67	1	33.3	t29	0	0.0	109.7
House, Kevin, Rams	0	0	—	0	—	0	—	0	0	—	0.0
Lofton, James, G.B.	1	0	0.0	0	0.00	0	0.0	0	0	0.0	39.6
Mitchell, Stump, St.L.	3	1	33.3	15	5.00	1	33.3	t15	0	0.0	90.3
Payton, Walter, Chi.	4	0	0.0	0	0.00	0	0.0	0	1	25.0	0.0

	Att	Comp	Pct Comp	Yds	Avg Gain	TD	Pct TD	Long	Int	Pct Int	Rating Points
Renfro, Mike, Dall.	1	1	100.0	23	23.00	0	0.0	23	0	0.0	118.8
Rice, Allen, Minn.	1	0	0.0	0	0.00	0	0.0	0	0	0.0	39.6
Rice, Jerry, S.F.	2	1	50.0	16	8.00	0	0.0	16	0	0.0	77.1
Riggs, Gerald, Atl.	1	0	0.0	0	0.00	0	0.0	0	0	0.0	39.6
Rutledge, Jeff, Giants	3	1	33.3	13	4.33	1	33.3	t13	0	0.0	87.5
Wattelet, Frank, N.O.	1	1	100.0	13	13.00	0	0.0	13	0	0.0	118.8
Williams, Doug, Wash.	1	0	0.0	0	0.00	0	0.0	0	0	0.0	39.6

t = touchdown
Leader based on rating points, minimum 224 attempts.

NFC — TEAM PASSING

	Att	Comp	Pct Comp	Gross Yards	Tkd	Yds Lost	Net Yards	Avg Yds Att	Avg Yds Comp	TD	Pct TD	Long	Int	Pct Int
San Francisco	582	353	60.7	4299	26	203	4096	7.39	12.18	21	3.6	t66	20	3.4
Minnesota	519	290	55.9	4185	44	272	3913	8.06	14.43	31	6.0	t76	15	2.9
Washington	542	276	50.9	4109	28	240	3869	7.58	14.89	22	4.1	t71	22	4.1
Dallas	547	319	58.3	4003	60	498	3505	7.32	12.55	21	3.8	t84	24	4.4
Green Bay	565	305	54.0	3708	37	261	3447	6.56	12.16	18	3.2	62	27	4.8
Giants	472	260	55.1	3500	46	367	3133	7.42	13.46	22	4.7	49	22	4.7
Detroit	500	286	57.2	3107	39	323	2784	6.21	10.86	18	3.6	73	20	4.0
Chicago	415	208	50.1	2912	24	153	2759	7.02	14.00	12	2.9	85	25	6.0
St. Louis	516	293	56.8	3140	59	424	2716	6.09	10.72	17	3.3	t48	19	3.7
New Orleans	425	232	54.6	2893	27	225	2668	6.81	12.47	13	3.1	84	25	5.9
Atlanta	452	246	54.4	3046	56	464	2582	6.74	12.38	14	3.1	65	17	3.8
Philadelphia	514	268	52.1	3248	104	708	2540	6.32	12.12	19	3.7	t75	17	3.3
Tampa Bay	459	245	53.4	2892	56	394	2498	6.30	11.80	13	2.8	46	25	5.4
Rams	403	194	48.1	2380	27	184	2196	5.91	12.27	15	3.7	t65	15	3.7
Conf. Total	6911	3775	—	47422	633	4716	42706	—	—	256	—	85	293	—
Conf. Average	493.6	269.6	54.6	3387.3	45.2	336.9	3050.4	6.86	12.56	18.3	3.7	—	20.9	4.2

NFC — INDIVIDUAL RECEIVERS

	No	Yards	Avg	Long	TD
Rice, Jerry, S.F.	86	1570	18.3	t66	15
Craig, Roger, S.F.	81	624	7.7	48	0
Smith, J.T., St.L.	80	1014	12.7	45	6
Walker, Herschel, Dall.	76	837	11.0	t84	2
Clark, Gary, Wash.	74	1265	17.1	55	7
Monk, Art, Wash.	73	1068	14.6	69	4
Bavaro, Mark, Giants	66	1001	15.2	41	4
Lofton, James, G.B.	64	840	13.1	36	4
Brown, Charlie, Atl.	63	918	14.6	42	4
Clark, Dwight, S.F.	61	794	13.0	t45	2
Quick, Mike, Phil.	60	939	15.7	t75	9
Jordan, Steve, Minn.	58	859	14.8	t68	6
Ferrell, Earl, St.L.	56	434	7.8	t30	3
Jones, James, Det.	54	334	6.2	21	1
Chadwick, Jeff, Det.	53	995	18.8	73	5
Nelson, Darrin, Minn.	53	593	11.2	34	3
Hill, Tony, Dall.	49	770	15.7	63	3
Epps, Phillip, G.B.	49	612	12.5	t53	4
Jones, Mike, N.O.	48	625	13.0	45	3
Newsome, Tim, Dall.	48	421	8.8	30	3
Magee, Calvin, T.B.	45	564	12.5	45	5
Bland, Carl, Det.	44	511	11.6	34	2
Bryant, Kelvin, Wash.	43	449	10.4	40	3
Wilder, James, T.B.	43	326	7.6	25	1
Gault, Willie, Chi.	42	818	19.5	t53	5
Carter, Gerald, T.B.	42	640	15.2	46	2
Dixon, Floyd, Atl.	42	617	14.7	65	2
Green, Roy, St.L.	42	517	12.3	t48	6
Sherrard, Mike, Dall.	41	744	18.1	t68	5
Francis, Russ, S.F.	41	505	12.3	52	1
Tautalatasi, Junior Phil.	41	325	7.9	56	2
Mitchell, Stump, St.L.	41	276	6.7	24	0
Spagnola, John, Phil	39	397	10.2	38	1
Carter, Anthony, Minn.	38	686	18.1	t60	7
Martin, Eric, N.O.	37	675	18.2	84	5
Payton, Walter, Chi.	37	382	10.3	57	3
Giles, Jimmie, T.B.-Det.	37	376	10.2	30	4
Tice, John, N.O.	37	330	8.9	t29	3
Stanley, Walter, G.B.	35	723	20.7	62	2
Cribbs, Joe, S.F.	35	346	9.9	33	0
Didier, Clint, Wash.	34	691	20.3	t71	4
Ellard, Henry, Rams	34	447	13.1	t34	4
James, Garry, Det.	34	219	6.4	26	0
Galbreath, Tony, Giant	33	268	8.1	19	0
Lewis, Leo, Minn.	32	600	18.8	t76	2

	No	Yards	Avg	Long	TD
Johnson, Bobby, Giants	31	534	17.2	t44	5
Ivery, Eddie Lee, G.B.	31	385	12.4	42	1
Jackson, Kenny, Phil.	30	506	16.9	49	6
Rice, Allen, Minn.	30	391	13.0	t32	3
Robinson, Stacy, Giants	29	494	17.0	49	2
Jones, Hassan, Minn.	28	570	20.4	t55	4
Cosbie, Doug, Dall.	28	312	11.1	t22	1
Redden, Barry, Rams	28	217	7.8	t24	1
Moorehead, Emery, Chi.	26	390	15.0	85	1
Dickerson, Eric, Rams	26	205	7.9	28	0
Haddix, Michael, Phil.	26	150	5.8	29	0
Brown, Ron, Rams	25	396	15.8	t65	3
Thompson, Leonard, Det.	25	320	12.8	t36	5
Marsh, Doug, St.L.	25	313	12.5	27	0
Dorsett, Tony, Dall.	25	267	10.7	t36	1
Hunter, Herman, Det.	25	218	8.7	t18	1
Cox, Arthur, Atl.	24	301	12.5	49	1
Ellis, Gerry, G.B.	24	258	10.8	29	0
Suhey, Matt, Chi.	24	235	9.8	58	0
Springs, Ron, T.B.	24	187	7.8	46	0
Riggs, Gerald, Atl.	24	136	5.7	11	0
Carruth, Paul, G.B.	24	134	5.6	19	2
Ortego, Keith, Chi.	23	430	18.7	t58	2
Renfro, Mike, Dall.	22	325	14.8	t30	3
Wrightman, Tim, Chi.	22	241	11.0	29	0
Morris, Joe, Giants	21	233	11.1	23	1
Davis, Kenneth, G.B.	21	142	6.8	18	1
Goodlow, Eugene, N.O.	20	306	15.3	t29	2
Stamps, Sylvester, Atl.	20	221	11.1	t39	1
Whisenhunt, Ken, Atl.	20	184	9.2	t23	3
Warren, Don, Wash.	20	164	8.2	20	1
Gentry, Dennis, Chi.	19	238	12.5	41	0
Anderson, Ottis, St.L.-Giants	19	137	7.2	19	0
House, Kevin, T.B.-Rams	18	384	21.3	t60	2
Brenner, Hoby, N.O.	18	286	15.9	34	0
Banks, Gordon, Dall.	17	202	11.9	23	0
Anderson, Alfred, Minn.	17	179	10.5	t37	2
Ross, Dan, G.B.	17	143	8.4	16	1
Hilliard, Dalton, N.O.	17	107	6.3	17	0
Mayes, Rueben, N.O.	17	96	5.6	18	0
McConkey, Phil, Giants	16	279	17.4	46	1
Carthon, Maurice, Giants	16	67	4.2	10	0
Hunter, Tony, Rams	15	206	13.7	42	0
West, Ed, G.B.	15	199	13.3	t46	1
Young, Mike, Rams	15	181	12.1	21	3
Brown, Ted, Minn.	15	132	8.8	20	0
Sanders, Ricky, Wash.	14	286	20.4	71	2

	No	Yards	Avg	Long	TD
Freeman, Phil, T.B.	14	229	16.4	t33	2
Johnson, Troy, St.L.	14	203	14.5	39	0
Hill, David, Rams	14	202	14.4	33	1
Little, David, Phil	14	132	9.4	26	0
Toney, Anthony, Phil.	13	177	13.6	47	0
Rathman, Tom, S.F.	13	121	9.3	14	0
Garrity, Gregg, Phil.	12	227	18.9	34	0
Williams, Keith, Atl.	12	164	13.7	t32	1
Ellerson, Gary, G.B.	12	130	10.8	32	0
Johnson, Ron, Phil.	11	207	18.8	39	1
Manuel, Lionel, Giants	11	181	16.5	35	3
Harris, Herbert, N.O.	11	148	13.5	27	0
Jordan, Buford, N.O.	11	127	11.5	37	0
Griffin, Keith, Wash.	11	110	10.0	28	0
Mularkey, Mike, Minn.	11	89	8.1	20	2
Byars, Keith, Phil.	11	44	4.0	17	0
Allen, Anthony, Atl.	10	156	15.6	32	2
Duckworth, Bobby, Rams-Phil.	10	148	14.8	32	1
Edwards, Kelvin, N.O.	10	132	13.2	24	0
Bell, Jerry, T.B.	10	120	12.0	25	0
Mowatt, Zeke, Giants	10	119	11.9	30	2
Sikahema, Vai, St.L.	10	99	9.9	27	1
Lewis, David, Det.	10	88	8.8	16	1
Miller, Solomon, Giants	9	144	16.0	t32	2
Wilson, Mike, S.F.	9	104	11.6	18	1
Guman, Mike, Rams	9	68	7.6	13	0
Frank, John, S.F.	9	61	6.8	17	2
Rouson, Lee, Giants	8	121	15.1	t37	1
Harmon, Derrick, S.F.	8	78	9.8	15	0
Wonsley, Nathan, T.B.	8	57	7.1	11	0
Moore, Alvin, Det.	8	47	5.9	8	0
Jones, Joey, Atl.	7	141	20.1	41	0
Mandley, Pete, Det.	7	106	15.1	51	0
Franklin, Pat, T.B.	7	29	4.1	9	1
Smith, Phil, Phil.	6	94	15.7	36	0
Williams, David, T.B.	6	91	15.2	25	0
Chandler, Thornton, Dall.	6	57	9.5	15	2
Johnson, Billy, Atl.	6	57	9.5	27	0
Clark, Jessie, G.B.	6	41	6.8	12	0
Middleton, Ron, Atl.	6	31	5.2	8	0
Scott, Chuck, Rams.	5	76	15.2	21	0
Crawford, Derrick, S.F.	5	70	14.0	42	0
Rubick, Rob, Det.	5	62	12.4	27	0
Gustafson, Jim, Minn.	5	61	12.2	18	2
Howard, Bobby, T.B.	5	60	12.0	29	0
Fox, Chas, St.L.	5	59	11.8	t38	1
Long, Darren, Rams	5	47	9.4	13	0

	No	Yards	Avg	Long	TD
Andrews, William, Atl..............	5	35	7.0	14	0
Lavette, Robert, Dall..................	5	31	6.2	9	1
Moffitt, Mike, G.B.	4	87	21.8	34	0
Anderson, Neal, Chi.	4	80	20.0	t58	1
Barnes, Lew, Chi...................	4	54	13.5	14	0
Thomas, Calvin, Chi.	4	18	4.5	18	0
Dunn, K.D., T.B......................	3	83	27.7	38	0
Harris, Leonard, T.B.	3	52	17.3	23	0
Tilley, Pat, St.L......................	3	51	17.0	18	0
Orr, Terry, Wash.	3	45	15.0	t22	1
Heflin, Vince, T.B.	3	42	14.0	15	0
Holman, Scott, St.L.	3	41	13.7	18	0
Bailey, Stacey, Atl.	3	39	13.0	21†	0
Rhymes, Buster, Minn.	3	25	8.3	12	0
Rogers, George, Wash.	3	24	8.0	13	0
Austin, Cliff, Atl.....................	3	21	7.0	9	0
Gray, Mel, N.O.......................	2	45	22.5	38	0
Wolfley, Ron, St.L...................	2	32	16.0	28	0
Waters, Mike, Phil.	2	27	13.5	19	0
Sanders, Thomas, Chi..............	2	18	9.0	18	0
Darby, Byron, Phil.	2	16	8.0	13	0
Margerum, Ken, S.F.................	2	12	6.0	6	0
Williams, Scott, Det.	2	9	4.5	6	0
Lewis, Mark, G.B.....................	2	7	3.5	t4	2
Monroe, Carl, S.F....................	2	6	3.0	5	0
Matthews, Aubrey, Atl..............	1	25	25.0	25	0
Fowler, Todd, Dall.	1	19	19.0	19	0
Clack, Darryl, Dall.	1	18	18.0	18	0
Gillespie, Willie, T.B.	1	18	18.0	18	0
Carson, Harry, Giants..............	1	13	13.0	t13	1
Waymer, Dave, N.O.	1	13	13.0	13	0
Mallory, Rick, T.B....................	1	9	9.0	9	0
Tyrrell, Tim, Rams...................	1	9	9.0	9	0
Bortz, Mark, Chi, ...	1	8	8.0	8	0
Ring, Bill, S.F.........................	1	8	8.0	8	0
Sargent, Broderick, St.L.	1	8	8.0	8	0
Franz, Nolan, G.B.	1	7	7.0	7	0
Holloway, Derek, Wash.	1	7	7.0	7	0
White, Charles, Rams...............	1	7	7.0	7	0
Williams, John, N.O..................	1	5	5.0	5	0
Novacek, Jay, St.L.	1	2	2.0	2	0
Hebert, Bobby, N.O..................	1	1	1.0	1	0
Heller, Ron, T.B.	1	1	1.0	t1	1
Wilson, Wayne, N.O.	1	-3	-3.0	-3	0

t = touchdown
Leader based on most passes caught

NFC — TOP 25 RECEIVERS BY YARDS

	Yards	No	Avg	Long	TD
Rice, Jerry, S.F.	1570	86	18.3	t66	15
Clark, Gary, Wash.	1265	74	17.1	55	7
Monk, Art, Wash	1068	73	14.6	69	4
Smith, J.T., St.L.	1014	80	12.7	45	6
Bavaro, Mark, Giants	1001	66	15.2	41	4
Chadwick, Jeff, Det.	995	53	18.8	73	5
Quick, Mike, Phil.	939	60	15.7	t75	9
Brown, Charlie, Atl.	918	63	14.6	42	4
Jordan, Steve, Minn.	859	58	14.8	t68	6
Lofton, James, G.B.	840	64	13.1	36	4
Walker, Herschel, Dall.	837	76	11.0	t84	2
Gault, Willie, Chi.	818	42	19.5	t53	5
Clark, Dwight, S.F.	794	61	13.0	t45	2
Hill, Tony, Dall.	770	49	15.7	63	3
Sherrard, Mike, Dall.	744	41	18.1	t68	5
Stanley, Walter, G.B.	723	35	20.7	62	2
Didier, Clint, Wash.	691	34	20.3	t71	4
Carter, Anthony, Minn.	686	38	18.1	t60	7
Martin, Eric, N.O.	675	37	18.2	84	5
Carter, Gerald, T.B.	640	42	15.2	46	2
Jones, Mike, N.O.	625	48	13.0	45	3
Craig, Roger, S.F.	624	81	7.7	48	0
Dixon, Floyd, Atl.	617	42	14.7	65	2
Epps, Phillip, G.B.	612	49	12.5	t53	4
Lewis, Leo, Minn.	600	32	18.8	t76	2

NFC — INDIVIDUAL INTERCEPTORS

	No	Yards	Avg	Long	TD
Lott, Ronnie, S.F.	10	134	13.4	t57	1
Waymer, Dave, N.O.	9	48	5.3	17	0
Lee, Mark, G.B.	9	33	3.7	11	0
Gray, Jerry, Rams	8	101	12.6	28	0
Holt, Issiac, Minn.	8	54	6.8	27	0
Richardson, Mike, Chi.	7	69	9.9	32	0
Irvin, LeRoy, Rams	6	150	25.0	t50	1
Duerson, Dave, Chi.	6	139	23.2	38	0
Downs, Michael, Dall.	6	54	9.0	31	0
Waters, Andre, Phil.	6	39	6.5	21	0
McKyer, Tim, S.F.	6	33	5.5	t21	1
Young, Roynell, Phil.	6	9	1.5	9	0
Cromwell, Nolan, Rams	5	101	20.2	t80	1
Clark, Bret, Atl.	5	94	18.8	34	0
Marshall, Wilber, Chi.	5	68	13.6	t58	1
Fellows, Ron, Dall.	5	46	9.2	t34	1
Mitchell, Devon, Det.	5	41	8.2	17	0
Green, Darrell, Wash.	5	9	1.8	7	0
Browner, Joey, Minn.	4	62	15.5	t39	1
Galloway, Duane, Det.	4	58	14.5	36	0
Fahnhorst, Jim, S.F.	4	52	13.0	46	0
Kinard, Terry, Giants	4	52	13.0	25	0
Fuller, Jeff, S.F.	4	44	11.0	26	0
Mack, Cedric, St.L.	4	42	10.5	24	0
Poe, Johnnie, N.O.	4	42	10.5	30	0
Case, Scott, Atl.	4	41	10.3	41	0
Williams, Perry, Giants	4	31	7.8	15	0
Cade, Mossy, G.B.	4	26	6.5	18	0
McNorton, Bruce, Det.	4	10	2.5	10	0
Holmoe, Tom, S.F.	3	149	49.7	t78	2
Harris, John, Minn.	3	69	23.0	28	0
Jordan, Curtis, Wash.	3	46	15.3	20	0
Walls, Everson, Dall.	3	46	15.3	24	0
Newsome, Vince, Rams	3	45	15.0	34	0
Fencik, Gary, Chi.	3	37	12.3	24	0
Wattelet, Frank, N.O.	3	34	11.3	22	0
Hill, Kenny, Giants	3	25	8.3	23	0
Cooper, Evan, Phil.	3	20	6.7	20	0
McKeever, Vito, T.B.	3	12	4.0	10	0
Lee, Carl, Minn.	3	10	3.3	10	0
Johnson, Alonzo, Phil.	3	6	2.0	9	0
Williamson, Carlton, S.F.	3	3	1.0	2	0
Griffin, Don, S.F.	3	0	0.0	0	0
Jackson, Vestee, Chi.	3	0	0.0	0	0
Nixon, Tory, S.F.	2	106	53.0	t88	1

	No	Yards	Avg	Long	TD
Brantley, Scot, T.B.	2	65	32.5	57	0
Gibson, Antonio, N.O.	2	43	21.5	43	0
Croudip, David, Atl.	2	35	17.5	29	0
Griffin, James, Det.	2	34	17.0	21	0
Solomon, Jesse, Minn.	2	34	17.0	18	0
Milot, Rich, Wash.	2	33	16.5	31	0
Wilson, Otis, Chi.	2	31	15.5	21	0
Reasons, Gary, Giants	2	28	14.0	18	0
Patterson, Elvis, Giants	2	26	13.0	26	0
Sutton, Mickey, Rams	2	25	12.5	20	0
Jerue, Mark, Rams	2	23	11.5	t22	1
Welch, Herb, Giants	2	22	11.0	16	0
Washington, Lionel, St.L.	2	19	9.5	19	0
Johnson, Demetrious, Det.	2	18	9.0	18	0
Williams, Joel, Atl.	2	18	9.0	t14	1
Maxie, Brett, N.O.	2	15	7.5	15	0
Wilburn, Barry, Wash.	2	14	7.0	14	0
Woodberry, Dennis, Atl.	2	14	7.0	9	0
Carter, Carl, St.L.	2	12	6.0	11	0
Williams, Jimmy, Det.	2	12	6.0	11	0
Wilkes, Reggie, Atl.	2	11	5.5	10	0
Jakes, Van, N.O.	2	6	3.0	4	0
Bowles, Todd, Wash.	2	0	0.0	0	0
Coffey, Ken, Wash.	2	0	0.0	0	0
Curry, Craig, T.B.	2	0	0.0	0	0
Greene, George, G.B.	2	0	0.0	0	0
Martin, George, Giants	1	78	78.0	t78	1
Doleman, Chris, Minn.	1	59	59.0	t59	1
Stills, Ken, G.B.	1	58	58.0	t58	1
Smith, Wayne, St.L.	1	35	35.0	35	0
Butler, Bobby, Atl.	1	33	33.0	t33	1
Curry, Buddy, Atl.	1	32	32.0	32	0
Scott, Victor, Dall.	1	31	31.0	31	0
Swoope, Craig, T.B.	1	23	23.0	23	0
Tuiasosopo, Manu, S.F.	1	22	22.0	22	0
Leopold, Bobby, G.B.	1	21	21.0	21	0
Carson, Harry, Giants	1	20	20.0	20	0
Cousineau, Tom, S.F.	1	18	18.0	18	0
Hoage, Terry, Phil.	1	18	18.0	18	0
Haynes, James, N.O.	1	17	17.0	17	0
Millard, Keith, Minn.	1	17	17.0	17	0
Browner, Keith, T.B.	1	16	16.0	16	0
Johnson, Vaughan, N.O.	1	15	15.0	15	0
Olkewicz, Neal, Wash.	1	15	15.0	15	0
Foules, Elbert, Phil.	1	14	14.0	14	0
Gary, Russell, N.O.	1	14	14.0	14	0
Gayle, Shaun, Chi.	1	13	13.0	13	0

	No	Yards	Avg	Long	TD
Johnson, Johnnie, Rams	1	13	13.0	13	0
Johnson, Pepper, Giants	1	13	13.0	13	0
Smith, Leonard, St.L.	1	13	13.0	13	0
Bess, Rufus, Minn.	1	12	12.0	12	0
Washington, Chris, T.B.	1	12	12.0	12	0
Schulz, Jody, Phil.	1	11	11.0	11	0
Cason, Wendell, Atl.	1	10	10.0	10	0
Turner, Keena, S.F.	1	9	9.0	9	0
Bostic, John, Det.	1	8	8.0	8	0
Haley, Charles, S.F.	1	8	8.0	8	0
Ferguson, Keith, Det.	1	7	7.0	7	0
Phillips, Reggie, Chi.	1	6	6.0	6	0
Rade, John, Atl.	1	6	6.0	6	0
Watts, Elbert, G.B.	1	6	6.0	6	0
Dean, Vernon, Wash.	1	5	5.0	5	0
Lockhart, Eugene, Dall.	1	5	5.0	5	0
McMichael, Steve, Chi.	1	5	5.0	5	0
Daniels, Calvin, Wash	1	4	4.0	4	0
Joyner, Seth, Phil.	1	4	4.0	4	0
Anderson, John, G.B.	1	3	3.0	3	0
Cobb, Garry, Phil.	1	3	3.0	3	0
Singletary, Mike, Chi.	1	3	3.0	3	0
Studwell, Scott, Minn.	1	2	2.0	2	0
Williams, Eric, Det.	1	2	2.0	2	0
Headen, Andy, Giants	1	1	1.0	1	0
Holloway, Johnny, Dall.	1	1	1.0	1	0
Jackson, Rickey, N.O.	1	1	1.0	1	0

t = touchdown
Leader based on most interceptions

NFC — TEAM INTERCEPTIONS

	Att	Yards	Avg	Long	TD
San Francisco	39	578	14.8	t88	5
Chicago	31	370	11.9	t58	1
Rams	28	458	16.4	t80	3
New Orleans	26	235	9.0	43	1
Minnesota	24	319	13.3	t59	2
Giants	24	296	12.3	t78	1
Philadelphia	23	124	5.4	21	0
Atlanta	22	294	13.4	41	2
Detroit	22	190	8.6	36	0
Green Bay	20	147	7.4	t58	1
Washington	19	126	6.6	31	0
Dallas	17	183	10.8	t34	1
Tampa Bay	13	128	9.8	57	0
St. Louis	10	121	12.1	35	0
Conference Total	318	3569	—	t88	17
Conference Average	22.7	254.9	11.2	—	1.2

NFC — INDIVIDUAL PUNTERS

	No	Yards	Long	Avg	Total Punts	TB	Blk	Opp Ret	Ret Yds	In 20	Net Avg
Landeta, Sean, Giants .	79	3539	61	44.8	79	11	0	41	386	24	37.1
Donnelly, Rick, Atl.	78	3421	71	43.9	79	9	1	47	477	19	35.0
Cox, Steve, Wash.	75	3271	58	43.6	75	16	0	36	220	21	36.4
Hansen, Brian, N.O......	81	3456	66	42.7	82	11	1	37	234	17	36.6
Teltschik, John, Phil.....	108	4493	62	41.6	109	10	1	62	631	20	33.6
Runager, Max, S.F.......	83	3450	62	41.6	85	8	2	49	373	23	34.3
Coleman, Greg, Minn...	67	2774	69	41.4	67	4	0	39	353	15	34.9
Buford, Maury, Chi.......	69	2850	59	41.3	70	8	1	23	110	20	36.9
Saxon, Mike, Dall.........	86	3498	58	40.7	87	10	1	41	301	28	34.4
Garcia, Frank, T.B.	77	3089	60	40.1	77	8	0	38	410	19	32.7
Bracken, Don, G.B.......	55	2203	63	40.1	57	5	2	33	235	6	32.8
Black, Mike, Det...........	46	1819	57	39.5	47	5	1	21	250	11	31.3
Hatcher, Dale, Rams....	97	3740	57	38.6	98	5	1	47	416	26	32.9
Cater, Greg, St.L.........	61	2271	52	37.2	62	4	1	24	130	16	33.2
(Non-Qualifiers)											
Arnold, Jim, Det.	36	1533	60	42.6	37	4	1	18	267	7	32.1
Arapostathis, E., St.L..	30	1140	50	38.0	30	0	0	20	166	5	32.5
Renner, Bill, G.B..........	15	622	50	41.5	18	1	3	11	52	2	30.6
Nelson, Chuck, Minn.....	3	72	31	24.0	3	0	0	0	0	0	24.0
Cunningham, R., Phil....	2	54	39	27.0	2	0	0	1	3	0	25.5
Wilson, Wade, Minn.	2	76	46	38.0	3	0	1	1	3	0	24.3
Murray, Ed, Det............	1	37	37	37.0	1	1	0	0	0	0	17.0
Springs, Ron, T.B.	1	43	43	43.0	1	0	0	1	4	0	39.0

Leader based on gross average, minimum 40 punts

NFC — TEAM PUNTING

	Total Punts	Yards	Long	Avg	TB	Blk	Opp Ret	Ret Yds	In 20	Net Avg
N.Y. Giants...............	79	3539	61	44.8	11	0	41	386	24	37.1
Washington...............	75	3271	58	43.6	16	0	36	220	21	36.4
Atlanta	79	3421	71	43.3	9	1	47	477	19	35.0
New Orleans..............	82	3456	66	42.1	11	1	37	234	17	36.6
Philadelphia..............	111	4547	62	41.0	10	1	63	634	20	33.5
Chicago	70	2850	59	40.7	8	1	23	110	20	36.9
San Francisco...........	85	3450	62	40.6	8	2	49	373	23	34.3
Dallas.......................	87	3498	58	40.2	10	1	41	301	28	34.4
Tampa Bay	78	3132	60	40.2	8	0	39	414	19	32.8
Minnesota	73	2922	69	40.0	4	1	40	356	15	34.1
Detroit......................	85	3389	60	39.9	10	2	39	517	18	31.4
Rams	98	3740	57	38.2	5	1	47	416	26	32.9
Green Bay	75	2825	63	37.7	6	5	44	287	8	32.2
St. Louis	92	3411	52	37.1	4	1	44	296	21	33.0
Conference Total	1169	47451	71	—	120	17	590	5021	279	—
Conference Average .	83.5	3389.4	—	40.6	8.6	1.2	42.1	358.6	19.9	34.2

NFC — INDIVIDUAL PUNT RETURNERS

	No	FC	Yards	Avg	Long	TD
Sikahema, Vai, St.L.	43	16	522	12.1	t71	2
Griffin, Don, S.F.	38	18	377	9.9	t76	1
Mandley, Pete, Det.	43	9	420	9.8	t81	1
Jenkins, Ken, Wash.	28	11	270	9.6	39	0
Stanley, Walter, G.B.	33	7	316	9.6	t83	1
Martin, Eric, N.O.	24	9	227	9.5	39	0
Barnes, Lew, Chi.	57	9	482	8.5	35	0
Sutton, Mickey, Rams	28	5	234	8.4	32	0
McConkey, Phil, Giants	32	12	253	7.9	22	0
Bess, Rufus, Minn.	23	10	162	7.0	15	0
Banks, Gordon, Dall.	27	14	160	5.9	20	0
Dixon, Floyd, Atl.	26	3	151	5.8	16	0
(Non-Qualifiers)						
Lavette, Robert, Dall.	18	3	92	5.1	28	0
Garrity, Gregg, Phil.	17	7	187	11.0	t76	1
Cooper, Evan, Phil.	16	7	139	8.7	58	0
Ellard, Henry, Rams	14	10	127	9.1	20	0
Futrell, Bobby, T.B.	14	5	67	4.8	12	0
Green, Darrell, Wash.	12	2	120	10.0	23	0
McLemore, Dana, N.O.	10	3	67	6.7	23	0
Yarber, Eric, Wash.	9	4	143	15.9	44	0
Walker, Kevin, T.B.	9	0	27	3.0	10	0
Johnson, Billy, Atl.	8	8	87	10.9	30	0
Poe, Johnnie, N.O.	8	3	71	8.9	17	0
Lewis, Leo, Minn.	7	4	53	7.6	13	0
Jones, Joey, Atl.	7	1	36	5.1	14	0
Waters, Mike, Phil.	7	1	30	4.3	13	0
Smith, Phil, Phil.	4	1	18	4.5	7	0
Crawford, Derrick, S.F.	4	0	15	3.8	9	0
Manuel, Lionel, Giants	3	6	22	7.3	12	0
Harris, Leonard, T.B.	3	0	16	5.3	8	0
Collins, Mark, Giants	3	1	11	3.7	6	0
Edwards, Kelvin, N.O.	3	0	2	0.7	5	0
Galbreath, Tony, Giants	3	1	1	0.3	1	0
Allen, Anthony, Atl.	2	0	10	5.0	9	0
Tullis, Willie, N.O.	2	0	10	5.0	7	0
Clark, Gary, Wash.	1	3	14	14.0	14	0
Stamps, Sylvester, Atl.	1	0	8	8.0	8	0
Smith, J.T., St.L.	1	0	6	6.0	6	0
McKyer, Tim, S.F.	1	1	5	5.0	5	0
Milot, Rich, Wash.	1	0	3	3.0	3	0
Carter, Carl, St.L.	1	0	0	0.0	0	0
Holloway, Johnny, Dall.	1	0	0	0.0	0	0
Rice, Allen, Minn.	1	0	0	0.0	0	0
Carter, Anthony, Minn.	0	1	0	—	0	0

	No	FC	Yards	Avg	Long	TD
Johnson, Johnnie, Rams	0	7	0	—	0	0
Morrell, Kyle, Minn....................	0	2	0	—	0	0

t = touchdown
Leader based on average return, minimum 20 returns

NFC — TEAM PUNT RETURNS

	Att	FC	Yards	Avg	Long	TD
St. Louis..................	45	16	528	11.7	t71	2
Washington	51	20	550	10.8	44	0
Detroit......................	43	9	420	9.8	t81	1
Green Bay................	33	7	316	9.6	t83	1
San Francisco	43	19	397	9.2	t76	1
Rams........................	42	22	361	8.6	32	0
Philadelphia.............	44	16	374	8.5	t76	1
Chicago...................	57	9	482	8.5	35	0
New Orleans	47	15	377	8.0	39	0
Giants	41	20	287	7.0	22	0
Minnesota................	31	17	215	6.9	15	0
Atlanta.....................	44	12	292	6.6	30	0
Dallas......................	46	17	252	5.5	28	0
Tampa Bay..............	26	5	110	4.2	12	0
Conference Total	593	204	4961	—	t83	6
Conference Average	42.4	14.6	354.4	8.4	—	0.4

NFC — INDIVIDUAL KICKOFF RETURNERS

	No	Yards	Avg	Long	TD
Gentry, Dennis, Chi.	20	576	28.8	t91	1
Gray, Mel, N.O.	31	866	27.9	t101	1
Sikahema, Vai, St.L.	37	847	22.9	44	0
Bess, Rufus, Minn.	31	705	22.7	43	0
Brown, Ron, Rams	36	794	22.1	55	0
Stamps, Sylvester, Atl.	24	514	21.4	35	0
Hunter, Herman, Det.	49	1007	20.6	54	0
Jenkins, Ken, Wash.	27	554	20.5	37	0
Stanley, Walter, G.B.	28	559	20.0	55	0
Elder, Donnie, Pitt.-Det.	22	435	19.8	36	0
McConkey, Phil, Giants	24	471	19.6	27	0
Lavette, Robert, Dall.	36	699	19.4	37	0
Freeman, Phil, T.B.	31	582	18.8	33	0
Crawford, Charles, Phil.	27	497	18.4	36	0
Sanders, Thomas, Chi.	22	399	18.1	44	0
(Non-Qualifiers)					
Clack, Darryl, Dall.	19	421	22.2	51	0
Tautalatasi, Junior, Phil.	18	344	19.1	51	0
Crawford, Derrick, S.F.	15	280	18.7	34	0
Williams, Keith, Atl.	14	255	18.2	32	0
Verdin, Clarence, Wash.	12	240	20.0	29	0
Watts, Elbert, G.B.	12	239	19.9	40	0
Davis, Kenneth, G.B.	12	231	19.3	35	0
White, Charles, Rams	12	216	18.0	28	0
Collins, Mark, Giants	11	204	18.5	26	0
Mayes, Rueben, N.O.	10	213	21.3	34	0
Stills, Ken, G.B.	10	209	20.9	38	0
Wonsley, Nathan, T.B.	10	208	20.8	29	0
Swanson, Eric, St.L.	10	206	20.6	40	0
Rhymes, Buster, Minn.	9	213	23.7	34	0
Griffin, Keith, Wash.	8	156	19.5	35	0
Walker, Kevin, T.B.	8	146	18.3	26	0
Monroe, Carl, S.F.	8	139	17.4	25	0
Ellerson, Gary, G.B.	7	154	22.0	57	0
Garner, Dwight, Wash.	7	142	20.3	26	0
Harris, Herbert, N.O.	7	122	17.4	22	0
Austin, Cliff, Atl.	7	120	17.1	25	0
Miller, Solomon, Giants	7	111	15.9	23	0
Mitchell, Stump, St.L.	6	203	33.8	53	0
Fox, Chas, St.L.	6	161	26.8	38	0
Bland, Carl, Det.	6	114	19.0	24	0
Futrell, Bobby, T.B.	5	115	23.0	30	0
Griffin, Don, S.F.	5	97	19.4	28	0
Sutton, Mickey, Rams	5	91	18.2	22	0
Rice, Allen, Minn.	5	88	17.6	23	0

	No	Yards	Avg	Long	TD
Smith, Oscar, Det.	5	81	16.2	30	0
Hill, Kenny, Giants	5	61	12.2	30	0
Harmon, Derrick, S.F.	4	82	20.5	28	0
Andrews, William, Atl.	4	71	17.8	22	0
Howard, Bobby, T.B.	4	71	17.8	24	0
Harris, Leonard, T.B.	4	63	15.8	23	0
Carruth, Paul, G.B.	4	40	10.0	20	0
Anderson, Neal, Chi.	4	26	6.5	13	0
Nelson, Darrin, Minn.	3	105	35.0	40	0
Barnes, Lew, Chi.	3	94	31.3	t85	1
Graham, William, Det.	3	72	24.0	27	0
Rathman, Tom, S.F.	3	66	22.0	22	0
Martin, Eric, N.O.	3	64	21.3	27	0
Johnson, Troy, St.L.	3	46	15.3	25	0
Holloway, Derek, Wash.	3	44	14.7	18	0
Matthews, Aubrey, Atl.	3	42	14.0	20	0
Ferrell, Earl, St.L.	3	41	13.7	27	0
Anderson, Alfred, Minn.	3	38	12.7	17	0
Franklin, Pat, T.B.	3	23	7.7	18	0
Byars, Keith, Phil.	2	47	23.5	31	0
Cooper, Evan, Phil.	2	42	21.0	24	0
McLemore, Dana, N.O.	2	39	19.5	22	0
Mandley, Pete, Det.	2	37	18.5	37	0
Wilson, Wayne, Minn.	2	33	16.5	26	0
Newsome, Tim, Dall.	2	32	16.0	18	0
Orr, Terry, Wash.	2	31	15.5	16	0
Cherry, Tony, S.F.	2	29	14.5	17	0
Williams, David, T.B.	2	29	14.5	15	0
Guman, Mike, Rams	2	28	14.0	16	0
Tullis, Willie, N.O.	2	28	14.0	19	0
Sargent, Broderick, St.L.	2	27	13.5	14	0
Frank, John, S.F.	2	24	12.0	16	0
Carter, Carl, St.L.	2	21	10.5	14	0
Magee, Calvin, T.B.	2	21	10.5	11	0
Rouson, Lee, Giants	2	21	10.5	12	0
Carpenter, Rob, Rams	2	19	9.5	11	0
Brown, Ted, Minn.	2	18	9.0	17	0
Quick, Mike, Phil.	2	6	3.0	6	0
Banks, Gordon, Dall.	1	56	56.0	56	0
Allen, Greg, T.B.	1	21	21.0	21	0
Epps, Phillip, G.B.	1	21	21.0	21	0
Croudip, David, Atl.	1	20	20.0	20	0
Gault, Willie, Chi.	1	20	20.0	20	0
Ellard, Henry, Rams	1	18	18.0	18	0
Berry, Ed, G.B.	1	16	16.0	16	0
Heflin, Vince, T.B.	1	15	15.0	15	0
McKyer, Tim, S.F.	1	15	15.0	15	0

	No	Yards	Avg	Long	TD
Ring, Bill, S.F.	1	15	15.0	15	0
Dixon, Floyd, Atl.	1	13	13.0	13	0
Wilson, Mike, S.F.	1	10	10.0	10	0
Schulz, Jody, Phil.	1	9	9.0	9	0
Krakoski, Joe, Wash.	1	8	8.0	8	0
Curry, Craig, T.B.	1	6	6.0	6	0
Boatner, Mack, T.B.	1	2	2.0	2	0
Holmes, Don, St.L.	1	2	2.0	2	0
Noble, Brian, G.B.	1	1	1.0	1	0
Dunn, K.D., T.B.	1	0	0.0	0	0
Evans, Leon, Det.	1	0	0.0	0	0
Irwin, Tim, Minn.	1	0	0.0	0	0
Lasker, Greg, Giants	1	0	0.0	0	0
Randle, Ervin, T.B.	1	0	0.0	0	0
Simmons, Clyde, Phil.	1	0	0.0	0	0
Tuinei, Mark, Dall.	1	0	0.0	0	0
Love, Duval, Rams	1	-6	-6.0	-6	0
Wolfley, Ron, St.L.	0	-6	—	-6	0

t = touchdown
Leader based on average return, minimum 20 returns

NFC — TEAM KICKOFF RETURNS

	No	Yards	Avg	Long	TD
New Orleans	55	1332	24.2	t101	1
Chicago	50	1115	22.3	t91	2
St. Louis	70	1548	22.1	53	0
Minnesota	56	1200	21.4	43	0
Dallas	59	1208	20.5	56	0
Detroit	67	1321	19.7	54	0
Rams	59	1160	19.7	55	0
Washington	60	1175	19.6	37	0
Green Bay	76	1470	19.3	57	0
Atlanta	54	1035	19.2	35	0
San Francisco	42	757	18.0	34	0
Philadelphia	53	945	17.8	51	0
Giants	50	868	17.4	30	0
Tampa Bay	75	1302	17.4	33	0
Conference Total	826	16436	—	t101	3
Conference Average	59.0	1174.0	19.9	—	0.2

NFC — INDIVIDUAL SCORERS

KICKERS

	XP	XPA	FG	FGA	PTS
Butler, Kevin, Chi.	36	37	28	41	120
Wersching, Ray, S.F.	41	42	25	35	116
Nelson, Chuck, Minn.	44	47	22	28	110
Andersen, Morten, N.O.	30	30	26	30	108
Allegre, Raul, Giants	33	33	24	32	105
Septien, Rafael, Dall.	43	43	15	21	88
McFadden, Paul, Phil.	26	27	20	31	86
Lansford, Mike, Rams	34	35	17	24	85
Murray, Ed, Det.	31	32	18	25	85
Del Greco, Al, G.B.	29	29	17	27	80
Igwebuike, Donald, T.B.	26	27	17	24	77
Luckhurst, Mick, Atl.	21	21	14	24	63
Zendejas, Max, Wash.	23	28	9	14	50
Lee, John, St.L.	14	17	8	13	38
Haji-Sheikh, Ali, Atl.	7	8	9	12	34
Schubert, Eric, St.L.	9	9	3	11	18
Cooper, Joe, Giants	4	4	2	4	10
Cox, Steve, Wash.	0	0	3	5	9
Thomas, Bob, Giants	4	4	0	1	4
Atkinson, Jess, Wash.	3	3	0	0	3
Donnelly, Rick, Atl.	1	1	0	0	1

NON-KICKERS

	TD	TDR	TDP	TDM	PTS
Rogers, George, Wash.	18	18	0	0	108
Rice, Jerry, S.F.	16	1	15	0	96
Morris, Joe, Giants	15	14	1	0	90
Walker, Herschel, Dall.	14	12	2	0	84
Dickerson, Eric, Rams	11	11	0	0	66
Payton, Walter, Chi.	11	8	3	0	66
Jones, James, Det.	9	8	1	0	54
Quick, Mike, Phil.	9	0	9	0	54
Riggs, Gerald, Atl.	9	9	0	0	54
Mayes, Rueben, N.O.	8	8	0	0	48
Bryant, Kelvin, Wash.	7	4	3	0	42
Carter, Anthony, Minn.	7	0	7	0	42
Clark, Gary, Wash.	7	0	7	0	42
Craig, Roger, S.F.	7	7	0	0	42
Nelson, Darrin, Minn.	7	4	3	0	42
Dorsett, Tony, Dall.	6	5	1	0	36
Green, Roy, St.L.	6	0	6	0	36
Jackson, Kenny, Phil.	6	0	6	0	36
Jordan, Steve, Minn.	6	0	6	0	36
Smith, J.T., St.L.	6	0	6	0	36

	TD	TDR	TDP	TDM	PTS
Chadwick, Jeff, Det.	5	0	5	0	30
Cribbs, Joe, S.F.	5	5	0	0	30
Cunningham, Randall, Phil.	5	5	0	0	30
Gault, Willie, Chi.	5	0	5	0	30
Hilliard, Dalton, N.O.	5	5	0	0	30
Johnson, Bobby, Giants	5	0	5	0	30
Magee, Calvin, T.B.	5	0	5	0	30
Martin, Eric, N.O.	5	0	5	0	30
Mitchell, Stump, St.L.	5	5	0	0	30
Newsome, Tim, Dall.	5	2	3	0	30
Redden, Barry, Rams	5	4	1	0	30
Rice, Allen, Minn.	5	2	3	0	30
Sanders, Thomas, Chi.	5	5	0	0	30
Sherrard, Mike, Dall.	5	0	5	0	30
Thompson, Leonard, Det.	5	0	5	0	30
Young, Steve, T.B.	5	5	0	0	30
Anderson, Alfred, Minn.	4	2	2	0	24
Bavaro, Mark, Giants	4	0	4	0	24
Brown, Charlie, Atl.	4	0	4	0	24
Brown, Ted, Minn.	4	4	0	0	24
Carruth, Paul, G.B.	4	2	2	0	24
Didier, Clint, Wash.	4	0	4	0	24
Ellard, Henry, Rams	4	0	4	0	24
Epps, Phillip, G.B.	4	0	4	0	24
Giles, Jimmie, T.B.-Det.	4	0	4	0	24
Jones, Hassan, Minn.	4	0	4	0	24
Lofton, James, G.B.	4	0	4	0	24
Monk, Art, Wash.	4	0	4	0	24
Anderson, Ottis, St.L.-Giants	3	3	0	0	18
Brown, Ron, Rams	3	0	3	0	18
Ellerson, Gary, G.B.	3	3	0	0	18
Ferrell, Earl, St.L.	3	0	3	0	18
Gentry, Dennis, Chi.	3	1	0	2	18
Hill, Tony, Dall.	3	0	3	0	18
Irvin, LeRoy, Rams	3	0	0	3	18
James, Garry, Det.	3	3	0	0	18
Jones, Mike, N.O.	3	0	3	0	18
Manuel, Lionel, Giants	3	0	3	0	18
Renfro, Mike, Dall.	3	0	3	0	18
Rouson, Lee, Giants	3	2	1	0	18
Sikahema, Vai, St.L.	3	0	1	2	18
Stanley, Walter, G.B.	3	0	2	1	18
Tice, John, N.O.	3	0	3	0	18
Tomczak, Mike, Chi.	3	3	0	0	18
Whisenhunt, Ken, Atl.	3	0	3	0	18
Wilder, James, T.B.	3	2	1	0	18
Wonsley, Nathan, T.B.	3	3	0	0	18

	TD	TDR	TDP	TDM	PTS
Young, Mike, Rams	3	0	3	0	18
Allen, Anthony, Atl.	2	0	2	0	12
Bland, Carl, Det.	2	0	2	0	12
Carter, Gerald, T.B.	2	0	2	0	12
Chandler, Thornton, Dall.	2	0	2	0	12
Clark, Dwight, S.F.	2	0	2	0	12
Dixon, Floyd, Atl.	2	0	2	0	12
Ellis, Gerry, G.B.	2	2	0	0	12
Frank, John, S.F.	2	0	2	0	12
Franklin, Pat, T.B.	2	0	1	1	12
Freeman, Phil, T.B.	2	0	2	0	12
Goodlow, Eugene, N.O.	2	0	2	0	12
Gustafson, Jim, Minn.	2	0	2	0	12
Holmoe, Tom, S.F.	2	0	0	2	12
House, Kevin, Rams	2	0	2	0	12
Lewis, Leo, Minn.	2	0	2	0	12
Lewis, Mark, G.B.	2	0	2	0	12
Marshall, Wilber, Chi.	2	0	0	2	12
Miller, Solomon, Giants	2	0	2	0	12
Mowatt, Zeke, Giants	2	0	2	0	12
Mularkey, Mike, Minn.	2	0	2	0	12
Ortego, Keith, Chi.	2	0	2	0	12
Robinson, Stacy, Giants	2	0	2	0	12
Sanders, Ricky, Wash.	2	0	2	0	12
Suhey, Matt, Chi.	2	2	0	0	12
Tautalatasi, Junior, Phil.	2	0	2	0	12
Williams, Scott, Det.	2	2	0	0	12
Anderson, Neal, Chi.	1	0	1	0	6
Andrews, William, Atl.	1	1	0	0	6
Austin, Cliff, Atl.	1	1	0	0	6
Barnes, Lew, Chi.	1	0	0	1	6
Britt, James, Atl.	1	0	0	1	6
Browner, Joey, Minn.	1	0	0	1	6
Butler, Bobby, Atl.	1	0	0	1	6
Byars, Keith, Phil.	1	1	0	0	6
Carson, Harry, Giants	1	0	1	0	6
Cosbie, Doug, Dall.	1	0	1	0	6
Cox, Arthur, Atl.	1	0	1	0	6
Crawford, Charles, Phil.	1	1	0	0	6
Cromwell, Nolan, Rams	1	0	0	1	6
Davis, Kenneth, G.B.	1	0	1	0	6
DeBerg, Steve, T.B.	1	1	0	0	6
Doleman, Chris, Minn.	1	0	0	1	6
Duckworth, Bobby, Rams	1	0	1	0	6
Everett, Jim, Rams	1	1	0	0	6
Fellows, Ron, Dall.	1	0	0	1	6
Flutie, Doug, Chi.	1	1	0	0	6

	TD	TDR	TDP	TDM	PTS
Flynn, Tom, Giants	1	0	0	1	6
Fox, Chas, St.L.	1	0	1	0	6
Francis, Russ, S.F.	1	0	1	0	6
Garrity, Gregg, Phil.	1	0	0	1	6
Gray, Mel, N.O.	1	0	0	1	6
Griffin, Don, S.F.	1	0	0	1	6
Harmon, Derrick, S.F.	1	1	0	0	6
Haynes, James, N.O.	1	0	0	1	6
Heflin, Vince, T.B.	1	0	0	1	6
Heller, Ron, T.B.	1	0	1	0	6
Hill, David, Rams	1	0	1	0	6
Holt, Issiac, Minn.	1	0	0	1	6
Howard, Bobby, T.B.	1	1	0	0	6
Hunter, Herman, Det.	1	0	1	0	6
Ivery, Eddie Lee, G.B.	1	0	1	0	6
Jerue, Mark, Rams	1	0	0	1	6
Johnson, Ron, Phil.	1	0	1	0	6
Jordan, Buford, N.O.	1	1	0	0	6
Kramer, Tommy, Minn.	1	1	0	0	6
Lavette, Robert, Dall.	1	0	1	0	6
Lewis, David, Det.	1	0	1	0	6
Lomax, Neil, St.L.	1	1	0	0	6
Lott, Ronnie, S.F.	1	0	0	1	6
Mandley, Pete, Det.	1	0	0	1	6
Manley, Dexter, Wash.	1	0	0	1	6
Martin, George, Giants	1	0	0	1	6
McConkey, Phil, Giants	1	0	1	0	6
McKyer, Tim, S.F.	1	0	0	1	6
McMahon, Jim, Chi.	1	1	0	0	6
Moorehead, Emery, Chi.	1	0	1	0	6
Moroski, Mike, S.F.	1	1	0	0	6
Newberry, Tom, Rams	1	0	0	1	6
Nixon, Tory, S.F.	1	0	0	1	6
Orr, Terry, Wash.	1	0	1	0	6
Pelluer, Steve, Dall.	1	1	0	0	6
Pitts, Mike, Atl.	1	0	0	1	6
Rathman, Tom, S.F.	1	1	0	0	6
Ross, Dan, G.B.	1	0	1	0	6
Schonert, Turk, Atl.	1	1	0	0	6
Schroeder, Jay, Wash.	1	1	0	0	6
Simmons, John, G.B.	1	0	0	1	6
Simms, Phil, Giants	1	1	0	0	6
Spagnola, John, Phil.	1	0	1	0	6
Stamps, Sylvester, Atl.	1	0	1	0	6
Stills, Ken, G.B.	1	0	0	1	6
Toney, Anthony, Phil.	1	1	0	0	6
Warren, Don, Wash.	1	0	1	0	6

	TD	TDR	TDP	TDM	PTS
West, Ed, G.B.	1	0	1	0	6
White, Danny, Dall.	1	1	0	0	6
Williams, Joel, Atl.	1	0	0	1	6
Williams, Keith, Atl.	1	0	1	0	6
Wilson, Dave, N.O.	1	1	0	0	6
Wilson, Mike, S.F.	1	0	1	0	6
Wilson, Wade, Minn.	1	1	0	0	6
Wright, Randy, G.B.	1	1	0	0	6
Brown, Greg, Phil.	0	0	0	0	*2
Gann, Mike, Atl.	0	0	0	0	*2
Hampton, Dan, Chi.	0	0	0	0	*2
Jeter, Gary, Rams.	0	0	0	0	*2
McMichael, Steve, Chi.	0	0	0	0	*2

* Safety

NFC — TEAM SCORING

	TD	TDR	TDP	TDM	XP	XPA	FG	FGA	SAF	PTS
Minnesota	48	14	31	3	44	48	22	28	0	398
San Francisco	43	16	21	6	41	43	25	35	0	374
Giants	42	18	22	2	41	42	26	37	0	371
Washington	46	23	22	1	38	45	18	32	0	368
Chicago	38	21	12	5	36	38	28	41	2	352
Dallas	43	21	21	1	43	43	15	21	0	346
Ran.s	37	16	15	6	34	36	17	24	1	309
New Orleans	30	15	13	2	30	30	26	30	0	288
Atlanta	30	12	14	4	29	30	23	36	1	280
Detroit	32	13	18	1	31	32	18	25	0	277
Philadelphia	28	8	19	1	26	27	20	31	1	256
Green Bay	29	8	18	3	29	29	17	27	0	254
Tampa Bay	27	12	13	2	26	27	17	24	0	239
St. Louis	27	8	17	2	23	27	11	24	0	218
Conf. Total	500	205	256	39	471	497	283	415	5	4330
Conf. Average	35.7	14.6	18.3	2.8	33.6	35.5	20.2	29.6	0.4	309.3

NFC — Team-by-Team Summary

NFC Offense	Atl.	Chi.	Dall.	Det.	G.B.
Rushes	578	606	447	470	424
Net Yds. Gained	2524	2700	1969	1771	1614
Avg. Gain	4.4	4.5	4.4	3.8	3.8
Avg. Yds. per Game	157.8	168.8	123.1	110.7	100.9
Passes Attempted	452	415	547	500	565
Completed	246	208	319	286	305
% Completed	54.4	50.1	58.3	57.2	54.0
Total Yds. Gained	3046	2912	4003	3107	3708
Times Sacked	56	24	60	39	37
Yds. Lost	464	153	498	323	261
Net Yds. Gained	2582	2759	3505	2784	3447
Avg. Yds. per Game	161.4	172.4	219.1	174.0	215.4
Net Yds. per Pass Play	5.08	6.28	5.77	5.17	5.73
Yds. Gained per Comp.	12.38	14.00	12.55	10.86	12.16
Combined Net Yds. Gained	5106	5459	5474	4555	5061
% Total Yds. Rushing	49.4	49.5	36.0	38.9	31.9
% Total Yds. Passing	50.6	50.5	64.0	61.1	68.1
Avg. Yds. per Game	319.1	341.2	342.1	284.7	316.3
Had Intercepted	17	25	24	20	27
Yds. Opp. Returned	198	115	331	311	357
Ret. by Opp. for TD	1	1	2	2	3
Punts	79	70	87	85	75
Yds. Punted	3421	2850	3498	3389	2825
Avg. Yds. per Punt	43.3	40.7	40.2	39.9	37.7
Punt Returns	44	57	46	43	33
Yds. Returned	292	482	252	420	316
Avg. Yds. per Return	6.6	8.5	5.5	9.8	9.6
Returned for TD	0	0	0	1	1
Kickoff Returns	54	50	59	67	76
Yds. Returned	1035	1115	1208	1321	1470
Avg. Yds. per Return	19.2	22.3	20.5	19.7	19.3
Returned for TD	0	2	0	0	0
Total Points Scored	280	352	346	277	254
Total TDs	30	38	43	32	29
TDs Rushing	12	21	21	13	8
TDs Passing	14	12	21	18	18
TDs on Ret. and Rec.	4	5	1	1	3
Extra Points	29	36	43	31	29
Safeties	1	2	0	0	0
Field Goals Made	23	28	15	18	17
Field Goals Attempted	36	41	21	25	27
% Successful	63.9	68.3	71.4	72.0	63.0

Rams	Minn.	N.O.	N.Y.G.	Phil.	St.L.	S.F.	T.B.	Wash.
578	461	505	558	499	419	510	455	474
2457	1738	2074	2245	2002	1787	1986	1863	1732
4.3	3.8	4.1	4.0	4.0	4.3	3.9	4.1	3.7
153.6	108.6	129.6	140.3	125.1	111.7	124.1	116.4	108.3
403	519	425	472	514	516	582	459	542
194	290	232	260	268	293	353	245	276
48.1	55.9	54.6	55.1	52.1	56.8	60.7	53.4	50.9
2380	4185	2893	3500	3248	3140	4299	2892	4109
27	44	27	46	104	59	26	56	28
184	272	225	367	708	424	203	394	240
2196	3913	2668	3133	2540	2716	4096	2498	3869
137.3	244.6	166.8	195.8	158.8	169.8	256.0	156.1	241.8
5.11	6.95	5.90	6.05	4.11	4.72	6.74	4.85	6.79
12.27	14.43	12.47	13.46	12.12	10.72	12.18	11.80	14.89
4653	5651	4742	5378	4542	4503	6082	4361	5601
52.8	30.8	43.7	41.7	44.1	39.7	32.7	42.7	30.9
47.2	69.2	56.3	58.3	55.9	60.3	67.3	57.3	69.1
290.8	353.2	296.4	336.1	283.9	281.4	380.1	272.6	350.1
15	15	25	22	17	19	20	25	22
128	88	362	218	192	271	205	236	186
0	0	0	1	1	2	0	1	0
98	73	82	79	111	92	85	78	75
3740	2922	3456	3539	4547	3411	3450	3132	3271
38.2	40.0	42.1	44.8	41.0	37.1	40.6	40.2	43.6
42	31	47	41	44	45	43	26	51
361	215	377	287	374	528	397	110	550
8.6	6.9	8.0	7.0	8.5	11.7	9.2	4.2	10.8
0	0	0	0	1	2	1	0	0
59	56	55	50	53	70	42	75	60
1160	1200	1332	868	945	1548	757	1302	1175
19.7	21.4	24.2	17.4	17.8	22.1	18.0	17.4	19.6
0	0	1	0	0	0	0	0	0
309	398	288	371	256	218	374	239	368
37	48	30	42	28	27	43	27	46
16	14	15	18	8	8	16	12	23
15	31	13	22	19	17	21	13	22
6	3	2	2	1	2	6	2	1
34	44	30	41	26	23	41	26	38
1	0	0	0	1	0	0	0	0
17	22	26	26	20	11	25	17	18
24	28	30	37	31	24	35	24	32
70.8	78.6	86.7	70.3	64.5	45.8	71.4	70.8	56.3

NFC Defense	Atl.	Chi.	Dall.	Det.	G.B.
Rushes	485	427	500	519	565
Net Yds. Gained	1916	1463	2200	2349	2095
Avg. Gain	4.0	3.4	4.4	4.5	3.7
Avg. Yds. per Game	119.8	91.4	137.5	146.8	130.9
Passes Attempted	453	513	464	468	448
Completed	241	243	226	279	267
% Completed	53.2	47.4	48.7	59.6	59.6
Total Yds. Gained	3169	3170	3149	3090	3142
Times Sacked	26	62	53	41	28
Yds. Lost	177	503	364	290	222
Net Yds. Gained	2992	2667	2785	2800	2920
Avg. Yds. per Game	187.0	166.7	174.1	175.0	182.5
Net Yds. per Pass Play	6.25	4.64	5.39	5.50	6.13
Yds. Gained per Comp.	13.15	13.05	13.93	11.08	11.77
Combined Net Yds. Gained	4908	4130	4985	5149	5015
% Total Yds. Rushing	39.0	35.4	44.1	45.6	41.8
% Total Yds. Passing	61.0	64.6	55.9	54.4	58.2
Avg. Yds. per Game	306.8	258.1	311.6	321.8	313.4
Intercepted by	22	31	17	22	20
Yds. Returned by	294	370	183	190	147
Returned for TD	2	1	1	0	1
Punts	83	100	87	68	70
Yds. Punted	3436	4090	3620	2836	2769
Avg. Yds. per Punt	41.4	40.9	41.6	41.7	39.6
Punt Returns	47	23	41	39	44
Yds. Returned	477	110	301	517	287
Avg. Yds. per Return	10.1	4.8	7.3	13.3	6.5
Returned for TD	3	0	0	2	0
Kickoff Returns	59	64	66	56	62
Yds. Returned	1190	1376	1358	1096	1181
Avg. Yds. per Return	20.2	21.5	20.6	19.6	19.0
Returned for TD	0	0	0	0	0
Total Points Scored	280	187	337	326	418
Total TDs	34	20	41	36	52
TDs Rushing	10	4	17	15	16
TDs Passing	19	12	21	14	31
TDs on Ret. and Rec.	5	4	3	7	5
Extra Points	31	19	39	36	48
Safeties	0	0	2	1	2
Field Goals Made	15	16	16	24	18
Field Goals Attempted	26	22	30	35	25
% Successful	57.7	72.7	53.3	68.6	72.0

Rams	Minn.	N.O.	N.Y.G.	Phil.	St.L.	S.F.	T.B.	Wash.
460	481	486	350	458	560	406	558	459
1681	1796	1559	1284	1989	2227	1555	2648	1805
3.7	3.7	3.2	3.7	4.3	4.0	3.8	4.7	3.9
105.1	112.3	97.4	80.3	124.3	139.2	97.2	165.5	112.8
539	494	576	587	532	436	604	484	532
313	276	331	334	260	215	324	289	302
58.1	55.9	57.5	56.9	48.9	49.3	53.6	59.7	56.8
3482	3475	3886	3887	3641	2992	3773	3838	3916
39	38	47	59	53	41	51	19	55
292	259	343	414	406	355	448	153	424
3190	3216	3543	3473	3235	2637	3325	3685	3492
199.4	201.0	221.4	217.1	202.2	164.8	207.8	230.3	218.3
5.52	6.05	5.69	5.38	5.53	5.53	5.08	7.33	5.95
11.12	12.59	11.74	11.64	14.00	13.92	11.65	13.28	12.97
4871	5012	5102	4757	5224	4864	4880	6333	5297
34.5	35.8	30.6	27.0	38.1	45.8	31.9	41.8	34.1
65.5	64.2	69.4	73.0	61.9	54.2	68.1	58.2	65.9
304.4	313.3	318.9	297.3	326.5	304.0	305.0	395.8	331.1
28	24	26	24	23	10	39	13	19
458	319	235	296	124	121	578	128	126
3	2	1	1	0	0	5	0	0
96	75	78	89	97	83	91	59	95
3975	3021	3315	3499	3751	3514	3765	2438	3923
41.4	40.3	42.5	39.3	38.7	42.3	41.4	41.3	41.3
47	40	37	41	63	44	49	39	36
416	356	234	386	634	296	373	414	220
8.9	8.9	6.3	9.4	10.1	6.7	7.6	10.6	6.1
0	0	0	0	2	0	0	3	0
64	79	35	70	62	50	71	46	50
1282	1532	662	1362	1261	886	1598	1009	1005
20.0	19.4	18.9	19.5	20.3	17.7	22.5	21.9	20.1
0	0	0	0	0	0	1	1	0
267	273	287	236	312	351	247	473	296
28	28	34	26	39	40	29	59	35
9	10	11	10	14	17	8	31	14
17	16	21	15	21	21	18	23	21
2	2	2	1	4	2	3	5	0
27	24	32	26	37	37	28	56	35
0	0	0	0	1	1	0	0	0
24	27	17	18	13	24	15	21	17
31	33	27	25	26	32	25	30	24
77.4	81.8	63.0	72.0	50.0	75.0	60.0	70.0	70.8

AFC, NFC AND NFL SUMMARY — 1986

	AFC Offense Total	AFC Offense Avg.	AFC Defense Total	AFC Defense Avg.
First Downs	4304	307.4	4368	312.0
Rushing	1400	100.0	1509	107.8
Passing	2537	181.2	2482	177.3
Penalty	367	26.2	377	26.9
Rushes	6525	466.1	6795	485.4
Net Yds. Gained	24,710	1765.0	26,605	1900.4
Avg. Gain	—	3.8	—	3.9
Avg. Yds. per Game	—	110.3	—	118.8
Passes Attempted	7558	539.9	7339	524.2
Completed	4239	302.8	4114	293.9
% Completed	—	56.1	—	56.1
Total Yds. Gained	53,706	3836.1	52,518	3751.3
Times Sacked	565	40.4	586	41.9
Yds. Lost	4331	309.4	4397	314.1
Net Yds. Gained	49,375	3526.8	48,121	3437.2
Avg. Yds. per Game	—	220.4	—	214.8
Net Yds. per Pass Play	—	6.08	—	6.07
Yds. Gained per Comp.	—	11.65	—	11.70
Combined Net Yds. Gained	74,085	5291.8	74,726	5337.6
% Total Yds. Rushing	—	33.4	—	35.6
% Total Yds. Passing	—	66.6	—	64.4
Avg. Yds. per Game	—	330.7	—	333.6
Ball Control Plays	14,648	1046.3	14,720	1051.4
Avg. Yds. per Play	—	5.1	—	5.1
Third Down Efficiency	—	38.7	—	38.0

NFC Offense Total	NFC Offense Avg.	NFC Defense Total	NFC Defense Avg.	NFL Total	NFL Avg.
4188	299.1	4124	294.6	8492	303.3
1639	117.1	1530	109.3	3039	108.5
2212	158.0	2267	161.9	4749	169.6
337	24.1	327	23.4	704	25.1
6984	498.9	6714	479.6	13,509	482.5
28,462	2033.0	26,567	1897.6	53,172	1899.0
—	4.1	—	4.0	—	3.9
—	127.1	—	118.6	—	118.7
6911	493.6	7130	509.3	14,469	516.8
3775	269.6	3900	278.6	8014	286.2
—	54.6	—	54.7	—	55.4
47,422	3387.3	48,610	3472.1	101,128	3611.7
633	45.2	612	43.7	1198	42.8
4716	336.9	4650	332.1	9047	323.1
42,706	3050.4	43,960	3140.0	92,081	3288.6
—	190.7	—	196.3	—	205.5
—	5.66	—	5.68	—	5.88
—	11.31	—	11.27	—	11.49
71,168	5083.4	70,527	5037.6	145,253	5187.6
—	40.0	—	37.7	—	36.6
—	60.0	—	62.3	—	63.4
—	317.7	—	314.9	—	324.2
14,528	1037.7	14,456	1032.6	29,176	1042.0
—	4.9	—	4.9	—	5.0
—	36.3	—	36.9	—	37.5

	AFC Offense Total	AFC Offense Avg.	AFC Defense Total	AFC Defense Avg.
Interceptions	263	18.8	288	20.6
Yds. Returned	3181	227.2	3552	253.7
Returned for TD	12	0.9	15	1.1
Punts	1142	81.6	1140	81.4
Yds. Punted	46,023	3287.4	45,522	3251.6
Avg. Yds. per Punt	—	40.3	—	39.9
Punt Returns	552	39.4	555	39.6
Yds. Returned	4859	347.1	4799	342.8
Avg. Yds. per Return	—	8.8	—	8.6
Returned for TD	8	0.6	4	0.3
Kickoff Returns	867	61.9	859	61.4
Yds. Returned	17,005	1214.6	16,643	1188.8
Avg. Yds. per Return	—	19.6	—	19.4
Returned for TD	4	0.3	5	0.4
Penalties	1479	105.6	1454	103.9
Yds. Penalized	12,025	858.9	11,692	835.1
Fumbles	444	31.7	465	33.2
Lost	221	15.8	220	15.7
Out of Bounds	46	3.3	47	3.4
Own Rec. for TD	5	0.4	5	0.4
Opp. Rec.	218	15.6	220	15.7
Opp. Rec. for TD	11	0.8	10	0.7
Total Points Scored	4863	347.4	4903	350.2
Total TDs	577	41.2	576	41.1
TDs Rushing	196	14.0	215	15.4
TDs Passing	330	23.6	316	22.6
TDs on Ret. and Rec.	51	3.6	45	3.2
Extra Points	555	39.6	551	39.4
Safeties	9	0.6	7	0.5
Field Goals Made	276	19.7	294	21.0
Field Goals Attempted	400	28.6	424	30.3
% Successful	—	69.0	—	69.3

NFC Offense Total	NFC Offense Avg.	NFC Defense Total	NFC Defense Avg.	NFL Total	NFL Avg.
318	22.7	293	20.9	581	20.8
3569	254.9	3198	228.4	6750	241.1
17	1.2	14	1.0	29	1.0
1169	83.5	1171	83.6	2311	82.5
47,451	3389.4	47,952	3425.1	93,474	3338.4
—	40.6	—	40.9	—	40.4
593	42.4	590	42.1	1145	40.9
4961	354.4	5021	358.6	9820	350.7
—	8.4	—	8.5	—	8.6
6	0.4	10	0.7	14	0.5
826	59.0	834	59.6	1693	60.5
16,436	1174.0	16,798	1199.9	33,441	1194.3
—	19.9	—	20.1	—	19.8
3	0.2	2	0.1	7	0.3
1396	99.7	1421	101.5	2875	102.7
11,202	800.1	11,535	823.9	23,227	829.5
466	33.3	445	31.8	910	32.5
210	15.0	211	15.1	431	15.4
28	2.0	27	1.9	74	2.6
1	0.1	1	0.1	6	0.2
211	15.1	209	14.9	429	15.3
7	0.5	8	0.6	18	0.6
4330	309.3	4290	306.4	9193	328.3
500	35.7	501	35.8	1077	38.5
205	14.6	186	13.3	401	14.3
256	18.3	270	19.3	586	20.9
39	2.8	45	3.2	90	3.2
471	33.6	475	33.9	1026	36.6
5	0.4	7	0.5	14	0.5
283	20.2	265	18.9	559	20.0
415	29.6	391	27.9	815	29.1
—	68.2	—	67.8	—	68.6

CLUB LEADERS

	Offense	Defense
First Downs	Mia. 351	Chi. 241
Rushing	Chi. 166	Chi. 67
Passing	Mia. 250	Hou. 137
Penalty	Den. 41	Rams 10
Rushes	Chi. 606	N.Y.G. 350
Net Yds. Gained	Chi. 2700	N.Y.G. 1284
Avg. Gain	Cin. 4.9	N.O. 3.2
Passes Attempted	Mia. 645	St. L. 436
Completed	Mia. 392	St. L. 215
% Completed	N.Y.J. 62.2	Hou. 46.5
Total Yds. Gained	Mia. 4898	St. L. 2992
Times Sacked	Mia. 17	Raiders 63
Yds. Lost	Mia. 119	Chi. 503
Net Yds. Gained	Mia. 4779	St. L. 2637
Net Yds. per Pass Play	Cin 7.54	Chi. 4.64
Yds. Gained per Comp.	Wash. 14.89	Det. 11.08
Combined Net Yds. Gained	Cin. 6490	Chi. 4130
% Total Yds. Rushing	Rams 52.8	N.Y.G. 27.0
% Total Yds. Passing	Mia. 75.6	St. L. 54.2
Ball Control Plays	S.F. 1118	Atl. 964
Avg. Yds. per Play	Mia 6.3	Chi. 4.1
Avg. Time of Poss.	Atl. 32:35	—
Third Down Efficiency	Mia. 50.8	S.F. 30.3
Interceptions	—	S.F. 39
Yds. Returned	—	S.F. 578
Returned for TD	—	S.F. 5
Punts	Phil. 111	—
Yds. Punted	Phil. 4547	—
Avg. Yds. per Punt	N.Y.G. 44.8	—
Punt Returns	Chi. 57	Cin. 19
Yds Returned	Den. 552	Chi. 110
Avg. Yds. per Return	St. L. 11.7	N.Y.J. 4.6
Returned for TD	Den. & St. L. 2	—
Kickoff Returns	G.B. 76	Hou. 32
Yds. Returned	St. L. 1548	N.O. 662
Avg. Yds. per Return	N.O. 24.2	Raiders 16.9
Returned for TD	Chi. & N.Y.J. 2	—
Total Points Scored	Mia. 430	Chi. 187
Total TDs	Mia. 56	Chi. 20
TDs Rushing	Cin. 24	Chi. 4
TD Passing	Mia. 46	Chi. 12
TDs on Ret. and Rec.	K.C. 10	Wash. 0
Extra Points	Mia. 52	Chi. 19
Safeties	Chi. & Den. 2	—
Field Goals Made	N.E. 32	Phil. 13
Field Goals Attempted	Chi. & N.E. 41	Raiders 21
% Successful	N.O. 86.7	Phil. 50.0

CLUB RANKINGS BY YARDS

Team	Offense			Defense		
	Total	Rush	Pass	Total	Rush	Pass
Atlanta	17	3	25	7	16	7
Buffalo	19	21	15	24	9	27
Chicago	7	*1	20	*1	2	2
Cincinnati	*1	2	3	20	22	10
Cleveland	9	22	8	19	18	15
Dallas	6	11	12	10	23	3
Denver	15	20	10	9	5	16
Detroit	24	15	19	15	26	4
Green Bay	18	23	14	12	21	5
Houston	16	19	13	13	20	8
Indianapolis	22	26	16	25	17	26
Kansas City	28	27	21	8	11	12
Los Angeles Raiders	14	13	11	3	10	9
Los Angeles Rams	23	4	28	5	8	11
Miami	2	25	*1	26t	27	22
Minnesota	4	16	5	11	13	13
New England	13	28	4	16	24	6
New Orleans	21	8	23	14	4	21
New York Giants	10	6	17	2	*1	19
New York Jets	11	18	9	26t	6	28
Philadelphia	25	9	26	17	19	14
Pittsburgh	20	7	24	18	15	18
St. Louis	26	14	22	4	25	*1
San Diego	12	24	7	23	7	25
San Francisco	3	10	2	6	3	17
Seattle	8	5	18	22	12	23
Tampa Bay	27	12	27	28	28	24
Washington	5	17	6	21	14	20

t = Tie for position
* = League leader

SUPER BOWL RECORDS

RESULTS

GAME	DATE	WINNER	LOSER	SITE	ATTENDANCE
XXI	1-25-87	N.Y. Giants (NFC) 39	Denver (AFC) 20	Pasadena	101,643
XX	1-26-86	Chicago Bears (NFC) 46	N.E. Patriots (AFC) 10	New Orleans	73,818
XIX	1-20-85	San Francisco (NFC) 38	Miami (AFC) 16	Stanford	84,059
XVIII	1-22-84	L.A. Raiders (AFC) 38	Washington (NFC) 9	Tampa	72,920
XVII	1-30-83	Washington (NFC) 27	Miami (AFC) 17	Pasadena	103,667
XVI	1-24-82	San Francisco (NFC) 26	Cincinnati (AFC) 21	Pontiac	81,270
XV	1-25-81	Oakland (AFC) 27	Philadelphia (NFC) 10	New Orleans	76,135
XIV	1-20-80	Pittsburgh (AFC) 31	Los Angeles (NFC) 19	Pasadena	103,985
XIII	1-21-79	Pittsburgh (AFC) 35	Dallas (NFC) 31	Miami	79,484
XII	1-15-78	Dallas (NFC) 27	Denver (AFC) 10	New Orleans	75,583
XI	1- 9-77	Oakland (AFC) 32	Minnesota (NFC) 14	Pasadena	103,438
X	1-18-76	Pittsburgh (AFC) 21	Dallas (NFC) 17	Miami	80,187
IX	1-12-75	Pittsburgh (AFC) 16	Minnesota (NFC) 6	New Orleans	80,997
VIII	1-13-74	Miami (AFC) 24	Minnesota (NFC) 7	Houston	71,882
VII	1-14-73	Miami (AFC) 14	Washington (NFC) 7	Los Angeles	90,182
VI	1-16-72	Dallas (NFC) 24	Miami (AFC) 3	New Orleans	81,023
V	1-17-71	Baltimore (AFC) 16	Dallas (NFC) 13	Miami	79,204
IV	1-11-70	Kansas City (AFL) 23	Minnesota (NFL) 7	New Orleans	80,562
III	1-12-69	N.Y. Jets (AFL) 16	Baltimore (NFL) 7	Miami	75,389
II	1-14-68	Green Bay (NFL) 33	Oakland (AFL) 14	Miami	75,546
I	1-15-67	Green Bay (NFL) 35	Kansas City (AFL) 10	Los Angeles	61,946

SUPER BOWL COMPOSITE STANDINGS

	W	L	Pct	Pts	OP
Pittsburgh Steelers	4	0	1.000	103	73
Green Bay Packers	2	0	1.000	68	24
San Francisco 49ers	2	0	1.000	64	37
New York Jets	1	0	1.000	16	7
Chicago Bears	1	0	1.000	46	10
New York Giants	1	0	1.000	39	20
Oakland/L.A. Raiders	3	1	.750	111	66
Baltimore Colts	1	1	.500	23	29
Kansas City Chiefs	1	1	.500	33	42
Dallas Cowboys	2	3	.400	112	85
Miami Dolphins	2	3	.400	74	103
Washington Redskins	1	2	.333	43	69
Cincinnati Bengals	0	1	.000	21	26
Los Angeles Rams	0	1	.000	19	31
New England Patriots	0	1	.000	10	46
Philadelphia Eagles	0	1	.000	10	27
Denver Broncos	0	2	.000	30	66
Minnesota Vikings	0	4	.000	34	95

SUPER BOWL RECORDS

1967: Super Bowl I   1974: Super Bowl VIII   1981: Super Bowl XV
1968: Super Bowl II   1975: Super Bowl IX   1982: Super Bowl XVI
1969: Super Bowl III   1976: Super Bowl X   1983: Super Bowl XVII
1970: Super Bowl IV   1977: Super Bowl XI   1984: Super Bowl XVIII
1971: Super Bowl V   1978: Super Bowl XII   1985: Super Bowl XIX
1972: Super Bowl VI   1979: Super Bowl XIII   1986: Super Bowl XX
1973: Super Bowl VII   1980: Super Bowl XIV   1987: Super Bowl XXI

INDIVIDUAL RECORDS

SERVICE

Most Games
5   Marv Fleming, Green Bay, 1967-68; Miami, 1972-74
     Larry Cole, Dallas, 1971-72, 1976, 1978-79
     Cliff Harris, Dallas, 1971-72, 1976, 1978-79
     D.D. Lewis, Dallas, 1971-72, 1976, 1978-79
     Preston Pearson, Baltimore, 1969; Pittsburgh, 1975; Dallas, 1976, 1978-79
     Charlie Waters, Dallas, 1971-72, 1976, 1978-79
     Rayfield Wright, Dallas, 1971-72, 1976, 1978-79
4   By many players

Most Games, Coach
6   Don Shula, Baltimore, 1969; Miami, 1972-74, 1983, 1985
5   Tom Landry, Dallas, 1971-72, 1976, 1978-79
4   Bud Grant, Minnesota, 1970, 1974-75, 1977
     Chuck Noll, Pittsburgh, 1975-76, 1979-80

Most Games, Winning Team, Coach
4   Chuck Noll, Pittsburgh, 1975-76, 1979-80
2   Vince Lombardi, Green Bay, 1967-68
     Tom Landry, Dallas, 1972, 1978
     Don Shula, Miami, 1973-74
     Tom Flores, Oakland, 1981; L.A. Raiders, 1984

SCORING

POINTS
Most Points, Career
24   Franco Harris, Pittsburgh, 4 games (4-td)
20   Don Chandler, Green Bay, 2 games (8-pat, 4-fg)

Most Points, Game
18   Roger Craig, San Francisco vs. Miami, 1985 (3-td)
15   Don Chandler, Green Bay vs. Oakland, 1968 (3-pat, 4-fg)

TOUCHDOWNS
Most Touchdowns, Career
4   Franco Harris, Pittsburgh, 4 games (4-r)
3   John Stallworth, Pittsburgh, 4 games (3-p)
     Lynn Swann, Pittsburgh, 4 games (3-p)
     Cliff Branch, Oakland/L.A. Raiders, 3 games (3-p)

Most Touchdowns, Game

3   Roger Craig, San Francisco vs. Miami, 1985 (2-p, 1-r)
2   Max McGee, Green Bay vs. Kansas City, 1967 (2-p)
    Elijah Pitts, Green Bay vs. Kansas City, 1967 (2-r)
    Bill Miller, Oakland vs. Green Bay, 1968 (2-p)
    Larry Csonka, Miami vs. Minnesota, 1974 (2-r)
    Pete Banaszak, Oakland vs. Minnesota, 1977 (2-r)
    John Stallworth, Pittsburgh vs. Dallas, 1979 (2-p)
    Franco Harris, Pittsburgh vs. Los Angeles, 1980 (2-r)
    Cliff Branch, Oakland vs. Philadelphia, 1981 (2-p)
    Dan Ross, Cincinnati vs. San Francisco, 1982 (2-p)
    Marcus Allen, L.A. Raiders vs. Washington, 1984 (2-r)

FIELD GOALS

Field Goals, Attempted, Career

7   Roy Gerela, Pittsburgh, 3 games
6   Jim Turner, N.Y. Jets/Denver, 2 games

Most Field Goals, Attempted, Game

5   Jim Turner, N.Y. Jets vs. Baltimore, 1969
    Efren Herrera, Dallas vs. Denver, 1978

Most Field Goals, Career

5   Ray Wersching, San Francisco, 2 games (5 att)
4   Don Chandler, Green Bay, 2 games (4 att)
    Jim Turner, N.Y. Jets/Denver, 2 games (6 att)

Most Field Goals, Game

4   Don Chandler, Green Bay vs. Oakland, 1968
    Ray Wersching, San Francisco vs. Cincinnati, 1982

Longest Field Goal

48 Jan Stenerud, Kansas City vs. Minnesota, 1970

RUSHING

ATTEMPTS

Most Attempts, Career

101 Franco Harris, Pittsburgh, 4 games
64   John Riggins, Washington, 2 games
57   Larry Csonka, Miami, 3 games

Most Attempts, Game

38 John Riggins, Washington vs. Miami, 1983

YARDS GAINED

Most Yards Gained, Career

354 Franco Harris, Pittsburgh, 4 games
297 Larry Csonka, Miami, 3 games

Most Yards Gained, Game

191 Marcus Allen, L.A. Raiders vs. Washington, 1984

Longest Run from Scrimmage

74 Marcus Allen, L.A. Raiders vs. Washington, 1984

PASSING

ATTEMPTS

Most Passes Attempted, Career
98 Roger Staubach, Dallas, 4 games
89 Fran Tarkenton, Minnesota, 3 games

Most Passes Attempted, Game
50 Dan Marino, Miami vs. San Francisco, 1985

COMPLETIONS

Most Passes Completed, Career
61 Roger Staubach, Dallas, 4 games
49 Terry Bradshaw, Pittsburgh, 4 games

Most Passes Completed, Game
29 Dan Marino, Miami vs. San Francisco, 1985

Most Consecutive Completions, Game
10 Phil Simms, N.Y. Giants vs. Denver, 1987

YARDS GAINED

Most Yards Gained, Career
932 Terry Bradshaw, Pittsburgh, 4 games
734 Roger Staubach, Dallas, 4 games

Most Yards Gained, Game
331 Joe Montana, San Francisco vs. Miami, 1985

Longest Pass Completion
80 Jim Plunkett (to King), Oakland vs. Philadelphia, 1981 (TD)

TOUCHDOWNS

Most Touchdown Passes, Career
9 Terry Bradshaw, Pittsburgh, 4 games
8 Roger Staubach, Dallas, 4 games

Most Touchdown Passes, Game
4 Terry Bradshaw, Pittsburgh vs. Dallas, 1979

HAD INTERCEPTED

Lowest Percentage, Passes Had Intercepted, Career (40 attempts)
0.00 Joe Montana, San Francisco, 2 games (57-0)
0.00 Jim Plunkett, Oakland/L.A. Raiders, 2 games (46-0)
2.13 Bart Starr, Green Bay, 2 games (47-1)

PASS RECEIVING

RECEPTIONS

Most Receptions, Career
16 Lynn Swann, Pittsburgh, 4 games
15 Chuck Foreman, Minnesota, 3 games

Most Receptions, Game
11 Dan Ross, Cincinnati vs. San Francisco, 1982

YARDS GAINED

Most Yards Gained, Career
364 Lynn Swann, Pittsburgh, 4 games
268 John Stallworth, Pittsburgh, 4 games

Most Yards Gained, Game
161 Lynn Swann, Pittsburgh vs. Dallas, 1976

Longest Reception
80 Kenny King (from Plunkett), Oakland vs. Philadelphia, 1981 (TD)

INTERCEPTIONS BY

Most Interceptions By, Career
3 Chuck Howley, Dallas, 2 games
   Rod Martin, Oakland/L.A. Raiders, 2 games
2 Randy Beverly, N.Y. Jets, 1 game
   Jake Scott, Miami, 3 games
   Mike Wagner, Pittsburgh, 3 games
   Mel Blount, Pittsburgh, 4 games

Most Interceptions By, Game
3 Rod Martin, Oakland vs. Philadelphia, 1981

YARDS GAINED

Longest Return
75 Willie Brown, Oakland vs. Minnesota, 1977 (TD)

PUNTING

Most Punts, Career
17 Mike Elscheid, Oakland/Minnesota, 3 games

Most Punts, Game
9 Ron Widby, Dallas vs. Baltimore, 1971

Longest Punt
62 Rich Camarillo, New England vs. Chicago, 1986

PUNT RETURNS

Most Punt Returns, Career
6 Willie Wood, Green Bay, 2 games
   Jake Scott, Miami, 3 games
   Theo Bell, Pittsburgh, 2 games
   Mike Nelms, Washington, 1 game

Most Punt Returns, Game
6 Mike Nelms, Washington vs. Miami, 1983

YARDS GAINED

Most Yards Gained, Career
52 Mike Nelms, Washington, 1 game
45 Jake Scott, Miami, 3 games

Most Yards Gained, Game
52 Mike Nelms, Washington vs. Miami, 1983

Longest Return
34   Darrell Green, Washington vs. L.A. Raiders, 1984

KICKOFF RETURNS

Most Kickoff Returns, Career
8   Larry Anderson, Pittsburgh, 2 games
7   Preston Pearson, Baltimore/Pittsburgh/Dallas, 5 games

Most Kickoff Returns, Game
7   Stephen Starring, New England vs. Chicago, 1986
5   Larry Anderson, Pittsburgh vs. Los Angeles, 1980
    Billy Campfield, Philadelphia vs. Oakland, 1981
    David Verser, Cincinnati vs. San Francisco, 1982

YARDS GAINED
Most Yards Gained Career
283   Fulton Walker, Miami, 2 games
207   Larry Anderson, Pittsburgh, 2 games

Most Yards Gained, Game
190   Fulton Walker, Miami vs. Washington, 1983

Longest Return
98   Fulton Walker, Miami vs. Washington, 1983 (TD)

COMBINED NET YARDS GAINED

ATTEMPTS
Most Attempts, Career
108   Franco Harris, Pittsburgh, 4 games
66   John Riggins, Washington, 2 games

Most Attempts, Game
39   John Riggins, Washington vs. Miami, 1983

YARDS GAINED
Most Yards Gained, Career
468   Franco Harris, Pittsburgh, 4 games
391   Lynn Swann, Pittsburgh, 4 games

Most Yards Gained, Game
209   Marcus Allen, L.A. Raiders vs. Washington, 1984

TEAM RECORDS

GAMES, VICTORIES, DEFEATS

Most Games
5   Dallas, 1971-72, 1976, 1978-79

Most Games Won
4   Pittsburgh, 1975-76, 1979-80

Most Games Lost
4   Minnesota, 1970, 1974-75, 1977

SCORING

Most Points, Game
46   Chicago vs. New England, 1986

Fewest Points, Game
3   Miami vs. Dallas, 1972

Most Points, Both Teams, Game
66   Pittsburgh (35) vs. Dallas (31), 1979

Fewest Points, Both Teams, Game
21   Washington (7) vs. Miami (14), 1973

TOUCHDOWNS
Most Touchdowns, Game
5   Green Bay vs. Kansas City, 1967
     Pittsburgh vs. Dallas, 1979
     L.A. Raiders vs. Washington, 1984
     San Francisco vs. Miami, 1985

Fewest Touchdowns, Game
0   Miami vs. Dallas, 1972

Most Touchdowns, Both Teams, Game
9   Pittsburgh (5) vs. Dallas (4), 1979

Fewest Touchdowns, Both Teams, Game
2   Baltimore (1) vs. N.Y. Jets (1), 1969

FIELD GOALS
Most Field Goals Attempted, Game
5   N.Y. Jets vs. Baltimore, 1969
     Dallas vs. Denver, 1978

Most Field Goals Attempted, Both Teams, Game
7   N.Y. Jets (5) vs. Baltimore (2), 1969

Fewest Field Goals Attempted, Both Teams, Game
1   Minnesota (0) vs. Miami (1), 1974

Most Field Goals, Game
4   Green Bay vs. Oakland, 1968
     San Francisco vs. Cincinnati, 1982

Most Field Goals, Both Teams, Game
4   Green Bay (4) vs. Oakland (0), 1968
     San Francisco (4) vs. Cincinnati (0), 1982
     Miami (3) vs. San Francisco (1), 1985

Fewest Field Goals, Both Teams, Game
0   Miami vs. Washington, 1973
     Pittsburgh vs. Minnesota, 1975

NET YARDS GAINED RUSHING AND PASSING

Most Yards Gained, Game
537 San Francisco vs. Miami, 1985

Fewest Yards Gained, Game
119 Minnesota vs. Pittsburgh, 1975

Most Yards Gained, Both Teams, Game
851   San Francisco (537) vs. Miami (314), 1985

Fewest Yards Gained, Both Teams, Game
452   Minnesota (119) vs. Pittsburgh (333), 1975

RUSHING

ATTEMPTS
Most Attempts, Game
57   Pittsburgh vs. Minnesota, 1975

Fewest Attempts, Game
9   Miami vs. San Francisco, 1985

Most Attempts, Both Teams, Game
81   Washington (52) vs. Miami (29), 1983

Fewest Attempts, Both Teams, Game
49   Miami (9) vs. San Francisco (40), 1985

YARDS GAINED
Most Yards Gained, Game
276   Washington vs. Miami, 1983

Fewest Yards Gained, Game
7   New England vs. Chicago, 1986

Most Yards Gained, Both Teams, Game
372   Washington (276) vs. Miami (96), 1983

Fewest Yards Gained, Both Teams, Game
171   Baltimore (69) vs. Dallas (102), 1971

PASSING

ATTEMPTS
Most Passes Attempted, Game
50   Miami vs. San Francisco, 1985

Fewest Passes Attempted, Game
7   Miami vs. Minnesota, 1974

Most Passes Attempted, Both Teams, Game
85   Miami (50) vs. San Francisco (35), 1985

Fewest Passes Attempted, Both Teams, Game
35   Miami (7) vs. Minnesota (28), 1974

COMPLETIONS
Most Passes Completed, Game
29   Miami vs. San Francisco, 1985

Fewest Passes Completed, Game
4   Miami vs. Washington, 1983

Most Passes Completed, Both Teams, Game
53   Miami (29) vs. San Francisco (24), 1985

Fewest Passes Completed, Both Teams, Game
19   Miami (4) vs. Washington (15), 1983

YARDS GAINED
Most Yards Gained, Game
326 San Francisco vs. Miami, 1985

Fewest Yards Gained, Game
35   Denver vs. Dallas, 1978

Most Yards Gained, Both Teams, Game
615 San Francisco (355) vs. Miami (294), 1985

Fewest Yards Gained, Both Teams, Game
156 Miami (69) vs. Washington (87), 1973

TIMES SACKED
Most Times Sacked, Game
7   Dallas vs. Pittsburgh, 1976

Fewest Times Sacked, Game
0   Baltimore vs. N.Y. Jets, 1969; vs. Dallas, 1971
     Minnesota vs. Pittsburgh, 1975
     Pittsburgh vs. Los Angeles, 1980
     Philadelphia vs. Oakland, 1981

Most Times Sacked, Both Teams, Game
10   Chicago (3) vs. New England (7), 1986

Fewest Times Sacked, Both Teams, Game
1   Philadelphia (0) vs. Oakland (1), 1981

INTERCEPTIONS BY

Most Interceptions By, Game
4   N.Y. Jets vs. Baltimore, 1969
     Dallas vs. Denver, 1978

Most Interceptions By, Both Teams, Game
6   Baltimore (3) vs. Dallas (3), 1971

PUNTING

Most Punts, Game
9   Dallas vs. Baltimore, 1971

Fewest Punts, Game
2   Pittsburgh vs. Los Angeles, 1980

Most Punts, Both Teams, Game
15   Washington (8) vs. L.A. Raiders (7), 1984

Fewest Punts, Both Teams, Game
5   N.Y. Giants (3) vs. Denver (2), 1987

PUNT RETURNS

Most Punt Returns, Game
6   Washington vs. Miami, 1983

Fewest Punt Returns, Game
0   Minnesota vs. Miami, 1974

Most Punt Returns, Both Teams, Game
9   Pittsburgh (5) vs. Minnesota (4), 1975

Fewest Punt Returns, Both Teams, Game
2   Dallas (1) vs. Miami (1), 1972

YARDS GAINED
Most Yards Gained, Game
52   Washington vs. Miami, 1983

Fewest Yards Gained, Game
– 1   Dallas vs. Miami, 1972

Most Yards Gained, Both Teams, Game
74   Washington (52) vs. Miami (22), 1983

Fewest Yards Gained, Both Teams, Game
13   Miami (4) vs. Washington (9), 1973

KICKOFF RETURNS

Most Kickoff Returns, Game
7   Oakland vs. Green Bay, 1968
     Minnesota vs. Oakland, 1977
     Cincinnati vs. San Francisco, 1982
     Washington vs. L.A. Raiders, 1984
     Miami vs. San Francisco, 1985

Fewest Kickoff Returns, Game
1   N.Y. Jets vs. Baltimore, 1969
     L.A. Raiders vs. Washington, 1984

Most Kickoff Returns, Both Teams, Game
11   Los Angeles (6) vs. Pittsburgh (5), 1980
      Miami (7) vs. San Francisco (4), 1985

Fewest Kickoff Returns, Both Teams, Game
5   N.Y. Jets (1) vs. Baltimore (4), 1969
     Miami (2) vs. Washington (3), 1973

YARDS GAINED
Most Yards Gained, Game
222   Miami vs. Washington, 1983

Fewest Yards Gained, Game
17   L.A. Raiders vs. Washington, 1984

Most Yards Gained, Both Teams, Game
279   Miami (222) vs. Washington (57), 1983

Fewest Yards Gained, Both Teams, Game
78   Miami (33) vs. Washington (45), 1973

AFC - NFC Pro Bowl Results — NFC leads series 10-7

YEAR	DATE	WINNER	LOSER	SITE	ATTENDANCE
1987	Feb. 1	AFC 10	NFC 6	Honolulu	50,101
1986	Feb. 2	NFC 28	AFC 24	Honolulu	50,101
1985	Jan. 27	AFC 22	NFC 14	Honolulu	50,385
1984	Jan. 29	NFC 45	AFC 3	Honolulu	50,445
1983	Feb. 6	NFC 20	AFC 19	Honolulu	47,201
1982	Jan. 31	AFC 16	NFC 13	Honolulu	49,521
1981	Feb. 1	NFC 21	AFC 7	Honolulu	47,879
1980	Jan. 27	NFC 37	AFC 27	Honolulu	48,060
1979	Jan. 29	NFC 13	AFC 7	Los Angeles	46,281
1978	Jan. 23	NFC 14	AFC 13	Tampa	51,337
1977	Jan. 17	AFC 24	NFC 14	Seattle	64,151
1976	Jan. 26	NFC 23	AFC 20	New Orleans	30,546
1975	Jan. 20	NFC 17	AFC 10	Miami	26,484
1974	Jan. 20	AFC 15	NFC 13	Kansas City	66,918
1973	Jan. 21	AFC 33	NFC 28	Dallas	37,091
1972	Jan. 23	AFC 26	NFC 13	Los Angeles	53,647
1971	Jan. 24	NFC 27	AFC 6	Los Angeles	48,222

NUMBER-ONE DRAFT CHOICES

Season	Team	Player	Pos.	College
1987	Tampa Bay	Vinny Testaverde	QB	Miami
1986	Tampa Bay	Bo Jackson	RB	Auburn
1985	Buffalo Bills	Bruce Smith	DE	Virginia Tech.
1984	New England	Irving Fryar	WR	Nebraska
1983	Baltimore	John Elway	QB	Stanford
1982	New England	Kenneth Sims	DT	Texas
1981	New Orleans	George Rogers	RB	South Carolina
1980	Detroit	Billy Sims	RB	Oklahoma
1979	Buffalo	Tom Cousineau	LB	Ohio State
1978	Houston	Earl Campbell	RB	Texas
1977	Tampa Bay	Ricky Bell	RB	So. California
1976	Tampa Bay	Lee Roy Selmon	DE	Oklahoma
1975	Atlanta	Steve Bartkowski	QB	California
1974	Dallas	Ed Jones	DE	Tennessee State
1973	Houston	John Matuszak	DE	Tampa
1972	Buffalo	Walt Patulski	DE	Notre Dame
1971	New England	Jim Plunkett	QB	Stanford
1970	Pittsburgh	Terry Bradshaw	QB	Louisiana Tech.
1969	Buffalo (AFL)	O.J. Simpson	RB	So. California
1968	Minnesota	Ron Yary	T	So. California
1967	Baltimore	Bubba Smith	DT	Michigan State
1966	Atlanta	Tommy Nobis	LB	Texas
	Miami (AFL)	Jim Grabowski	RB	Illinois
1965	N.Y. Giants	Tucker Frederickson	RB	Auburn
	Houston (AFL)	Lawrence Elkins	E	Baylor
1964	San Francisco	Dave Parks	E	Texas Tech.
	Boston (AFL)	Jack Concannon	QB	Boston College

Season	Team	Player	Pos.	College
1963	Los Angeles Rams	Terry Baker	QB	Oregon State
	Kansas City (AFL)	Buck Buchanan	DT	Grambling
1962	Washington	Ernie Davis	RB	Syracuse
	Oakland (AFL)	Roman Gabriel	QB	N. Carolina State
1961	Minnesota	Tommy Mason	RB	Tulane
	Buffalo (AFL)	Ken Rice	G	Auburn
1960	Los Angeles Rams	Billy Cannon	RB	LSU
	(AFL had no formal first pick)			
1959	Green Bay	Randy Duncan	QB	Iowa
1958	Chi. Cardinals	King Hill	QB	Rice
1957	Green Bay	Paul Hornung	HB	Notre Dame
1956	Pittsburgh	Gary Glick	DB	Colorado A&M
1955	Baltimore	George Shaw	QB	Oregon
1954	Cleveland	Bobby Garrett	QB	Stanford
1953	San Francisco	Harry Babcock	E	Georgia
1952	Los Angeles Rams	Bill Wade	QB	Vanderbilt
1951	N.Y. Giants	Kyle Rote	HB	SMU
1950	Detroit	Leon Hart	E	Notre Dame
1949	Philadelphia	Chuck Bednarik	C	Pennsylvania
1948	Washington	Harry Gilmer	QB	Alabama
1947	Chi. Bears	Bob Fenimore	HB	Oklahoma A&M
1946	Boston	Frank Dancewicz	QB	Notre Dame
1945	Chi. Cardinals	Charley Trippi	HB	Georgia
1944	Boston	Angelo Bertelli	QB	Notre Dame
1943	Detroit	Frank Sinkwich	HB	Georgia
1942	Pittsburgh	Bill Dudley	HB	Virginia
1941	Chi. Bears	Tom Harmon	HB	Michigan
1940	Chi. Cardinals	George Cafego	HB	Tennessee
1939	Chi. Cardinals	Ki Aldrich	C	TCU
1938	Cleveland	Corbett Davis	FB	Indiana
1937	Philadelphia	Sam Francis	FB	Nebraska
1936	Philadelphia	Jay Berwanger	HB	Chicago

1987 COLLEGIATE DRAFT

ROUND 1

No. Team	Name	Pos.	College
Start of Round: 8:05am			
1 TAMPA BAY	Vinny Testaverde	QB	Miami (Florida)
2 INDIANAPOLIS	Cornelius Bennett	LB	Alabama
3 HOUSTON from Buffalo	Alonzo Highsmith	RB	Miami (Florida)
4 GREEN BAY	Brent Fullwood	RB	Auburn
5 CLEVELAND from San Diego	Mike Junkin	LB	Duke
6 ST. LOUIS	Kelly Stouffer	QB	Colorado State
7 DETROIT	Reggie Rogers	DE	Washington
8 BUFFALO from Houston	Shane Conlan	LB	Penn State
9 PHILADELPHIA	Jerome Brown	DT	Miami (Florida)
10 PITTSBURGH	Rod Woodson	DB	Purdue
11 NEW ORLEANS	Shawn Knight	DL	Brigham Young
12 DALLAS	Danny Noonan	DL	Nebraska
13 ATLANTA	Chris Miller	QB	Oregon
14 MINNESOTA from Miami	D.J. Dozier	RB	Penn State
15 L.A. RAIDERS	John Clay	OT	Missouri
16 MIAMI from Minnesota	John Bosa	DE	Boston College
17 CINCINNATI	Jason Buck	DE	Brigham Young
18 SEATTLE	Tony Woods	LB	Pittsburgh
19 KANSAS CITY	Paul Palmer	RB	Temple
20 HOUSTON from L.A. Rams	Haywood Jeffires	WR	North Carolina State
21 N.Y. JETS	Roger Vick	RB	Texas A&M
22 SAN FRANCISCO	Harris Barton	OT	North Carolina
23 NEW ENGLAND	Bruce Armstrong	OT	Louisville
24 SAN DIEGO from Cleveland	Rod Bernstine	TE	Texas A&M
25 SAN FRANCISCO from Washington	Terrence Flagler	RB	Clemson
26 CHICAGO	Jim Harbaugh	QB	Michigan
27 DENVER	Ricky Nattiel	WR	Florida
28 N.Y. GIANTS	Mark Ingram	WR	Michigan State

End of Round: 12:13pm Time of Round: 4 hrs, 8 mins Total Time: 4 hrs, 8 mins

ROUND 2

Start of Round: 12:13pm			
1 BUFFALO from Tampa Bay	Nate Odomes	DB	Wisconsin
2 WASHINGTON from Indianapolis	Brian Davis	DB	Nebraska
3 ATLANTA from Green Bay	Kenny Flowers	RB	Clemson
4 CLEVELAND from San Diego	Gregg Rakoczy	C	Miami (Florida)
5 BUFFALO	Roland Mitchell	DB	Texas Tech
6 ST. LOUIS	Tim McDonald	DB	Southern California
7 KANSAS CITY from Houston	Christian Okoye	RB	Azusa Pacific
8 TAMPA BAY from Detroit through Houston & Buffalo	Ricky Reynolds	DB	Washington State
9 SAN FRANCISCO from Philadelphia	Jeff Bregel	OG	Southern California
10 PITTSBURGH	Delton Hall	DB	Clemson
11 DALLAS	Ron Francis	DB	Baylor
12 NEW ORLEANS	Lonzell Hill	WR	Washington
13 GREEN BAY from Atlanta	Johnny Holland	LB	Texas A&M
14 N.Y. JETS from L.A. Raiders	Alex Gordon	LB	Cincinnati
15 MIAMI	Rick Graf	LB	Wisconsin
16 MINNESOTA	Ray Berry	LB	Baylor
17 SEATTLE	Dave Wyman	LB	Stanford
18 HOUSTON from Kansas City	Walter Johnson	LB	Louisiana Tech
19 L.A. RAMS	Donald Evans	DE	Winston-Salem State

No.	Team	Name	Pos.	College
20	WASHINGTON from N.Y.			
	Jets through L.A. Raiders	Wally Kleine	OT	Notre Dame
21	CINCINNATI	Eric Thomas	DB	Tulane
22	TAMPA BAY			
	from San Francisco	Winston Moss	LB	Miami (Florida)
23	TAMPA BAY			
	from New England	Don Smith	QB-RB	Mississippi State
24	L.A. RAIDERS			
	from Washington	Bruce Wilkerson	OT	Tennessee
25	SAN DIEGO from Cleveland	Louis Brock, Jr.	DB	Southern California
26	CHICAGO	Ron Morris	WR	SMU
27	N.Y. GIANTS from Denver	Adrian White	DB	Florida
28	MIAMI from N.Y. Giants			
	through St. Louis	Scott Schwedes	WR	Syracuse

End of Round: 2:48pm Time of Round: 2 hrs, 35 mins Total Time: 6 hrs, 43 mins

ROUND 3

Start of Round: 2:48pm

No.	Team	Name	Pos.	College
1	TAMPA BAY	Mark Carrier	WR	Nicholls State
2	INDIANAPOLIS	Chris Gambol	OT	Iowa
3	SAN DIEGO	Karl Wilson	DE	LSU
4	BUFFALO	David Brandon	LB	Memphis State
5	GREEN BAY	Dave Croston	OT	Iowa
6	ST. LOUIS	Robert Await	TE	San Diego State
7	DETROIT	Jerry Ball	DT	SMU
8	HOUSTON	Cody Carlson	QB	Baylor
9	PHILADELPHIA	Ben Tamburello	C	Auburn
10	PITTSBURGH	Charles Lockett	WR	Long Beach State
11	NEW ORLEANS	Mike Adams	DB	Arkansas State
12	DALLAS	Jeff Zimmerman	OG	Florida
13	GREEN BAY from Atlanta	Scott Stephen	LB	Arizona State
14	ST. LOUIS from Miami	Colin Scotts	DT	Hawaii
15	GREEN BAY			
	from L.A. Raiders	Frankie Neal	WR	Fort Hays State
16	MINNESOTA	Henry Thomas	DL	LSU
17	KANSAS CITY	Todd Howard	LB	Texas A&M
18	L.A. RAMS	Clifford Hicks	DB	Oregon
19	N.Y. JETS	Onzy Elam	LB	Tennessee State
20	CINCINNATI	Leonard Bell	DB	Indiana
21	CINCINNATI from Seattle	Skip McClendon	DE	Arizona State
22	BUFFALO			
	from San Francisco	Jamie Mueller	RB	Benedictine College
23	NEW ENGLAND	Bob Perryman	RB	Michigan
24	CLEVELAND	Tim Manoa	RB	Penn State
25	L.A. RAIDERS			
	from Washington through			
	New England	Steve Smith	RB	Penn State
26	CLEVELAND from Chicago			
	through L.A. Rams	Jeff Jaeger	PK	Washington
27	DENVER	Michael Brooks	LB	LSU
28	N.Y. GIANTS	Stephen Baker	WR	Fresno State

End of Round: 4:15pm Time of Round: 1 hr, 27 mins Total Time: 8 hrs, 10 mins

ROUND 4

No. Team	Name	Pos.	College
Start of Round: 4:15pm			
1 TAMPA BAY	Don Graham	LB	Penn State
2 INDIANAPOLIS	Randy Dixon	OT	Pittsburgh
3 TAMPA BAY from Buffalo	Ron Hall	TE	Hawaii
4 GREEN BAY	Lorenzo Freeman	DT	Pittsburgh
5 SAN DIEGO	Mark Vlasic	QB	Iowa
6 ST. LOUIS	Rod Saddler	DL	Texas A&M
7 L.A. RAMS from Houston	Doug Bartlett	NT	Northern Illinois
8 DETROIT	Garland Rivers	DB	Michigan
9 PHILADELPHIA	Byron Evans	LB	Arizona
10 PITTSBURGH	Thomas Everett	DB	Baylor
11 DALLAS	Kelvin Martin	WR	Boston College
12 NEW ORLEANS	Steve Trapilo	OG	Boston College
13 ATLANTA	Ralph Van Dyke	OT	Southern Illinois
14 NEW ENGLAND from L.A. Raiders	Rich Gannon	QB-RB	Delaware
15 MIAMI	Troy Stradford	WR	Boston College
16 MINNESOTA	Reginald Rutland	DB	Georgia Tech
17 CHICAGO from L.A. Rams	Sean Smith	DL	Grambling State
18 NEW ENGLAND from N.Y. Jets through L.A. Raiders	Derrick Beasley	DB	Winston-Salem State
19 CINCINNATI	Jim Riggs	TE	Clemson
20 SEATTLE	Mark Moore	DB	Oklahoma State
21 HOUSTON from Kansas City	Mark Dusbabek	LB	Minnesota
22 TAMPA BAY from San Francisco	Bruce Hill	WR	Arizona State
23 NEW ENGLAND	Tim Jordan	LB	Wisconsin
24 BUFFALO from Washington	Leon Seals	DL	Jackson State
25 L.A. RAMS from Cleveland	Larry Kelm	LB	Texas A&M
26 L.A. RAIDERS from Chicago	Steve Beuerlein	QB	Notre Dame
27 DENVER	Marc Munford	LB	Nebraska
28 N.Y. GIANTS	Odessa Turner	WR	Northwestern Louisiana

End of Round: 5:35 pm Time of Round: 1 hr, 20 mins Total Time: 9 hrs, 30 mins

ROUND 5

	Name	Pos.	College
Start of Round: 5:35 pm			
1 NEW ENGLAND from Tampa Bay	Danny Villa	OT	Arizona State
2 INDIANAPOLIS	Roy Banks	WR	Eastern Illinois
3 SAN DIEGO from Green Bay	Nelson Jones	DB	North Carolina State
4 NEW ENGLAND from San Diego	Tom Gibson	DE	Northern Arizona
5 WASHINGTON from Buffalo	Tim Smith	RB	Texas Tech
6 ST. LOUIS	George Swarn	RB	Miami (Ohio)
7 SEATTLE from Detroit	Tommie Agee	RB	Auburn
8 CHICAGO from Houston through Washington & L.A. Raiders	Steve Bryan	DE	Oklahoma
9 PHILADELPHIA	David Alexander	OG	Tulsa
10 PITTSBURGH	Hardy Nickerson	LB	California
11 NEW ORLEANS	Milton Mack	DB	Alcorn State
12 DALLAS	Everett Gay	WR	Texas
13 ATLANTA	Mark Mraz	DE	Utah State
14 ST. LOUIS from Miami	John Bruno	P	Penn State

No.	Team	Name	Pos.	College
15	ST. LOUIS from L.A. Raiders	Ilia Jarostchuk	LB	New Hampshire
16	KANSAS CITY from Minnesota through Miami	Kitrick Taylor	WR	Washington State
17	N.Y. JETS	Kirby Jackson	DB	Mississippi State
18	CINCINNATI	Mark Logan	RB	Kentucky
19	SEATTLE	Ruben Rodriguez	P	Arizona
20	MIAMI from Kansas City	Chris Conlin	OT	Penn State
21	HOUSTON from L.A. Rams	Spencer Tillman	RB	Oklahoma
22	SAN FRANCISCO	Paul Jokisch	TE	Michigan
23	TAMPA BAY from New England	Henry Rolling	LB	Nevada-Reno
24	L.A. RAMS from Cleveland	Scott Mersereau	DT	Southern Connecticut
25	TAMPA BAY from Washington	Tony Mayes	DB	Kentucky
26	CHICAGO	Will Johnson	LB	Northeast Louisiana
27	CINCINNATI from Denver	Greg Horne	P	Arkansas
28	N.Y. GIANTS	Paul O'Connor	OG	Miami (Florida)

End of Round: 6:48 pm Time of Round: 1 hr, 13 mins Total Time: 10 hrs, 43 mins

ROUND 6
Start of Round: 6:48 pm

No.	Team	Name	Pos.	College
1	PITTSBURGH from Tampa Bay	Tim Johnson	NT	Penn State
2	INDIANAPOLIS	Freddie Robinson	DB	Alabama
3	TAMPA BAY from San Diego	Steve Bartalo	RB	Colorado State
4	WASHINGTON from Buffalo	Steve Gage	DB	Tulsa
5	GREEN BAY	Willie Marshall	WR	Temple
6	ST. LOUIS	Mark Garalczyk	DT	Western Michigan
7	HOUSTON	Al Smith	LB	Utah State
8	DETROIT	Danny Lockett	LB	Arizona
9	PHILADELPHIA	Ron Moten	LB	Florida
10	PITTSBURGH	Greg Lloyd	LB	Fort Valley State
11	DALLAS	Joe Onosai	OL	Hawaii
12	NEW ORLEANS	Thomas Henley	WR	Stanford
13	ATLANTA	Paul Kiser	OG	Wake Forest
14	CHICAGO from L.A. Raiders	John Adickes	C	Baylor
15	MIAMI	Lance Sellers	LB	Boise State
16	MINNESOTA	Greg Richardson	WR-KR	Alabama
17	CINCINNATI	Sonny Gordon	DB	Ohio State
18	PHILADELPHIA from Seattle	Chris Pike	DT	Tulsa
19	HOUSTON from Kansas City	Toby Caston	LB	LSU
20	N.Y. GIANTS from L.A. Rams	Tim Richardson	RB	Pacific
21	N.Y. JETS	Tracy Martin	WR	North Dakota
22	SAN FRANCISCO	Bob White	LB	Penn State
23	NEW ENGLAND	Gene Taylor	WR	Fresno State
24	WASHINGTON	Ed Simmons	OT	Eastern Washington
25	CLEVELAND	Stephen Braggs	DB	Texas
26	L.A. RAMS from Chicago	Jon Embree	TE	Colorado
27	DENVER	Warren Marshall	RB	James Madison
28	N.Y. GIANTS	Doug Riesenberg	OT	California

End of Round: 7:52 pm Time of Round: 1 hr, 4 mins Total Time: 11 hrs, 47 mins

ROUND 7

No.	Team	Name	Pos.	College
Start of Round: 7:52 pm				
1	TAMPA BAY	Curt Jarvis	NT	Alabama
2	INDIANAPOLIS	Mark Bellini	WR	Brigham Young
3	BUFFALO	Kerry Porter	RB	Washington State
4	GREEN BAY	Tony Leiker	DT	Stanford
5	SAN DIEGO	Jamie Holland	WR	Ohio State
6	ST. LOUIS	Tim Peoples	DB	Washington
7	DETROIT	Dan Saleaumua	DT	Arizona State
8	HOUSTON	Robert Banks	LB	Notre Dame
9	PHILADELPHIA	Brian Williams	OT	Central Michigan
10	PITTSBURGH	Chris Kelley	TE	Akron
11	NEW ORLEANS	Gene Atkins	DB	Florida A&M
12	DALLAS	Kevin Sweeney	QB	Fresno State
13	ATLANTA	Michael Reid	LB	Wisconsin
14	MIAMI	Tom Brown	RB	Pittsburgh
15	L.A. RAIDERS	Bo Jackson	RB	Auburn
16	SEATTLE from Minnesota	Roland Barbay	DT	LSU
17	SEATTLE	Derek Tennell	TE	UCLA
18	KANSAS CITY	Doug Hudson	QB	Nicholls State
19	PHILADELPHIA from L.A. Rams			
	choice exercised in 1986 Supplemental Draft (RB Charles Crawford)			
20	N.Y. JETS	Gerald Nichols	NT	Florida State
21	CINCINNATI	Chris Thatcher	OG	Lafayette
22	SAN FRANCISCO	Steve DeLine	PK	Colorado State
23	TAMPA BAY from New England	Harry Swayne	DL	Rutgers
24	GREEN BAY from Cleveland	Bill Smith	P	Mississippi
25	WASHINGTON	Johnny Thomas	DB	Baylor
26	CHICAGO	Archie Harris	OT	William & Mary
27	DENVER	Wilbur Strozier	TE-G	Georgia
28	ST. LOUIS from N.Y. Giants	William Harris	TE	Bishop

End of Round: 8:47 pm Time of Round: 0 hrs, 55 mins Total Time: 12 hrs, 42 mins

ROUND 8

Start of Round: 8:47 pm

No.	Team	Name	Pos.	College
1	N.Y. JETS from Tampa Bay	Eddie Hunter	RB	Virginia Tech
2	TAMPA BAY from Indianapolis	Stan Mataele	NT	Arizona
3	GREEN BAY	Jeff Drost	DT	Iowa
4	SAN DIEGO	Joe MacEsker	OT	Texas-El Paso
5	INDIANAPOLIS from Buffalo	Chuckie Miller	DB	UCLA
6	ST. LOUIS	Steve Alvord	DT	Washington
7	HOUSTON	Michel James	WR	Washington State
8	DETROIT	Dennis Gibson	LB	Iowa State
9	SAN DIEGO from Philadelphia	Ron Brown	LB	Southern California
10	PITTSBURGH	Charles Buchanan	DE	Tennessee State
11	DALLAS	Kevin Gogan	OT	Washington
12	NEW ORLEANS	Toi Cook	DB	Stanford
13	ATLANTA	Curtis Taliaferro	LB	Virginia Tech
14	BUFFALO from L.A. Raiders	Bruce Mesner	DE	Maryland
15	MIAMI	Joel Williams	TE	Notre Dame
16	MINNESOTA	Rick Fenney	RB	Washington

No.	Team	Name	Pos.	College
17	MIAMI from Kansas City	Mark Dennis	OT	Illinois
18	L.A. RAMS	Michael Stewart	DB	Fresno State
19	N.Y. JETS	Mike Rice	P	Montana
20	CINCINNATI	Solomon Wilcots	DB	Colorado
21	SEATTLE	Sammy Garza	QB	Texas-El Paso
22	SAN FRANCISCO	David Grayson	LB	Fresno State
23	KANSAS CITY from New England	Michael Clemons	RB	William & Mary
24	WASHINGTON	Clarence Vaughn	LB	Northern Illinois
25	CLEVELAND	Steve Bullitt	LB	Texas A&M
26	CHICAGO	Paul Migliazzo	LB	Oklahoma
27	DENVER	Dan Morgan	OG	Penn State
28	N.Y. GIANTS	Rod Jones	TE	Washington

End of Round: 9:56 pm Time of Round: 1 hr, 9 mins Total Time: 13 hrs, 51 mins

ROUND 9
Start of Round: 9:56 pm

No.	Team	Name	Pos.	College
1	TAMPA BAY	Joe Armentrout	RB	Wisconsin
2	N.Y. GIANTS from Indianapolis	Stan Parker	OL	Nebraska
3	SAN DIEGO	Thomas Wilcher	RB	Michigan
4	BUFFALO	Keith McKeller	TE	Jacksonville State
5	GREEN BAY	Gregg Harris	OG	Wake Forest
6	ST. LOUIS	Wayne Davis	LB	Alabama
7	DETROIT	Rick Calhoun	RB	Fullerton State
8	HOUSTON	Wes Neighbors	C	Alabama
9	PHILADELPHIA	Ken Lambiotte	QB	William & Mary
10	PITTSBURGH	Joey Clinkscales	WR	Tennessee
11	NEW ORLEANS	Scott Leach	LB	Ohio State
12	DALLAS	Alvin Blount	RB	Maryland
13	ATLANTA	Terrence Anthony	DB	Iowa State
14	MIAMI	Tim Pidgeon	LB	Syracuse
15	L.A. RAIDERS	Scott Eccles	TE	Eastern New Mexico
16	MINNESOTA	Leonard Jones	DB	Texas Tech
17	L.A. RAMS	Tracy Ham	RB	Georgia Southern
18	N.Y. JETS	Ron McLean	DE	Fullerton State
19	CINCINNATI	Craig Raddatz	LB	Wisconsin
20	SEATTLE	M.L. Johnson	LB	Hawaii
21	KANSAS CITY	Randy Watts	DE	Catawba
22	SAN FRANCISCO	Jonathan Shelley	DB	Mississippi
23	TAMPA BAY from New England	Greg Davis	P	Citadel
24	INDIANAPOLIS from Cleveland	Bob Ontko	LB	Penn State
25	WASHINGTON	Alfred Jenkins	RB	Arizona
26	CHICAGO	Lakei Heimuli	RB	Brigham Young
27	DENVER	Bruce Plummer	DB	Mississippi State
28	N.Y. GIANTS	Dana Wright	RB	Findlay

End of Round: 11:00 pm Time of Round: 1 hr, 4 mins Total Time: 14 hrs, 55 mins

ROUND 10

No.	Team	Name	Pos.	College
	Start of Round: 11:00 pm			
1	TAMPA BAY	Mike Simmonds	OG	Indiana State
2	INDIANAPOLIS	Chris Goode	DB	Alabama
3	L.A. RAIDERS from Buffalo	Rob Harrison	RB	Sacramento State
4	GREEN BAY	Don Majkowski	QB	Virginia
5	SAN DIEGO	Anthony Anderson	DB	Grambling State
6	ST. LOUIS	Charles Wright	DB	Tulsa
7	HOUSTON	Curtis Duncan	WR	Northwestern
8	DETROIT	Raynard Brown	WR	South Carolina
9	PHILADELPHIA	Paul Carberry	DT	Oregon State
10	PITTSBURGH	Merril Hoge	RB	Idaho State
11	DALLAS	Dale Jones	LB	Tennessee
12	NEW ORLEANS	Robert Clark	WR	North Carolina Central
13	ATLANTA	Jerry Reese	TE	Illinois
14	L.A. RAIDERS	John Gesek	OT	Sacramento State
15	MIAMI	Bobby Taylor	DB	Wisconsin
16	MINNESOTA	Bob Riley	OT	Indiana
17	N.Y. JETS	Sid Lewis	DB	Penn State
18	CINCINNATI	David McCluskey	RB	Georgia
19	SEATTLE	Louis Clark	TE	Mississippi State
20	KANSAS CITY	James Evans	RB	Southern University
21	L.A. RAMS	David Smith	LB	Northern Arizona
22	L.A. RAIDERS from San Francisco through Buffalo	Jim Ellis	LB	Boise State
23	SAN FRANCISCO from New England through L.A. Raiders	John Paye	QB	Stanford
24	WASHINGTON	Ted Wilson	WR	Central Florida
25	CLEVELAND	Frank Winters	C	Western Illinois
26	CHICAGO	Dick Chapura	DT	Missouri
27	DENVER	Rafe Wilkinson	LB	Richmond
28	N.Y. GIANTS	Chuck Faucette	LB	Maryland

End of Round: 12:03 am Time of Round: 1 hr, 3 mins Total Time: 15 hrs, 58 mins

ROUND 11

No.	Team	Name	Pos.	College
	Start of Round: 12:03 am			
1	TAMPA BAY	Reggie Taylor	RB	Cincinnati
2	INDIANAPOLIS	Jim Reynosa	DE	Arizona State
3	GREEN BAY	Patrick Scott	WR	Grambling State
4	SAN DIEGO	Joe Goebel	C	UCLA
5	BUFFALO	Howard Ballard	OT	Alabama A&M
6	ST. LOUIS	Todd Peat	OG	Northern Illinois
7	DETROIT	Brian Silverling	TE	Penn State
8	HOUSTON	John Davis	OG	Georgia Tech
9	L.A. RAIDERS from Philadelphia through San Francisco	Chris McLemore	RB	Arizona
10	PITTSBURGH	Paul Oswald	C	Kansas
11	NEW ORLEANS	Arthur Wells	TE	Grambling State
12	DALLAS	Jeff Ward	PK	Texas

No.	Team	Name	Pos.	College
13	ATLANTA	Elbert Shelley	DB	Arkansas State
14	MIAMI	Terence Mann	DT	SMU
15	L.A. RAIDERS	Mario Perry	TE	Mississippi
16	MINNESOTA	Brent Pease	QB	Montana
17	CINCINNATI	Jim Warne	OT	Arizona State
18	SEATTLE	Darryl Oliver	RB	Miami (Florida)
19	KANSAS CITY	Craig Richardson	WR	Eastern Washington
20	DENVER from L.A. Rams	Steve Roberts	DE	Washington
21	N.Y. JETS	Kirk Timmer	LB	Montana State
22	SAN FRANCISCO	Calvin Nicholas	WR	Grambling State
23	NEW ENGLAND	Carlos Reveiz	PK	Tennessee
24	CLEVELAND	Larry Brewton	DB	Temple
25	WASHINGTON	Laron Brown	WR	Texas
26	CHICAGO	Tim Jessie	WR	Auburn
27	DENVER	Tommy Neal	RB	Maryland
28	N.Y. GIANTS	Dave Walter	QB	Michigan Tech

End of Round: 1:05 am Time of Round: 1 hr, 2 mins Total Time: 17 hrs, 0 mins

ROUND 12

Start of Round: 1:05 am

No.	Team	Name	Pos.	College
1	TAMPA BAY	Scott Cooper	DT	Kearney State
2	INDIANAPOLIS	David Adams	RB	Arizona
3	SAN DIEGO	Marcus Greenwood	RB	UCLA
4	BUFFALO	Joe McGrail	DT	Delaware
5	SEATTLE from Green Bay	Wes Dove	DE	Syracuse
6	TAMPA BAY from St. Louis	Mike Shula	QB	Alabama
7	HOUSTON	Ira Valentine	RB	Texas A&M
8	DETROIT	Gary Lee	WR	Georgia Tech
9	PHILADELPHIA	Bobby Morse	RB	Michigan State
10	PITTSBURGH	Theo Young	TE	Arkansas
11	DALLAS	Scott Armstrong	LB	Florida
12	NEW ORLEANS	Tyrone Sorrells	OG	Georgia Tech
13	ATLANTA	Larry Emery	RB	Wisconsin
14	N.Y. GIANTS from L.A. Raiders	Bill Berthusen	DT	Iowa State
15	MIAMI	Jim Karsatos	QB	Ohio State
16	MINNESOTA	Keith Williams	DT	Florida
17	SEATTLE	Tony Burse	RB	Middle Tennessee State
18	KANSAS CITY	Bruce Holmes	LB	Minnesota
19	L.A. RAMS	Alonzo Williams	RB	Mesa College
20	N.Y. JETS	Bill Ransdell	QB	Kentucky
21	CINCINNATI	John Holifield	RB	West Virginia
22	N.Y. GIANTS from San Francisco through L.A. Raiders	Chad Stark	RB	North Dakota State
23	NEW ENGLAND	Elgin Davis	RB	Central Florida
24	WASHINGTON	Ray Hitchcock	C	Minnesota
25	L.A. RAMS from Cleveland	Fred Stokes	DE	Georgia Southern
26	CHICAGO	Eric Jeffries	DB	Texas
27	DENVER	Tyrone Braxton	DB	North Dakota State
28	GREEN BAY from N.Y. Giants	Norman Jefferson	DB	LSU

End of Round: 2:05 am Time of Round: 1 hr, 0 mins Total Time: 18 hrs, 0 mins

NCAA FOOTBALL STATISTICS

Division 1A NCAA Statistics (Seniors only)

Passing

	Att.	Comp.	Yds.	TDs.	Int.	Rtg
Vinny Testaverde (Miami, Florida)	276	175	2557	26	9	165.8
Jim Harbaugh (Michigan)	239	158	2432	10	8	158.7
Dave Yarema (Michigan State)	297	200	2581	16	11	150.7
Shawn Halloran (Boston College)	258	159	2090	17	6	146.8
Mark Vlasic (Iowa)	152	93	1234	9	4	143.7
Lee Saltz (Temple)	203	117	1727	12	7	141.7
Jeff Van Raaphorst (Arizona State)	239	144	1988	15	11	141.6
Ned James (New Mexico)	215	125	1777	14	8	141.6
Steve Beuerlein, (Notre Dame)	259	151	2211	13	7	141.2
Terry Morris, (Miami, Ohio)	308	193	2365	19	10	141.0
Kevin Sweeney, (Fresno State)	284	160	2363	15	9	137.3
Larry Egger, (Utah)	382	233	2761	21	9	135.1
Sammy Garza, (UTEP)	410	258	3140	21	19	134.9

Rushing

	Games	Att.	Yds.	Avg.	TDs.	Yds/Game
Paul Palmer (Temple)	11	346	1866	5.4	15	169.64
Kelvin Farmer (Toledo)	11	299	1532	5.1	16	139.27
Steve Bartalo (Colorado State)	11	366	1419	3.9	19	129.00
Brent Fullwood (Auburn)	11	167	1391	8.3	10	126.45
Reggie Taylor (Cincinnati)	11	256	1325	5.2	11	120.45
Troy Stradford (Boston College)	10	218	1188	5.4	10	118.80
Rick Calhoun (California St. Fullerton)	12	259	1398	5.4	11	116.50
Terrence Flagler, (Clemson)	11	180	1176	6.5	10	106.91
David Adams, (Arizona)	11	238	1175	4.9	7	106.82
George Swarn (Miami, Ohio)	11	251	1112	4.4	5	101.09
Roger Vick, (Texas A&M)	10	220	960	4.4	10	96.00

Receiving

	Games	No.	Yds.	Avg.	TDs.	Receptions per game
Mark Templeton (Long Beach St.)	11	99	685	6.9	2	9.00
Dave Montagne (Oregon State)	11	78	862	11.0	2	7.09
James Brim (Wake Forest)	11	66	930	14.0	5	6.00
Rod Bernstine (Texas A&M)	11	65	710	10.9	5	5.91
Craig McEwan (Utah)	11	54	721	13.4	7	5.82
Tom Compernolle, (Ohio)	11	61	626	10.3	4	5.55
Lafo Malauulu, (San Jose St.)	11	56	832	14.9	5	5.09
Ricky George, (Ball State)	11	55	569	10.3	4	5.00
Kelly Spielmaker, (Western Mich.)	9	43	585	13.6	3	4.78

Scoring

	Games	TDs.	EP/Att	FG/Att	Pts.	Points/ Game
Steve Bartalo (Colorado State)	11	19	0	0	114	10.36
Tim Lashar (Oklahoma)	11	0	60	12	96	8.73
Kelvin Farmer (Toledo)	11	16	0	0	96	8.73
Jeff Jaeger, (Washington)	11	0	42	17	93	8.45
Paul Palmer, (Temple)	11	15	0	0	90	8.18
Tom Graham, (Miami, Ohio)	11	15	0	0	90	8.18
John Carney, (Notre Dame)	11	0	24	21	87	7.91

Total Offense

	Yds. Rushing	Yds. Passing	Total Yards	Yds/ Play	Yds/ Game
Cody Carlson (Baylor)	356	2284	2640	6.70	264.00
Sammy Garza (UTEP)	−138	3140	3002	5.97	250.17
Vinny Testaverde (Miami, Florida)	−103	2557	2454	7.62	245.40
Larry Egger (Utah)	−136	2761	2625	6.13	238.64
Chris Miller, (Oregon)	46	2503	2549	5.93	231.73
Jim Harbaugh, (Michigan)	99	2432	2531	7.98	230.09
Kelly Stouffer, (Colorado St.)	−214	2604	2390	5.56	217.27
Dave Yarema, (Michigan St.)	−222	2581	2359	6.96	214.45
Don Smith, (Mississippi St.)	740	1609	2349	5.83	213.55
Ned James, (New Mexico)	527	1777	2304	6.31	209.45

Interceptions

	Games	No.	Yds.	TD	No./ Game
Toi Cook, (Stanford)	9	7	115	0	0.78
Ron Francis, (Baylor)	11	8	25	0	0.73
Elton Slater, (Southwestern La.)	11	8	1	0	0.73
Jim King, (Colorado St.)	11	7	83	0	0.64
Ed Hulbert, (Oregon)	11	7	48	0	0.64
Derrick Taylor, (North Caro. St.)	11	6	164	1	0.55
Jeff Wilcox, (Brigham Young)	11	6	110	0	0.55
K.C. Clark, (San Jose State)	11	6	107	0	0.55
Craig Rutledge, (UCLA)	11	6	104	1	0.55
Stephen Braggs, (Texas)	11	6	84	0	0.55
Thomas Everett, (Baylor)	11	6	77	1	0.55
Troy White, (Miami, Ohio)	11	6	59	0	0.55
Alvin Horn, (Nevada-Las Vegas)	11	6	35	0	0.55

Field Goals

	Games	FGAtt	FG	Pct.	FG/ Game
John Carney, (Notre Dame)	11	28	21	.750	1.91
John Duvic, (Northwestern)	11	23	19	.826	1.73
Steve Deline, (Colorado State)	11	24	19	.792	1.73
Jeff Jaeger, (Washington)	11	21	17	.810	1.55
John Diettrich, (Ball State)	11	23	17	.739	1.55
Dave Franey, (UCLA)	11	19	15	.789	1.36

Punting

	No.	Yds.	Avg.
Greg Horne, (Arkansas)	49	2313	47.20
Bill Smith, (Mississippi)	57	2522	44.25
Mike Preacher, (Oregon)	49	2143	43.73

COLLEGE BOWL RESULTS

December 20
Independence Bowl
Mississippi 20 — Texas Tech 17

December 23
Hall of Fame Bowl
Boston College 27 — Georgia 24

December 25
Sun Bowl
Alabama 28 — Washington 6

December 27
Gator Bowl
Clemson 27 — Stanford 21

Aloha Bowl
Arizona 30 — North Carolina 21

December 29
Liberty Bowl
Tennessee 21 — Minnesota 14

December 30
Freedom Bowl
UCLA 31 — Brigham Young 10

Holiday Bowl
Iowa 39 — San Diego State 38

December 31
All-American Bowl
Florida State 27 — Indiana 13

Bluebonnet Bowl
Baylor 21 — Colorado 9

Peach Bowl
Virginia Tech 25 — North Carolina State 24

January 1
Cotton Bowl
Ohio State 28 — Texas A&M 12

Florida Citrus Bowl
Auburn 16 — USC 7

Orange Bowl
Oklahoma 42 — Arkansas 8

Rose Bowl
Arizona State 22 — Michigan 15

Sugar Bowl
Nebraska 30 — LSU 15

January 2
Fiesta Bowl
Penn State 14 — Miami 10

HEISMAN TROPHY WINNERS

1986 — Vinny Testaverde, Miami, QB
1985 — Bo Jackson, Auburn, RB
1984 — Doug Flutie, Boston, QB
1983 — Mike Rozier, Nebraska, TB
1982 — Herschel Walker, Georgia, TB
1981 — Marcus Allen, Southern California, TB
1980 — George Rogers, South Carolina, HB
1979 — Charles White, Southern California, TB
1978 — Billy Sims, Oklahoma, HB
1977 — Earl Campbell, Texas, FB
1976 — Tony Dorsett, Pittsburgh, HB
1975 — Archie Griffin, Ohio State, HB
1974 — Archie Griffin, Ohio State, HB
1973 — John Cappelletti, Penn State, HB
1972 — Johnny Rogers, Nebraska, FL
1971 — Pat Sullivan, Auburn, QB
1970 — Jim Plunkett, Stanford, QB
1969 — Steve Owens, Oklahoma, HB
1968 — O.J. Simpson, Southern California, TB
1967 — Gary Beban, UCLA, QB
1966 — Steve Spurrier, Florida, QB
1965 — Mike Garrett, Southern California, TB
1964 — John Huarte, Notre Dame, QB
1963 — Roger Staubach, Navy, QB
1962 — Terry Baker, Oregon State, QB
1961 — Ernie Davis, Syracuse, HB
1960 — Joe Bellino, Navy, HB
1959 — Billy Cannon, LSU, HB
1958 — Pete Dawkins, Army, HB
1957 — John David Crow, Texas A&M, HB
1956 — Paul Hornung, Notre Dame, QB
1955 — Howard Cassady, Ohio State, HB
1954 — Alan Ameche, Wisconsin, FB
1953 — John Lattner, Notre Dame, HB
1952 — Billy Vessels, Oklahoma, HB
1951 — Dick Kazmaier, Princeton, HB
1950 — Vic Janowicz, Ohio State, HB
1949 — Leon Hart, Notre Dame, HB
1948 — Doak Walker, SMU, HB
1947 — John Lujack, Notre Dame, QB
1946 — Glenn Davis, Army, HB
1945 — Doc Blanchard, Army, HB
1944 — Les Horvath, Ohio State, QB
1943 — Angelo Bertelli, Notre Dame, QB
1942 — Frank Sinkwich, Georgia, HB
1941 — Bruce Smith, Minnesota, HB
1940 — Tom Harmon, Michigan, HB
1939 — Nile Kinnick, Iowa, HB
1938 — Davey O'Brien, TCU, QB
1937 — Clint Frank, Yale, HB
1936 — Larry Kelley, Yale, E
1935 — Jay Berwanger, Chicago, HB

1986 SEASON RESULTS

WEEK 1

Sunday, September 7

Atlanta Falcons at New Orleans Saints...31—10
Cincinnati Bengals at Kansas City Chiefs ....14—24
Cleveland Browns at Chicago Bears...31—41
Detroit Lions at Minnesota Vikings...13—10
Houston Oilers at Green Bay Packers ....31— 3
Indianapolis Colts at New England Patriots.. 3—33
Los Angeles Raiders at Denver Broncos..36—38
Los Angeles Rams at St. Louis Cardinals..16—10
Miami Dolphins at San Diego Chargers..28—50
New York Jets at Buffalo Bills...28—24
Philadelphia Eagles at Washington Redskins ....14—41
Pittsburgh Steelers at Seattle Seahawks... 0—30
San Francisco 49ers at Tampa Bay Buccaneers ....31— 7

Monday, September 8

New York Giants at Dallas Cowboys...28—31

WEEK 2

Thursday, September 11

New England Patriots at New York Jets ....20— 6

Sunday, September 14

Buffalo Bills at Cincinnati Bengals ....(OT) 33—36
Cleveland Browns at Houston Oilers...23—20
Dallas Cowboys at Detroit Lions..31— 7
Green Bay Packers at New Orleans Saints...10—24
Indianapolis Colts at Miami Dolphins..10—30
Kansas City Chiefs at Seattle Seahawks..17—23
Los Angeles Raiders at Washington Redskins...................................... 6—10
Minnesota Vikings at Tampa Bay Buccaneers......................................23—10
Philadelphia Eagles at Chicago Bears......................................(OT) 10—13
St. Louis Cardinals at Atlanta Falcons...13—33
San Diego Chargers at New York Giants.. 7—20
San Francisco 49ers at Los Angeles Rams...13—16

Monday, September 15

Denver Broncos at Pittsburgh Steelers ....21—10

WEEK 3

Thursday, September 18

Cincinnati Bengals at Cleveland Browns..30—13

Sunday, September 21

Atlanta Falcons at Dallas Cowboys...37—35
Denver Broncos at Philadelphia Eagles ....33— 7
Houston Oilers at Kansas City Chiefs..13—27
Los Angeles Rams at Indianapolis Colts...24— 7
Miami Dolphins at New York Jets...(OT) 45—51
New Orleans Saints at San Francisco 49ers...17—26
New York Giants at Los Angeles Raiders...14— 9
Pittsburgh Steelers at Minnesota Vikings.. 7—31
St. Louis Cardinals at Buffalo Bills...10—17
Seattle Seahawks at New England Patriots...38—31
Tampa Bay Buccaneers at Detroit Lions..24—20
Washington Redskins at San Diego Chargers ....30—27

Monday, September 22

Chicago Bears at Green Bay Packers...25—12

WEEK 4

Sunday, September 28
Atlanta Falcons at Tampa Bay Buccaneers ....(OT) 23—20
Chicago Bears at Cincinnati Bengals...44— 7
Detroit Lions at Cleveland Browns...21—24
Green Bay Packers at Minnesota Vikings .... 7—42
Kansas City Chiefs at Buffalo Bills..20—17
Los Angeles Rams at Philadelphia Eagles..20—34
New England Patriots at Denver Broncos...20—27
New Orleans Saints at New York Giants ....17—20
New York Jets at Indianapolis Colts...26— 7
Pittsburgh Steelers at Houston Oilers ....(OT) 22—16
San Diego Chargers at Los Angeles Raiders.....................................13—17
San Francisco 49ers at Miami Dolphins...31—16
Seattle Seahawks at Washington Redskins ....14—19

Monday, September 29
Dallas Cowboys at St. Louis Cardinals ....31— 7

WEEK 5

Sunday, October 5
Buffalo Bills at New York Jets ....13—14
Cincinnati Bengals vs. Green Bay Packers at Milwaukee.......................34—28
Cleveland Browns at Pittsburgh Steelers...27—24
Dallas Cowboys at Denver Broncos..14—29
Houston Oilers at Detroit Lions..13—24
Indianapolis Colts at San Francisco 49ers..14—35
Los Angeles Raiders at Kansas City Chiefs.......................................24—17
Miami Dolphins at New England Patriots .... 7—34
Minnesota Vikings at Chicago Bears .... 0—23
New York Giants at St. Louis Cardinals...13— 6
Philadelphia Eagles at Atlanta Falcons..16— 0
Tampa Bay Buccaneers at Los Angeles Rams ....(OT) 20—26
Washington Redskins at New Orleans Saints......................................14— 6

Monday, October 6
San Diego Chargers at Seattle Seahawks .... 7—33

WEEK 6

Sunday, October 12
Buffalo Bills at Miami Dolphins ....14—27
Chicago Bears at Houston Oilers..20— 7
Denver Broncos at San Diego Chargers...31—14
Detroit Lions at Green Bay Packers...21—14
Kansas City Chiefs at Cleveland Browns.. 7—20
Los Angeles Rams at Atlanta Falcons...14—26
Minnesota Vikings at San Francisco 49ers...................................(OT) 27—24
New Orleans Saints at Indianapolis Colts...17—14
New York Jets at New England Patriots ....31—24
Philadelphia Eagles at New York Giants... 3—35
St. Louis Cardinals at Tampa Bay Buccaneers....................................30—19
Seattle Seahawks at Los Angeles Raiders...10—14
Washington Redskins at Dallas Cowboys .... 6—30

Monday, October 13
Pittsburgh Steelers at Cincinnati Bengals...22—24

WEEK 7

Sunday, October 19
Chicago Bears at Minnesota Vikings .... 7—23
Dallas Cowboys at Philadelphia Eagles ....17—14
Detroit Lions at Los Angeles Rams..10—14
Green Bay Packers at Cleveland Browns ....17—14
Houston Oilers at Cincinnati Bengals...28—31
Indianapolis Colts at Buffalo Bills...13—24
Los Angeles Raiders at Miami Dolphins ....30—28
New England Patriots at Pittsburgh Steelers ....34— 0
New York Giants at Seattle Seahawks..12—17
St. Louis Cardinals at Washington Redskins ....21—28
San Diego Chargers at Kansas City Chiefs..41—42
San Francisco 49ers at Atlanta Falcons......................................(OT) 10—10
Tampa Bay Buccaneers at New Orleans Saints...................................... 7—38

Monday, October 20
Denver Broncos at New York Jets..10—22

WEEK 8

Sunday, October 26
Atlanta Falcons at Los Angeles Rams .... 7—14
Cincinnati Bengals at Pittsburgh Steelers.. 9—30
Cleveland Browns at Minnesota Vikings ....23—20
Detroit Lions at Chicago Bears .... 7—13
Los Angeles Raiders at Houston Oilers ....28—17
Miami Dolphins at Indianapolis Colts ....17—13
New England Patriots at Buffalo Bills ....23— 3
New Orleans Saints at New York Jets ....23—28
St. Louis Cardinals at Dallas Cowboys .... 6—37
San Diego Chargers at Philadelphia Eagles .... 7—23
San Francisco 49ers vs. Green Bay Packers at Milwaukee ....31—17
Seattle Seahawks at Denver Broncos ....13—20
Tampa Bay Buccaneers at Kansas City Chiefs.......................................20—27

Monday, October 27
Washington Redskins at New York Giants..20—27

WEEK 9

Sunday, November 2
Atlanta Falcons at New England Patriots...17—25
Buffalo Bills at Tampa Bay Buccaneers...28—34
Cincinnati Bengals at Detroit Lions ....24—17
Cleveland Browns at Indianapolis Colts ....24— 9
Dallas Cowboys at New York Giants..14—17
Denver Broncos at Los Angeles Raiders...21—10
Green Bay Packers at Pittsburgh Steelers.. 3—27
Houston Oilers at Miami Dolphins.. 7—28
Kansas City Chiefs at San Diego Chargers...24—23
Minnesota Vikings at Washington Redskins ....(OT) 38—44
New York Jets at Seattle Seahawks ....38— 7
Philadelphia Eagles at St. Louis Cardinals ....10—13
San Francisco 49ers at New Orleans Saints..10—23

Monday, November 3
Los Angeles Rams at Chicago Bears...20—17

WEEK 10

Sunday, November 9

Chicago Bears at Tampa Bay Buccaneers...23— 3
Cincinnati Bengals at Houston Oilers ....28—32
Los Angeles Raiders at Dallas Cowboys..17—13
Los Angeles Rams at New Orleans Saints.. 0— 6
Minnesota Vikings at Detroit Lions...24—10
New England Patriots at Indianapolis Colts...30—21
New York Giants at Philadelphia Eagles..17—14
New York Jets at Atlanta Falcons...28—14
Pittsburgh Steelers at Buffalo Bills..12—16
St. Louis Cardinals at San Francisco 49ers..17—43
San Diego Chargers at Denver Broncos .... 9— 3
Seattle Seahawks at Kansas City Chiefs.. 7—27
Washington Redskins at Green Bay Packers..16— 7

Monday, November 10

Miami Dolphins at Cleveland Browns...16—26

WEEK 11

Sunday, November 16

Chicago Bears at Atlanta Falcons...13—10
Cleveland Browns at Los Angeles Raiders ....14—27
Dallas Cowboys at San Diego Chargers...24—21
Detroit Lions at Philadelphia Eagles...13—11
Houston Oilers at Pittsburgh Steelers...10—21
Indianapolis Colts at New York Jets ....16—31
Kansas City Chiefs at Denver Broncos ....17—38
New England Patriots at Los Angeles Rams..30—28
Miami Dolphins at Buffalo Bills...34—24
New York Giants at Minnesota Vikings ....22—20
New Orleans Saints at St. Louis Cardinals...16— 7
Seattle Seahawks at Cincinnati Bengals.. 7—34
Tampa Bay Buccaneers vs. Green Bay Packers at Milwaukee .... 7—31

Monday, November 17

San Francisco 49ers at Washington Redskins .... 6—14

WEEK 12

Thursday, November 20

Los Angeles Raiders at San Diego Chargers.......................................(OT) 37—31

Sunday, November 23

Atlanta Falcons at San Francisco 49ers... 0—20
Buffalo Bills at New England Patriots ....19—22
Dallas Cowboys at Washington Redskins...14—41
Denver Broncos at New York Giants ....16—19
Detroit Lions at Tampa Bay Buccaneers..38—17
Green Bay Packers at Chicago Bears..10—12
Indianapolis Colts at Houston Oilers...17—31
Kansas City Chiefs at St. Louis Cardinals ....14—23
Minnesota Vikings at Cincinnati Bengals...20—24
New Orleans Saints at Los Angeles Rams..13—26
Philadelphia Eagles at Seattle Seahawks ....20—24
Pittsburgh Steelers at Cleveland Browns ....(OT) 31—37

Monday, November 24

New York Jets at Miami Dolphins... 3—45

WEEK 13

Thursday, November 27

Green Bay Packers at Detroit Lions..44—40
Seattle Seahawks at Dallas Cowboys ....31—14

Sunday, November 30

Atlanta Falcons at Miami Dolphins...20—14
Buffalo Bills at Kansas City Chiefs...17—14
Cincinnati Bengals at Denver Broncos...28—34
Houston Oilers at Cleveland Browns......................................(OT) 10—13
Los Angeles Rams at New York Jets...17— 3
New England Patriots at New Orleans Saints................................21—20
Philadelphia Eagles at Los Angeles Raiders.........................(OT) 33—27
Pittsburgh Steelers at Chicago Bears....................................(OT) 10—13
San Diego Chargers at Indianapolis Colts ....17— 3
Tampa Bay Buccaneers at Minnesota Vikings ....13—45
Washington Redskins at St. Louis Cardinals ....20—17

Monday, December 1

New York Giants at San Francisco 49ers ....21—17

WEEK 14

Sunday, December 7

Cincinnati Bengals at New England Patriots..................................31— 7
Cleveland Browns at Buffalo Bills...21—17
Dallas Cowboys at Los Angeles Rams..10—29
Denver Broncos at Kansas City Chiefs..10—37
Detroit Lions at Pittsburgh Steelers..17—27
Houston Oilers at San Diego Chargers... 0—27
Indianapolis Colts at Atlanta Falcons..28—23
Miami Dolphins at New Orleans Saints..31—27
Minnesota Vikings at Green Bay Packers ....32— 6
New York Giants at Washington Redskins.....................................24—14
New York Jets at San Francisco 49ers...10—24
St. Louis Cardinals at Philadelphia Eagles ....(OT) 10—10
Tampa Bay Buccaneers at Chicago Bears......................................14—48

Monday, December 8

Los Angeles Raiders at Seattle Seahawks...................................... 0—37

WEEK 15

Saturday, December 13

Pittsburgh Steelers at New York Jets ....45—24
Washington Redskins at Denver Broncos ....30—31

Sunday, December 14

Buffalo Bills at Indianapolis Colts...14—24
Cleveland Browns at Cincinnati Bengals.......................................34— 3
Green Bay Packers at Tampa Bay Buccaneers ....21— 7
Kansas City Chiefs at Los Angeles Raiders...................................20—17
Miami Dolphins at Los Angeles Rams ....(OT) 37—31
Minnesota Vikings at Houston Oilers...10—23
New Orleans Saints at Atlanta Falcons..14— 9
Philadelphia Eagles at Dallas Cowboys ....23—21
St. Louis Cardinals at New York Giants... 7—27
San Francisco 49ers at New England Patriots................................29—24
Seattle Seahawks at San Diego Chargers ....34—24

Monday, December 15

Chicago Bears at Detroit Lions ....16—13

WEEK 16

Friday, December 19
Los Angeles Rams at San Francisco 49ers ....14—24
Saturday, December 20
Denver Broncos at Seattle Seahawks...16—41
Green Bay Packers at New York Giants ....24—55
Sunday, December 21
Atlanta Falcons at Detroit Lions ....20— 6
Buffalo Bills at Houston Oilers .... 7—16
Chicago Bears at Dallas Cowboys ....24—10
Indianapolis Colts at Los Angeles Raiders..30—24
Kansas City Chiefs at Pittsburgh Steelers ....24—19
New Orleans Saints at Minnesota Vikings ....17—33
New York Jets at Cincinnati Bengals ....21—52
San Diego Chargers at Cleveland Browns ....17—47
Tampa Bay Buccaneers at St. Louis Cardinals..17—21
Washington Redskins at Philadelphia Eagles ....21—14
Monday, December 22
New England Patriots at Miami Dolphins...34—27

FIRST ROUND PLAYOFF GAMES

SUNDAY, DECEMBER 28

American Football Conference
Kansas City Chiefs at New York Jets ....15—35
National Football Conference
Los Angeles Rams at Washington Redskins.. 7—19

DIVISIONAL PLAYOFF GAMES

SATURDAY, JANUARY 3

American Football Conference
New York Jets at Cleveland Browns ....(OT) 20—23

National Football Conference
Washington Redskins at Chicago Bears ....27—13

SUNDAY, JANUARY 4

American Football Conference
New England Patriots at Denver Broncos ....17—22

National Football Conference
San Francisco 49ers at New York Giants .... 3—49

CONFERENCE CHAMPIONSHIP GAMES, SUPER BOWL XX, AND AFC-NFC PRO BOWL

SUNDAY, JANUARY 11

American Football Conference Championship Game
Denver Broncos at Cleveland Browns..(OT) 23—20

National Football Conference Championship Game
Washington Redskins at New York Giants 0-17
SUNDAY, JANUARY 25
Super Bowl XXI Denver Broncos vs New York Giants ....20—39
SUNDAY, FEBRUARY 1
AFC-NFC Pro Bowl at Honolulu, Hawaii ....10— 6

1986 FINAL STANDINGS

AMERICAN FOOTBALL CONFERENCE (AFC)

EASTERN DIVISION

	W	L	T	PF	PA
New England Patriots	11	5	0	412	307
New York Jets	10	6	0	364	386
Miami Dolphins	8	8	0	430	405
Buffalo Bills	4	12	0	287	348
Indianapolis Colts	3	13	0	229	400

CENTRAL DIVISION

	W	L	T	PF	PA
Cleveland Browns	12	4	0	391	310
Cincinnati Bengals	10	6	0	409	394
Pittsburgh Steelers	6	10	0	307	336
Houston Oilers	5	11	0	274	329

WESTERN DIVISION

	W	L	T	PF	PA
Denver Broncos	11	5	0	378	327
Kansas City Chiefs	10	6	0	358	326
Seattle Seahawks	10	6	0	366	293
Los Angeles Raiders	8	8	0	323	346
San Diego Chargers	4	12	0	335	396

NATIONAL FOOTBALL CONFERENCE (NFC)

EASTERN DIVISION

	W	L	T	PF	PA
New York Giants	14	2	0	371	236
Washington Redskins	12	4	0	368	296
Dallas Cowboys	7	9	0	346	337
Philadelphia Eagles	5	10	1	256	312
St. Louis Cardinals	4	11	1	218	351

CENTRAL DIVISION

	W	L	T	PF	PA
Chicago Bears	14	2	0	352	187
Minnesota Vikings	9	7	0	398	273
Detroit Lions	5	11	0	277	326
Green Bay Packers	4	12	0	254	418
Tampa Bay Buccaneers	2	14	0	239	473

WESTERN DIVISION

	W	L	T	PF	PA
San Francisco 49ers	10	5	1	374	247
Los Angeles Rams	10	6	0	309	267
Atlanta Falcons	7	8	1	280	280
New Orleans Saints	7	9	0	288	287

1987 SEASON SCHEDULE

WEEK 1   **Result**

Sunday, September 13
Atlanta Falcons at Tampa Bay Buccaneers .... ____—____
Cincinnati Bengals at Indianapolis Colts .... ____—____
Cleveland Browns at New Orleans Saints .... ____—____
Dallas Cowboys at St. Louis Cardinals .... ____—____
Detroit Lions at Minnesota Vikings .... ____—____
Los Angeles Raiders at Green Bay Packers .... ____—____
Los Angeles Rams at Houston Oilers .... ____—____
Miami Dolphins at New England Patriots .... ____—____
New York Jets at Buffalo Bills .... ____—____
Philadelphia Eagles at Washington Redskins .... ____—____
San Diego Chargers at Kansas City Chiefs .... ____—____
San Francisco 49ers at Pittsburgh Steelers .... ____—____
Seattle Seahawks at Denver Broncos .... ____—____

Monday, September 14
New York Giants at Chicago Bears .... ____—____

WEEK 2

Sunday, September 20
Dallas Cowboys at New York Giants .... ____—____
Denver Broncos vs. Green Bay Packers at Milwaukee .... ____—____
Detroit Lions at Los Angeles Raiders .... ____—____
Houston Oilers at Buffalo Bills .... ____—____
Kansas City Chiefs at Seattle Seahawks .... ____—____
Miami Dolphins at Indianapolis Colts .... ____—____
Minnesota Vikings at Los Angeles Rams .... ____—____
New Orleans Saints at Philadelphia Eagles .... ____—____
Pittsburgh Steelers at Cleveland Browns .... ____—____
St. Louis Cardinals at San Diego Chargers .... ____—____
San Francisco 49ers at Cincinnati Bengals .... ____—____
Tampa Bay Buccaneers at Chicago Bears .... ____—____
Washington Redskins at Atlanta Falcons .... ____—____

Monday, September 21
New England Patriots at New York Jets .... ____—____

WEEK 3

Sunday, September 27
Atlanta Falcons at New Orleans Saints .... ____—____
Buffalo Bills at Dallas Cowboys .... ____—____
Chicago Bears at Detroit Lions .... ____—____
Cincinnati Bengals at Los Angeles Rams .... ____—____
Green Bay Packers at Tampa Bay Buccaneers .... ____—____
Indianapolis Colts at St. Louis Cardinals .... ____—____
Los Angeles Raiders at Houston Oilers .... ____—____
Minnesota Vikings at Kansas City Chiefs .... ____—____
New York Jets at Pittsburgh Steelers .... ____—____
New York Giants at Miami Dolphins .... ____—____
New England Patriots at Washington Redskins .... ____—____
Philadelphia Eagles at San Francisco 49ers .... ____—____
Seattle Seahawks at San Diego Chargers .... ____—____

Monday, September 28
Denver Broncos at Cleveland Browns .... ____—____

WEEK 4
Sunday, October 4
Chicago Bears at Philadelphia Eagles .... ___—___
Cleveland Browns at New England Patriots .... ___—___
Dallas Cowboys at New York Jets .... ___—___
Green Bay Packers at Minnesota Vikings .... ___—___
Houston Oilers at Denver Broncos .... ___—___
Indianapolis Colts at Buffalo Bills .... ___—___
Kansas City Chiefs at Los Angeles Raiders .... ___—___
Los Angeles Rams at New Orleans Saints .... ___—___
Miami Dolphins at Seattle Seahawks .... ___—___
Pittsburgh Steelers at Atlanta Falcons .... ___—___
St. Louis Cardinals at Washington Redskins .... ___—___
San Diego Chargers at Cincinnati Bengals .... ___—___
Tampa Bay Buccaneers at Detroit Lions .... ___—___
Monday, October 5
San Francisco 49ers at New York Giants .... ___—___

WEEK 5
Sunday, October 11
Atlanta Falcons at San Francisco 49ers .... ___—___
Buffalo Bills at New England Patriots .... ___—___
Cincinnati Bengals at Seattle Seahawks .... ___—___
Detroit Lions at Green Bay Packers .... ___—___
Houston Oilers at Cleveland Browns .... ___—___
Kansas City Chiefs at Miami Dolphins .... ___—___
Minnesota Vikings at Chicago Bears .... ___—___
New Orleans Saints at St. Louis Cardinals .... ___—___
New York Jets at Indianapolis Colts .... ___—___
Philadelphia Eagles at Dallas Cowboys .... ___—___
Pittsburgh Steelers at Los Angeles Rams .... ___—___
San Diego Chargers at Tampa Bay Buccaneers .... ___—___
Washington Redskins at New York Giants .... ___—___
Monday, October 12
Los Angeles Raiders at Denver Broncos .... ___—___

WEEK 6
Sunday, October 18
Cleveland Browns at Cincinnati Bengals .... ___—___
Denver Broncos at Kansas City Chiefs .... ___—___
Indianapolis Colts at Pittsburgh Steelers .... ___—___
Los Angeles Rams at Atlanta Falcons .... ___—___
Miami Dolphins at New York Jets .... ___—___
New England Patriots at Houston Oilers .... ___—___
New Orleans Saints at Chicago Bears .... ___—___
New York Giants at Buffalo Bills .... ___—___
Philadelphia Eagles at Green Bay Packers .... ___—___
St. Louis Cardinals at San Francisco 49ers .... ___—___
San Diego Chargers at Los Angeles Raiders .... ___—___
Seattle Seahawks at Detroit Lions .... ___—___
Tampa Bay Buccaneers at Minnesota Vikings .... ___—___
Monday, October 19
Washington Redskins at Dallas Cowboys .... ___—___

WEEK 7   Result
Sunday, October 25
Atlanta Falcons at Houston Oilers .... ____—____
Buffalo Bills at Miami Dolphins .... ____—____
Chicago Bears at Tampa Bay Buccaneers .... ____—____
Cincinnati Bengals at Pittsburgh Steelers .... ____—____
Dallas Cowboys at Philadelphia Eagles .... ____—____
Denver Broncos at Minnesota Vikings .... ____—____
Green Bay Packers at Detroit Lions .... ____—____
Kansas City Chiefs at San Diego Chargers .... ____—____
New England Patriots at Indianapolis Colts .... ____—____
New York Jets at Washington Redskins .... ____—____
St. Louis Cardinals at New York Giants .... ____—____
San Francisco 49ers at New Orleans Saints .... ____—____
Seattle Seahawks at Los Angeles Raiders .... ____—____
Monday, October 26
Los Angeles Rams at Cleveland Browns .... ____—____

WEEK 8
Sunday, November 1
Cleveland Browns at San Diego Chargers .... ____—____
Detroit Lions at Denver Broncos .... ____—____
Houston Oilers at Cincinnati Bengals .... ____—____
Indianapolis Colts at New York Jets .... ____—____
Kansas City Chiefs at Chicago Bears .... ____—____
Los Angeles Raiders at New England Patriots .... ____—____
Minnesota Vikings at Seattle Seahawks .... ____—____
New Orleans Saints at Atlanta Falcons .... ____—____
Philadelphia Eagles at St. Louis Cardinals .... ____—____
Pittsburgh Steelers at Miami Dolphins .... ____—____
San Francisco 49ers at Los Angeles Rams .... ____—____
Tampa Bay Buccaneers vs. Green Bay Packers at Milwaukee ..... ____—____
Washington Redskins at Buffalo Bills .... ____—____
Monday, November 2
New York Giants at Dallas Cowboys .... ____—____

WEEK 9
Sunday, November 8
Atlanta Falcons at Cleveland Browns .... ____—____
Chicago Bears at Green Bay Packers .... ____—____
Dallas Cowboys at Detroit Lions .... ____—____
Denver Broncos at Buffalo Bills .... ____—____
Houston Oilers at San Francisco 49ers .... ____—____
Los Angeles Raiders at Minnesota Vikings .... ____—____
Miami Dolphins at Cincinnati Bengals .... ____—____
New England Patriots at New York Giants .... ____—____
New Orleans Saints at Los Angeles Rams .... ____—____
Pittsburgh Steelers at Kansas City Chiefs .... ____—____
San Diego Chargers at Indianapolis Colts .... ____—____
Tampa Bay Buccaneers at St. Louis Cardinals .... ____—____
Washington Redskins at Philadelphia Eagles .... ____—____
Monday, November 9
Seattle Seahawks at New York Jets .... ____—____

WEEK 10   **Result**
Sunday, November 15
Buffalo Bills at Cleveland Browns ....____—____
Cincinnati Bengals at Atlanta Falcons ....____—____
Dallas Cowboys at New England Patriots ....____—____
Detroit Lions at Washington Redskins ....____—____
Green Bay Packers at Seattle Seahawks ....____—____
Houston Oilers at Pittsburgh Steelers ....____—____
Indianapolis Colts at Miami Dolphins ....____—____
Los Angeles Raiders at San Diego Chargers ....____—____
Los Angeles Rams at St. Louis Cardinals ....____—____
Minnesota Vikings at Tampa Bay Buccaneers ....____—____
New Orleans Saints at San Francisco 49ers ....____—____
New York Giants at Philadelphia Eagles ....____—____
New York Jets at Kansas City Chiefs ....____—____
Monday, November 16
Chicago Bears at Denver Broncos ....____—____

WEEK 11
Sunday, November 22
Atlanta Falcons at Minnesota Vikings ....____—____
Buffalo Bills at New York Jets ....____—____
Cleveland Browns at Houston Oilers ....____—____
Detroit Lions at Chicago Bears ....____—____
Denver Broncos at Los Angeles Raiders ....____—____
Green Bay Packers at Kansas City Chiefs ....____—____
Indianapolis Colts at New England Patriots ....____—____
Miami Dolphins at Dallas Cowboys ....____—____
New York Giants at New Orleans Saints ....____—____
Pittsburgh Steelers at Cincinnati Bengals ....____—____
St. Louis Cardinals at Philadelphia Eagles ....____—____
San Diego Chargers at Seattle Seahawks ....____—____
San Francisco 49ers at Tampa Bay Buccaneers ....____—____
Monday, November 23
Los Angeles Rams at Washington Redskins ....____—____

WEEK 12
Thursday, November 26
Kansas City Chiefs at Detroit Lions ....____—____
Minnesota Vikings at Dallas Cowboys ....____—____
Sunday, November 29
Cincinnati Bengals at New York Jets ....____—____
Cleveland Browns at San Francisco 49ers ....____—____
Denver Broncos at San Diego Chargers ....____—____
Green Bay Packers at Chicago Bears ....____—____
Houston Oilers at Indianapolis Colts ....____—____
Miami Dolphins at Buffalo Bills ....____—____
New Orleans Saints at Pittsburgh Steelers ....____—____
New York Giants at Washington Redskins ....____—____
Philadelphia Eagles at New England Patriots ....____—____
St. Louis Cardinals at Atlanta Falcons ....____—____
Tampa Bay Buccaneers at Los Angeles Rams ....____—____
Monday, November 30
Los Angeles Raiders at Seattle Seahawks ....____—____

WEEK 13   Result
Sunday, December 6
Atlanta Falcons at Dallas Cowboys................................____—____
Buffalo Bills at Los Angeles Raiders.............................____—____
Chicago Bears at Minnesota Vikings.............................____—____
Indianapolis Colts at Cleveland Browns.........................____—____
Kansas City Chiefs at Cincinnati Bengals.......................____—____
Los Angeles Rams at Detroit Lions...............................____—____
New England Patriots at Denver Broncos........................____—____
Philadelphia Eagles at New York Giants.........................____—____
San Diego Chargers at Houston Oilers...........................____—____
San Francisco 49ers at Green Bay Packers.....................____—____
Seattle Seahawks at Pittsburgh Steelers........................____—____
Tampa Bay Buccaneers at New Orleans Saints.................____—____
Washington Redskins at St. Louis Cardinals....................____—____
Monday, December 7
New York Jets at Miami Dolphins.................................____—____

WEEK 14
Sunday, December 13
Atlanta Falcons at Los Angeles Rams............................____—____
Buffalo Bills at Indianapolis Colts.................................____—____
Cincinnati Bengals at Cleveland Browns.........................____—____
Dallas Cowboys at Washington Redskins........................____—____
Denver Broncos at Seattle Seahawks............................____—____
Detroit Lions at Tampa Bay Buccaneers.........................____—____
Houston Oilers at New Orleans Saints...........................____—____
Los Angeles Raiders at Kansas City Chiefs.....................____—____
Miami Dolphins at Philadelphia Eagles...........................____—____
Minnesota Vikings vs. Green Bay Packers at Milwaukee.......____—____
New York Giants at St. Louis Cardinals..........................____—____
New York Jets at New England Patriots..........................____—____
Pittsburgh Steelers at San Diego Chargers......................____—____
Monday, December 14
Chicago Bears at San Francisco 49ers..........................____—____

WEEK 15
Saturday, December 19
Green Bay Packers at New York Giants..........................____—____
Kansas City Chiefs at Denver Broncos...........................____—____
Sunday, December 20
Cleveland Browns at Los Angeles Raiders.......................____—____
Indianapolis Colts at San Diego Chargers........................____—____
Minnesota Vikings at Detroit Lions................................____—____
New England Patriots at Buffalo Bills.............................____—____
New Orleans Saints at Cincinnati Bengals.......................____—____
Philadelphia Eagles at New York Jets............................____—____
Pittsburgh Steelers at Houston Oilers............................____—____
St. Louis Cardinals at Tampa Bay Buccaneers..................____—____
San Francisco 49ers at Atlanta Falcons.........................____—____
Seattle Seahawks at Chicago Bears.............................____—____
Washington Redskins at Miami Dolphins.........................____—____
Monday, December 21
Dallas Cowboys at Los Angeles Rams...........................____—____

WEEK 16 Result

Saturday, December 26
Cleveland Browns at Pittsburgh Steelers...____—____
Washington Redskins at Minnesota Vikings ....____—____
Sunday, December 27
Buffalo Bills at Philadelphia Eagles ....____—____
Chicago Bears at Los Angeles Raiders ....____—____
Cincinnati Bengals at Houston Oilers ....____—____
Detroit Lions at Atlanta Falcons ....____—____
Green Bay Packers at New Orleans Saints ....____—____
Los Angeles Rams at San Francisco 49ers................................____—____
New York Jets at New York Giants ....____—____
St. Louis Cardinals at Dallas Cowboys ....____—____
San Diego Chargers at Denver Broncos......................................____—____
Seattle Seahawks at Kansas City Chiefs ....____—____
Tampa Bay Buccaneers at Indianapolis Colts..............................____—____
Monday, December 28
New England Patriots at Miami Dolphins......................................____—____

FIRST ROUND PLAYOFF GAMES
Sunday, January 3, 1988
American Football Conference

_____at_____
National Football Conference

_____at_____

DIVISIONAL PLAYOFF GAMES
Saturday, January 9, 1988
American Football Conference

_____at_____
National Football Conference

_____at_____
Sunday, January 10, 1988
American Football Conference

_____at_____
National Football Conference

_____at_____

CONFERENCE CHAMPIONSHIP GAMES, SUPER BOWL XXII, AND AFC-NFC PRO BOWL
Sunday, January 17, 1988
American Football Conference Championship Game

_____at_____
National Football Conference Championship Game

_____at_____
Sunday, January 31, 1988
Super Bowl XXII at San Diego Jack Murphy Stadium, San Diego, California

_____vs_____
Sunday, February 7, 1988
AFC-NFC Pro Bowl at Honolulu, Hawaii

AFC _____vs.NFC _____